THE·CORE·KNOWLEDGE
SERIES

What Your Kindergartner Needs to Know

PREPARING YOUR CHILD FOR A LIFETIME OF LEARNING

Edited by

E. D. HIRSCH, JR., and JOHN HOLDREN

A Delta Book
Published by
Dell Publishing
a division of
Bantam Doubleday Dell Publishing Group, Inc.
1540 Broadway
New York, New York 10036

ISBN: 0-385-31841-3

Book Design by Bonni Leon-Berman

Reprinted by arrangement with Doubleday

Manufactured in the United States of America
Published simultaneously in Canada

September 1997

10   9   8   7

EDUCATORS PRAISE
The Core Knowledge Series

"Though I have twenty-five years' teaching experience, this is my first year as a **Core Knowledge** teacher. Now, for the first time in a long time, I am excited about teaching again. As for my students, I seriously believe that many of them would eliminate summer vacation to get on with the business of learning!"

—Joan Falbey, Teacher,
Three Oaks Elementary, Fort Myers, Florida

"Our school hired a curriculum specialist. He introduced me to **Core Knowledge.** With *What Your First Grader Needs to Know,* I have found hope and excitement for my Crow Indian students. I thank you for believing in the best for our children."

—Jennifer Flatlip, Teacher,
St. Charles School, Pryor, Montana

"For three years, we have been using elements of the **Core Knowledge** program, and I have watched as it invigorated our students. These books should be in every classroom in America."

—Richard E. Smith, Principal,
Northside Elementary School, Palestine, Texas

"Hirsch made it quite clear (in *Cultural Literacy*) that respect for cultural diversity is important but is best achieved when young people have adequate background knowledge of mainstream culture. In order for a truly democratic and economically sound society to be maintained, young people must have access to the best knowledge available so that they can understand the issues, express their viewpoints, and act accordingly."

—James P. Comer, M.D., Professor,
Child Study Center, Yale University
(in *Parents* magazine)

The
Core Knowledge™
Series

Resource Books for
Kindergarten Through Grade Six

Delta
Trade Paperbacks

Editor-in-Chief of the Core Knowledge Series: E. D. Hirsch, Jr.

Editor: John Holdren

Project Manager and Art Editor: Tricia Emlet

Writers: Curriculum Concepts, Inc. (Mathematics, Music); Diane Darst (Visual Arts); Susan Hitchcock (Science); John Holdren (Literature and Language, History and Geography, Music, Mathematics, Science); Mary Beth Klee (History and Geography)

Artists: Special thanks to Gail McIntosh for exceptional color art and other fine pieces. Leslie Evans, Julie Grant, Steve Henry, Bob Kirchman, Michael McCurdy, Giuseppe Trogu

Art and Photo Research and Permissions: Martha Clay Sullivan

Research Assistant: Deborah Hyland

Acknowledgments

This series has depended on the help, advice, and encouragement of two thousand people. Some of those singled out here already know the depth of our gratitude; others may be surprised to find themselves thanked publicly for help they gave quietly and freely for the sake of the enterprise alone. To helpers named and unnamed we are deeply grateful.

Advisers on Multiculturalism: Minerva Allen, Barbara Carey, Frank de Varona, Mick Fedullo, Dorothy Fields, Elizabeth Fox-Genovese, Marcia Galli, Dan Garner, Henry Louis Gates, Cheryl Kulas, Joseph C. Miller, Gerry Raining Bird, Connie Rocha, Dorothy Small, Sharon Stewart-Peregoy, Sterling Stuckey, Marlene Walking Bear, Lucille Watahomigie, Ramona Wilson

Advisers on Elementary Education: Joseph Adelson, Isobel Beck, Paul Bell, Carl Bereiter, David Bjorklund, Constance Jones, Elizabeth LaFuze, J. P. Lutz, Sandra Scarr, Nancy Stein, Phyllis Wilkin

Advisers on Technical Subject Matter: Marilyn Jager Adams, Diane Alavi, Richard Anderson, Judith Birsh, Cheryl Cannard, Paul Gagnon, David Geary, Andrew Gleason, Blair Jones, Connie Juel, Eric Karell, Joseph Kett, Mary Beth Klee, Michael Lynch, Joseph C. Miller, Jean Osborne, Margaret Redd, Nancy Royal, Mark Rush, Janet Smith, Ralph Smith, Nancy Strother, Nancy Summers, James Trefil, Nancy Wayne, Linda Williams, Lois Williams

Conferees, March 1990: Nola Bacci, Joan Baratz-Snowden, Thomasyne Beverley, Thomas Blackton, Angela Burkhalter, Monty Caldwell, Thomas M. Carroll, Laura Chapman, Carol Anne Collins, Lou Corsaro, Henry Cotton, Anne Coughlin, Arletta Dimberg, Debra P. Douglas, Patricia Edwards, Janet Elenbogen, Mick Fedullo, Michele Fomalont, Mamon Gibson, Jean Haines, Barbara Hayes, Stephen Herzog, Helen Kelley, Brenda King, John King, Elizabeth LaFuze, Diana Lam, Nancy Lambert, Doris Langaster, Richard LaPointe, Lloyd Leverton, Madeline Long, Allen Luster, Joseph McGeehan, Janet McLin, Gloria McPhee, Marcia Mallard, William J. Maloney, Judith Matz, John Morabito, Robert Morrill, Roberta Morse, Karen Nathan, Dawn Nichols, Valeta Paige, Mary Perrin, Joseph Piazza, Jeanne Price, Marilyn Rauth, Judith Raybern, Mary Reese, Richard Rice, Wallace Saval, John Saxon, Jan Schwab, Ted Sharp, Diana Smith, Richard Smith, Trevanian Smith, Carol Stevens, Nancy Summers, Michael Terry, Robert Todd, Elois Veltman, Sharon Walker, Mary Ann Ward, Penny Williams, Charles Whiten, Clarke Worthington, Jane York

Schools: Special thanks to Three Oaks Elementary for piloting the original Core Knowledge Sequence in 1990. And thanks to the schools that have offered their advice and suggestions for improving the Core Knowledge Sequence, including (in alphabetical order): Academy Charter School (CO); Coleman Elementary (TX); Coral Reef Elementary (FL); Coronado Village Elementary (TX); Crooksville Elementary (OH); Crossroads Academy (NH); Gesher Jewish Day School (VA); Hawthorne Elementary (TX); Highland Heights Elementary (IN); Joella Good Elementary (FL); Mohegan School–CS 67 (NY); The Morse School (MA); Nichols Hills Elementary (OK); Ridge View Elementary (WA); R. N. Harris Elementary (NC); Southside Elementary (FL); Three Oaks Elementary (FL); Washington Core Knowledge School (CO). And to the many other schools teaching Core Knowledge—too many to name here, and some of whom we have yet to discover—our heartfelt thanks for "sharing the knowledge"!

Benefactors: The Brown Foundation, The Challenge Foundation, Mrs. E. D. Hirsch, Sr., The Walton Family Foundation.

Our grateful acknowledgment to these persons does not imply that we have taken their (sometimes conflicting) advice in every case, or that each of them endorses all aspects of this project. Responsibility for final decisions must rest with the editors alone. Suggestion for improvements are very welcome, and we wish to thank in advance those who send advice for revising and improving this series.

With Love to Francesco,
who will enter kindergarten in the year 2000.
EDH

To my mother and father.
JH

A Note to Teachers

We hope you will find this book useful, especially those of you who are teaching in the growing national network of Core Knowledge schools. Throughout the book, we have addressed the suggested activities and explanations to "Parents," since you as teachers know your students and will have ideas about how to use the content of this book in relation to the lessons and activities you plan. If you are interested in the ideas of teachers in Core Knowledge schools, please write or call the Core Knowledge Foundation (2012-B Morton Drive, Charlottesville, VA 22903; [804] 977-7550) for information on ordering collections of lessons created and shared by teachers in Core Knowledge schools. Also, you can get access to more lessons and ideas shared by teachers through the Core Knowledge Home Page on the Internet at the following address:

http://www.coreknowledge.org

Contents

I. Language and Literature

Stories

Sayings

II. History and Geography

Introduction 115

World History and Geography

American History and Geography

III. Visual Arts

Introduction 155

IV. Music

Introduction 175

Do You Like Music?

Favorite Songs

V. Mathematics

Introduction 195

Patterns and Classifications

VI. Science
Introduction 243

CONTENTS

Introduction

Kindergarten: The Big First Step

For many children and parents, the beginning of kindergarten is a time of great expectations and great hopes—and a little anxiety. Even families in which children have attended day care or preschool perceive kindergarten as the beginning of something different—as the big first step on a path that, if navigated successfully, can lead to a lifetime of learning.

What kind of knowledge and skills can your child be expected to learn in a good kindergarten program? How can you help your child at home? These are questions we try to answer in this book.

This book also responds to the many parents and teachers who have written to us since 1991, when we published *What Your First Grader Needs to Know*. Ever since that book came out as the first of a six-grade series, we have received many calls and letters from parents and teachers, both thanking us and asking, "Where is the book for *kindergartners*? Kindergarten deserves separate attention."

Those parents and teachers are right. Although not all fifty states legally require children to begin schooling in kindergarten, for a great many children kindergarten represents their first formal schooling. And until such time as American policymakers see the wisdom and justice of offering, as in France, free public education for children as young as three, kindergarten is, for most of our children, the big first step.

Kindergarten is the year during which children learn what it means to "go to school." In part, this means that they learn social skills, such as taking turns, waiting to speak until called on, and working and playing cooperatively with fellow students.

While such skills are a vital part of kindergarten, they can be addressed directly only in the social setting of the classroom, and we do not discuss them in this book. Rather, this book presents a range of knowledge and skills—in literature, reading and writing, history and geography, visual arts, music, mathematics, and science—of the sort that should constitute the core of an enriching, challenging kindergarten program.

Some educators insist that "the real work of kindergartners is play." Like many an educational slogan, this appealing one does express at least a half-truth. No one would want to heap upon a five-year-old a burden of drudgery and ceaseless labor. We all want our children's early experience in school to be full of activity, imagination, and wonder.

At the same time, kindergarten must be more than extended day care, more than puzzles and Legos and cut-and-paste and "circle time" and recess and snack. Kindergarten is an extraordinary opportunity to *engage* children—when they are young, eager, and curious, and when their minds are absorbing knowledge like sponges—and also to *challenge* them by setting reasonable goals and helping them achieve those goals as they develop habits of attention and effort that will stand them in good stead throughout life.

The word "kindergarten" comes from the German—"children's garden." It is a nice image, though it needs to be examined carefully. Children are not flowers: they do not simply "blossom" if left alone to develop according to their own predilections. Gardens do not just happen: they need to be cultivated, watered, cared for.

When our children enter school, we want them to be respected and recognized as unique individuals. We want their particular gifts to be nurtured; we want their weaknesses to be treated with gentleness and encouragement in hopes of turning them, with time and effort, into strengths. Because individual children differ, and because localities across this big and diverse country also differ, kindergarten classrooms will offer different experiences. But classrooms do not, or should not, exist in isolation. In our public school system, classrooms are part of, and should prepare our children for life in, larger communities. Thus, even as we want kindergarten teachers to bring out the best in our children as individual learners and the kindergarten classroom to reflect our particular local community, we also look to kindergarten to prepare our children to be part of a larger community, or rather, communities: the town, the state, the nation, the world.

All communities require some common ground. What we have attempted to do in this book is give a concrete and specific sense of a common ground of learning for American kindergartners: *not* a comprehensive prescription for "everything every kindergartner needs to know," since such a prescription is undesirable, given individual and local differences, but a common ground for being an active, successful learner who is ready for the next big step, that is, first grade.

All children should enter school "ready to learn." So said the President and governors at the education summit held in 1989. This book attempts to give substance and meaning to that goal.

We hope you and your kindergartner will enjoy this book, and that it will help you get a good start on the path to a lifetime of learning.

E. D. Hirsch, Jr., and John Holdren

General Introduction
to the Core Knowledge Series

I. WHAT IS YOUR CHILD LEARNING IN SCHOOL?

A parent of identical twins sent me a letter in which she expressed concern that her children, who are in the same grade in the same school, are being taught completely different things. How can this be? Because they are in different classrooms; because the teachers in these classrooms have only the vaguest guidelines to follow; in short, because the school, like many in the United States, lacks a definite, specific curriculum.

Many parents would be surprised if they were to examine the curriculum of their child's elementary school. Ask to see your school's curriculum. Does it spell out, in clear and concrete terms, a core of specific content and skills all children at a particular grade level are expected to learn by the end of the school year?

Many curricula speak in general terms of vaguely defined skills, processes, and attitudes, often in an abstract, pseudotechnical language that calls, for example, for children to "analyze patterns and data," or "investigate the structure and dynamics of living systems," or "work cooperatively in a group." Such vagueness evades the central question: what is your child learning in school? It places unreasonable demands upon teachers, and often results in years of schooling marred by repetitions and gaps. Yet another unit on dinosaurs or "pioneer days." *Charlotte's Web* for the third time. "You've never heard of the Bill of Rights?" "You've never been taught how to add two fractions with unlike denominators?"

When identical twins in two classrooms of the same school have few academic experiences in common, that is cause for concern. When teachers in that school do not know what children in other classrooms are learning on the same grade level, much less in earlier and later grades, they cannot reliably predict that children will come prepared with a shared core of knowledge and skills. For an elementary school to be successful, teachers need a common vision of what they want their students to know and be able to do. They need to have *clear, specific learning goals*, as well as the sense of mutual accountability that comes from shared commitment to helping all children achieve those goals. Lacking both specific goals and mutual accountability, too many schools exist in a state of curricular incoherence, one result of which is that they fall far short of developing the full potential of our children.

To address this problem, I started the nonprofit Core Knowledge Foundation in 1986. This book and its companion volumes in the Core Knowledge Series are designed to give parents, teachers—and through them, children—a guide to clearly defined learning goals in the form of a carefully sequenced body of knowledge, based upon the specific content guidelines developed by the Core Knowledge Foundation (see below, "The Consensus Behind the Core Knowledge Sequence").

Core Knowledge is an attempt to define, in a coherent and sequential way, a body of widely used knowledge taken for granted by competent writers and speakers in the United States. Because this knowledge is taken for granted rather than being explained when it is used, it forms a necessary foundation for the higher-order reading, writing, and thinking skills that children need for academic and vocational success. The universal attainment of such knowledge should be a central aim of curricula in our elementary schools, just as it is currently the aim in all world-class educational systems.

For reasons explained in the next section, making sure that all young children in the United States possess a core of shared knowledge is a necessary step in developing a first-rate educational system.

II. WHY CORE KNOWLEDGE IS NEEDED

Learning builds on learning: children (and adults) gain new knowledge only by building on what they already know. It is essential to begin building solid foundations of knowledge in the early grades when children are most receptive because, for the vast majority of children, academic deficiencies from the first six grades can *permanently* impair the success of later learning. Poor performance of American students in middle and high school can be traced to shortcomings inherited from elementary schools that have not imparted to children the knowledge and skills they need for further learning.

All of the highest-achieving and most egalitarian elementary school systems in the world (such as those in Sweden, France, and Japan) teach their children a specific core of knowledge in each of the first six grades, thus enabling all children to enter each new grade with a secure foundation for further learning. It is time American schools did so as well, for the following reasons:

(1) Commonly shared knowledge makes schooling more effective.

We know that the one-on-one tutorial is the most effective form of schooling, in part because a parent or teacher can provide tailor-made instruction for the individual child. But in a nontutorial situation—in, for example, a typical classroom with twenty-five or more students—the instructor cannot effectively impart new knowledge to all the students unless each one shares the background knowledge that the lesson is being built upon.

Consider this scenario: In third grade, Ms. Franklin is about to begin a unit on early explorers—Columbus, Magellan, and others. In her class she has some students who were in Mr. Washington's second-grade class last year and some students who were in Ms. Johnson's second-grade class. She also has a few students who have moved in from other towns. As Ms. Franklin begins the unit on explorers, she asks the children to look at a globe and use their fingers to trace a route across the Atlantic Ocean from Europe to North American. The students who had Mr. Washington look blankly at her: they didn't learn that last year. The students who had Ms. Johnson, however, eagerly point to the proper places on the globe, while two of the students who came from other towns pipe up and say, "Columbus and Magellan again? We did that last year."

When all the students in a class *do* share the relevant background knowledge, a classroom can begin to approach the effectiveness of a tutorial. Even when some children in a class do not have elements of the knowledge they were supposed to acquire in previous grades, the existence of a specifically defined core makes it possible for the teacher or parent to identify and fill the gaps, thus giving all students a chance to fulfill their potentials in later grades.

(2) Commonly shared knowledge makes schooling more fair and democratic.

When all the children who enter a grade can be assumed to share some of the same building blocks of knowledge, and when the teacher knows exactly what those building blocks are, then all the students are empowered to learn. In our current system, children from disadvantaged backgrounds too often suffer from unmerited low expectations that translate into watered-down curricula. But if we specify the core of knowledge that all children should share, then we can guarantee equal access to that knowledge and compensate for the academic advantages some students are offered at home. In a Core Knowledge school *all* children enjoy the benefits of important, challenging knowledge that will provide the foundation for successful later learning.

(3) Commonly shared knowledge helps create cooperation and solidarity in our schools and nation.

Diversity is a hallmark and strength of our nation. American classrooms are usually made up of students from a variety of cultural backgrounds, and those different cultures should be honored by all students. At the same time, education should create a *school-based* culture that is common and welcoming to all because it includes knowledge of many cultures and gives all students, no matter what their background, a common foundation for understanding our cultural diversity.

In the next section, I will describe the steps taken by the Core Knowledge Foundation to develop a model of the commonly shared knowledge our children need (which forms the basis for this series of books).

III. THE CONSENSUS BEHIND THE CORE KNOWLEDGE SEQUENCE

The content in this and other volumes in the Core Knowledge Series is based on a document called the *Core Knowledge Sequence*, a grade-by-grade sequence of specific content guidelines in history, geography, mathematics, science, language arts, and fine arts. The *Sequence* is not meant to outline the whole of the school curriculum; rather, it offers specific guidelines to knowledge that can reasonably be expected to make up about *half* of any school's curriculum, thus leaving ample room for local requirements and emphases. Teaching a common core of knowledge, such as that articulated in the *Core Knowledge Sequence*, is compatible with a variety of instructional methods and additional subject matters.

The *Core Knowledge Sequence* is the result of a long process of research and consensus-building undertaken by the Core Knowledge Foundation. Here is how we achieved the consensus behind the *Core Knowledge Sequence*.

First we analyzed the many reports issued by state departments of education and by professional organizations—such as the National Council of Teachers of Mathematics and the American Association for the Advancement of Science—that recommend general outcomes for elementary and secondary education. We also tabulated the knowledge and skills through grade six specified in the successful educational systems of several other countries, including France, Japan, Sweden, and West Germany.

In addition, we formed an advisory board on multiculturalism that proposed a specific knowledge of diverse cultural traditions that American children should all share as part of their school-based common culture. We sent the resulting materials to three independent groups of teachers, scholars, and scientists around the country, asking them to create a master list of the knowledge children should have by the end of grade six. About 150 teachers (including college professors, scientists, and administrators) were involved in this initial step.

These items were amalgamated into a master plan, and further groups of teachers and specialists were asked to agree on a grade-by-grade sequence of the items. That sequence was then sent to some one hundred educators and specialists who participated in a national conference that was called to hammer out a working agreement on an appropriate core of knowledge for the first six grades.

This important meeting took place in March 1990. The conferees were elementary school teachers, curriculum specialists, scientists, science writers, officers of national organizations, representatives of ethnic groups, district superintendents, and school principals from across the country. A total of twenty-four working groups decided on revisions in the *Core Knowledge Sequence*. The resulting provisional *Sequence* was further fine-tuned during a year of implementation at a pioneering school, Three Oaks Elementary in Lee County, Florida.

In only a few years many more schools—urban and rural, rich and poor, public and private—joined in the effort to teach Core Knowledge. Based largely on suggestions from these schools, the *Core Knowledge Sequence* was revised in 1995: separate guidelines were added for kindergarten, and a few topics in other grades were added, omitted, or moved from one grade to another, in order to create an even more coherent sequence for learning. Revised editions of the books in the Core Knowledge Series reflect the revisions in the *Sequence*. Based on the principle of learning from experience, the Core Knowledge Foundation continues to work with schools and advisors to "fine-tune" the *Sequence*, and is also conducting research that will lead to the publication of guidelines for grades seven and eight, as well as for preschool. (The *Core Knowledge Sequence* may be ordered from the Core Knowledge Foundation; see the end of this Introduction for the address.)

IV. THE NATURE OF THIS SERIES

The books in this series are designed to give a convenient and engaging introduction to the knowledge specified in the *Core Knowledge Sequence*. These are resource books, addressed primarily to parents, but which we hope will be useful tools for both parents and teachers. These books are not intended to replace the local curriculum or school textbooks, but rather to serve as aids to help children gain some of the important knowledge they will need to make progress in school and be effective in society.

Although we have made these books as accessible and useful as we can, parents and teachers should understand that they are not the only means by which the *Core Knowledge Sequence* can be imparted. The books represent a single version of the possibilities inherent in the *Sequence*, and a first step in the Core Knowledge reform effort. We hope that publishers will be stimulated to offer educational videos, computer software, games, alternative books, and other imaginative vehicles based on the *Core Knowledge Sequence*.

These books are not textbooks or workbooks, though when appropriate they do suggest a variety of activities you can do with your child. In these books we address your child directly, and occasionally ask questions for him to think about. The earliest books in the series are intended to be read aloud to children. Even as children become able to read the books on their own, we encourage parents to help their children read more actively by reading along with them and talking about what they are reading.

You and your child can read the sections of this book in any order, depending on your child's interests or depending on the topics your child is studying in school, which this book may sometimes complement or reinforce. You can skip from section to section and reread as much as your child likes.

We encourage you to think of this book as a guidebook that opens the way to many paths you and your child can explore. These paths may lead to the library, to many other good books, and, if possible, to plays, museums, concerts, and other opportunities for knowledge and enrichment. In short, this guidebook recommends places to visit and describes what is important in those places, but only you and your child can make the actual visit, travel the streets, and climb the steps.

V. WHAT YOU CAN DO TO HELP IMPROVE AMERICAN EDUCATION

The first step for parents and teachers who are committed to reform is to be skeptical about oversimplified slogans like "critical thinking" and "learning to learn." Such slogans are everywhere, and unfortunately for our schools, their partial insights have been elevated to the level of universal truths. For example: "What students learn is not important; rather, we must teach students to learn *how* to learn." "The child, not the academic subject, is the true focus of education." "Do not impose knowledge on children before they are developmentally ready to receive it." "Do not bog children down in mere facts, but rather, teach critical-thinking skills."

Who has not heard these sentiments, so admirable and humane, and—up to a point—so true? But these positive sentiments in favor of "thinking skills" and "higher understanding" have been turned into negative sentiments against the teaching of important knowledge. Those who have entered the teaching profession over the past forty years have been taught to scorn important knowledge as "mere facts," and to see the imparting of this knowledge as somehow injurious to children. Thus it has come about that many educators, armed with partially true slogans, have seemingly taken leave of common sense.

Many parents and teachers have come to the conclusion that elementary education must strike a better balance between the development of the "whole child" and the more limited but fundamental duty of the school to ensure that all children master a core of knowledge and skills essential to their competence as learners in later grades. But these parents and teachers cannot act on their convictions without access to an agreed-upon, concrete sequence of knowledge. Our main motivation in developing the *Core Knowledge Sequence* and this book series has been to give parents and teachers something concrete to work with.

It has been encouraging to see how many teachers, since the first volume in this series was published, have responded to the Core Knowledge reform effort. If you would like more information about the growing network of Core Knowledge schools, please call or write the Director of School Programs at the Core Knowledge Foundation.

Parents and teachers are urged to join in a grass-roots effort to strengthen our elementary schools. The place to start is in your own school and district. Insist that your school clearly state the core of *specific* knowledge and skills that each child in a grade must learn. Whether your school's core corresponds exactly to the Core Knowledge model is less important than the existence of *some* core—which, we hope, will be as solid, coherent, and challenging as the *Core Knowledge Sequence* has proven to be. Inform members of your community about the need for such a specific curriculum, and help make sure that the people who are elected or appointed to your local school board are independent-minded people who will insist that our children have the benefit of a solid, specific, world-class curriculum in each grade.

You are invited to become a member of the Core Knowledge Network by writing the Core Knowledge Foundation, 2012-B Morton Drive, Charlottesville, VA 22903.

Share the knowledge!

E. D. Hirsch, Jr.
Charlottesville, Virginia

I.

Language
and
Literature

Reading, Writing, and Your Kindergartner

PARENTS: Before we present a selection of poems and stories for your child, we want to address you directly. This section, Reading, Writing, and Your Kindergartner, is intended to help you understand how children are—or should be—taught to read and write in a good kindergarten classroom, and to suggest a few ways that you can help at home.

Teaching Children to Read: The Need for a Balanced Approach

In kindergarten through third grade, schools must attend, first and foremost, to the crucial mission of early education: teaching children to read. To emphasize reading is not to suggest that the other two R's—'riting and 'rithmetic—are any less important, only to distinguish reading as, in many ways, the skill of skills, the critical ability required for most other learning.

Everyone agrees that children should learn to read. But, as suggested by the subtitle of a classic study of the teaching of reading—Jeanne Chall's *Learning to Read: The Great Debate*—not everyone agrees about how to achieve that goal. Many studies have demonstrated, however, that while fashions come and go in education, pulling schools toward one extreme or another, there is a reasonable middle ground that is best for children.*

This middle ground *balances* two approaches that some educators, who advocate the use of either one approach or the other, mistakenly see as mutually exclusive. The first approach emphasizes the systematic teaching of the "nuts and bolts" of written language: phonics and decoding skills (turning written letters into spoken sounds), spelling, handwriting, punctuation, grammar, vocabulary, sentence structure, paragraph form, and other rules and conventions. The second approach emphasizes the need for children to be nourished on a rich diet of poetry, fiction, and nonfiction. It focuses attention on the meanings and messages conveyed by written words, and insists that children be given frequent opportunities to use language in creative and expressive ways.

*See, for example, Marilyn Jager Adams, *Beginning to Read: Thinking and Learning About Print* (Cambridge: MIT Press, 1990). A convenient summary of this authoritative analysis of research on early reading is available from the Center for the Study of Reading, University of Illinois, 51 Gerty Drive, Champaign, IL 61820. (Call 217-244-4083 for current pricing.)

Schools need to embrace *both* of these approaches. In particular, at the time of this writing, many elementary schools need to pay much more attention to the "nuts and bolts": they need to take steps to balance a worthwhile emphasis on literature and creative expression with an equally necessary emphasis on the basic how-to skills of reading and writing.

While parents can support a child's growth as a reader and a writer, especially by reading aloud regularly at home, schools, not parents, are responsible for teaching children to read and write. We will now discuss what it means to learn to read and write, as well as appropriate goals for reading and writing in kindergarten.

Learning to Read and Write

To learn to read is to learn to understand and use our language, specifically our *written* language. Learning to read is not like learning to speak. When children learn to talk, it all seems to happen so *naturally*. With apparently little explicit instruction, children learn—just by hearing others talk—to understand the meaning of the sounds communicated to them: "Time to brush your teeth." "Look at the butterfly!" "I love you." They learn to make specific sounds that convey certain meanings: "Pretty!" "I'm thirsty." "Can we go to the park today?"

While speech seems to come naturally, reading is a very different story. It is not enough just to see or hear others reading. Learning to read takes effort and instruction, because reading is not a natural process. While children do have a natural hunger to understand the meanings and messages conveyed by written words, our written language is not a natural thing—it is an artificial code. There is no natural reason why when you see this mark—A—you should hear in your mind a sound that rhymes with "day." But you do, because you have learned the code. A few children seem to figure out this code for themselves, but most children need organized, systematic, direct instruction in how to decode the words on the page, that is, to turn the written symbols, the letters, into the speech sounds they represent.

All codes follow certain rules or conventions. In the code of written English, individual letters represent certain sounds. The letter "t" makes the sound heard at the beginning of "turtle," the letter "m" makes the sound heard at the beginning of "mitten." Groups of letters can be combined in particular ways to make other sounds. The letters "ea" can make the sound heard in "*team*" and "*each*." Letter-sound patterns written in a precise left-to-right order make words: "team" means something different than "meat."

The key to helping children unlock the code of our written language is to help them understand the relationships between individual letters, and combinations of letters, and the sounds they make. True, sometimes these relationships seem odd: consider, for example, the different sounds of the letters "ough" in "though" and "enough." Despite these occasional oddities, there is a logic to the written English alphabet: its basic symbols, the letters, represent the basic speech sounds, or "phonemes," of our spoken language. The relationships between letters and sounds exhibit many regular patterns, as in, for example, "cat," "hat," "sat," "mat," "fat," "rat."

So, part of learning to read means learning the predictable letter-sound patterns in written words. Learning these letter-sound patterns enables a child who confronts a page of print to *decode* the written words into the sounds of spoken language they represent. The other side of the coin here is learning the basic skills of writing, which enable a child who faces a blank page to *encode* the sounds of spoken language by putting on paper the corresponding written letters to form words, and by following other conventions of writing (such as capitalization and punctuation) that allow us to get across our meanings, even when the person to whom we are communicating is not present before us.

All of this talk about decoding and encoding may sound very mechanical and a little intimidating. It should be kept in mind that instruction in decoding and encoding is all in the service of meaning and understanding. If children are to communicate their ideas, thoughts, and desires in writing, as well as to understand what others are saying in print—whether it's a traffic sign, a movie poster, a letter from a relative, or a story by Dr. Seuss or Beverly Cleary—then they need to have the tools to encode and decode written English.

A Goal for Kindergarten

Upon entering kindergarten, some children will learn to read and write more readily than others. This is to be expected, since prior to kindergarten, children have had different degrees of exposure to language and literature. Some have rarely seen a book. Others know the alphabet, have been read to nightly, and play language games on home computers. Yet, even given the best of opportunities, some children will not learn to read and write as easily as others. Parents should not get anxious about who reads "first." Learning to read is not a race: no medals are given to the earliest reader.

Regardless of precisely when a child starts to read and write, all children need early instruction, and some may need extra guidance. Part of what a good kindergarten program does is to provide challenging tasks for advanced students as well as extra practice and assistance for the children who need it. If a child is having difficulty, a school should not rationalize his difficulty by saying that the child is "not developmentally ready." You do not wait for readiness to happen. Rather, the child who is less ready should be given appropriate preliminary experiences to help him benefit from formal reading instruction, followed up by even *more* support, encouragement, and practice in the areas posing difficulty.

In reading and writing, a reasonable goal for kindergarten is to have *all children beginning to read and write on their own by the end of the kindergarten year.* To achieve that goal, schools need to take a balanced approach that emphasizes both meaning and decoding. A good kindergarten program motivates children by offering them many occasions to communicate in speech and writing, and by giving them many opportunities to hear meaningful and well-told literature, including poetry, fiction, and nonfiction. Such literature gives children insight into a world of meaning expressed in words which they may not be able to read on their own but which they understand when the words are read aloud and discussed by an adult.

But for children to learn to read, it's not enough just to have good books read aloud to them. Listening to books does help children acquire a sense of what makes up a story, and it motivates them to want to read. But it will not teach them how to read the words on the page.

If children are to gain access on their own to the world of meaning, they must first be given the keys. Schools can give them these keys by providing explicit and systematic instruction in decoding written language. Children need repeated practice in working with letters and sounds in order to develop a good initial understanding of how language works. This does not mean mindless drill; rather, it means providing repeated and varied opportunities for children to work and play with letters and sounds.

What Does a Good Kindergarten Program Do?

Here are some things a good kindergarten program does to help children meet the goal of beginning to read and write on their own.

- A good program helps children develop their oral language, including speaking and listening. Children are asked to talk about books that have been read to them, to ask and answer questions, and sometimes to retell or summarize the story.
- A good program provides a classroom environment in which children are surrounded by written language that is meaningful to them, such as posters with the children's names and birthdays, name labels on desks or storage cubbies, and word labels on objects in the classroom ("door," "blackboard," "map," etc.). Children also

have their attention drawn to familiar uses of written language in everyday life, such as signs, recipes, invitations, and announcements of upcoming events.

- A good program develops children's knowledge of the alphabet so that early in the kindergarten year they can readily recognize and name the letters, both capital (uppercase) and small (lowercase). Children are also given regular practice throughout the year in writing all the letters. (See the handwriting chart on pages 7–8.)

- A good program explicitly and systematically develops children's phonemic awareness, that is, the understanding that the sound of a word can be thought of as a string of smaller, individual sounds. For example, you can say and hear the word "mat" as a single sound; but if you say it very slowly, you can recognize three separate sounds: *mmm-aaa-ttt*.

Here are accepted models for writing the small (lowercase) letters and the capital (uppercase) letters. Your child's school may offer models that differ in minor details from these; if so, follow the school's models. The directional arrows indicate a sequence of pencil strokes to follow. Have your child begin at the dot and form small letters in one continuous stroke, without lifting the pencil from the paper (except to cross the "f," "t," and "x" and to dot the "i" and "j").

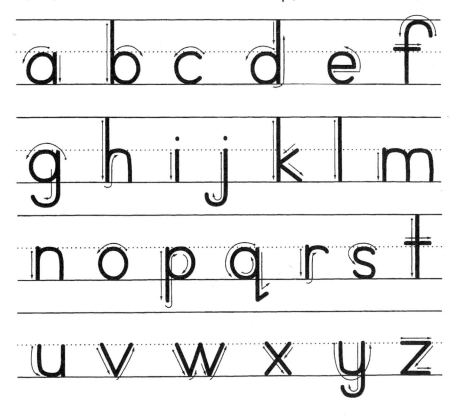

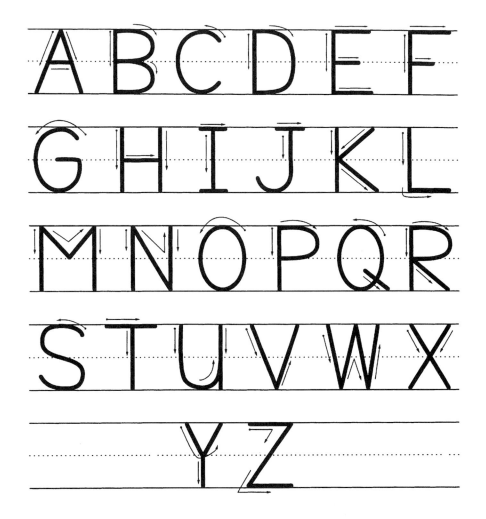

Here is how a left-handed child should hold a pencil.

Here is how a right-handed child should hold a pencil.

- Through a variety of listening activities, a good program regularly asks children to pay attention to the sounds in words so that they begin to distinguish the smaller units of sound that make up a single word. For example, they may be asked to clap along with the separate syllables as they say a word: "happy—hap[clap]-py[clap]; yesterday—yes[clap]-ter[clap]-day[clap]." They may be asked to listen to the syllables of a word, then blend them together and say the whole word aloud; for example, they hear "pic-nic," and say "picnic." They are asked to listen to and compare words, and recognize similarities and differences in their sounds. For example, does "mat" rhyme with "mate"? Does "mat" rhyme with "bat"? Does "moon" start with the same sound as "soon"? Does "moon" start with the same sound as "mop"?

  At the kindergarten level, these are initially listening activities, not accompanied by written letters or words. This initial fine-tuning of listening skills develops children's ability to hear and identify the sequences of sounds in spoken words, and leads directly to the decoding skills necessary to "sound out" words when reading or writing. (*Parents take note:* Some schools discourage children from sounding out words and urge them instead to "guess" the words based on "clues" from pictures or what's going on in the story. This is a serious mistake. Children need to learn a systematic, reliable way to figure out words they don't know, and this can come only from giving them explicit instruction in the code of our written language.)

- A good program provides a solid understanding of the basic principle underlying our written language—the *alphabetic principle*: that the sounds we hear in words are represented by letters written from left to right. Individual letters represent specific sounds, and groups of letters may also be combined to form specific letter-sound patterns (such as the letters "ch" in "check," "chick," and "chimp"). While there is no single universally accepted sequence for teaching the letter-sound patterns of the English language, a good kindergarten program gives children regular practice with the initial consonant letter-sound patterns (for example, the *mmm* sound made by the letter "m" in "mitten," or the *sss* sound made by the letter "s" in "sun"), and at least some of the short vowel letter-sounds (for example, the sound made by the letter "a" in "apple" and the letter "o" in "olive"). For more examples, see the typical "Letter-Keyword Chart" pictured on page 11.

- Whatever sequence a school follows, it is important that the instruction be systematically organized to make *explicit* the letter-sound patterns and present them in a way that builds logically and sequentially, *not* in a haphazard or occasional fashion. Phonics instruction is most effective when it is regular, if not daily, with one skill building on another and with plenty of practice and review.

- As children master individual letter-sound patterns and become able to sound out words like "bat," "cat," "ham," and "Sam," a good program provides phonetically controlled reading materials. These are simple stories written in a controlled vocabulary that corresponds to the letter-sound patterns a child has been taught in preparation for reading the story. For example, after being taught some consonants and the short *a* sound (as in "apple"), a child might read a simple story about "Mat and Sam" or "Mac and Tab and the Hat." While such stories are of course not literature, they are very helpful in teaching children to read, especially in providing the early and tremendously satisfying experience of being able "to read it all by myself." In preparation for reading these stories, children also need to be taught to recognize some "sight words," words that occur frequently in books but do not conform to the usual letter-sound patterns, such as "of," "was," "do," "the."

Mat sat. Sam sat.

Letter—Keyword Chart

Keywords are often used to introduce children to some basic letter sounds. If your child can recognize and name the letters of the alphabet, then you can use this chart by following this pattern: letter name/keyword/sound. For example, point to the ball and say the letter name, "b," then the word, "ball," then the sound, *buh*. Have your child repeat after you: "m"—"mitten"—*mmm*; "s"—"sun"—*sss*; and so on. Note that for the vowels—"a," "e," "i," "o," "u"—this chart presents keywords with short vowel sounds, as in "igloo" and "olive." You can tell your child that the vowels are special letters that can make different sounds. In some words the vowels have long sounds and "say their own names," for example "a" as in "hay," "e" as in "see," "i" as in "pie," "o" as in "no," and "u" as in "unicorn."

- A good program recognizes that reading and writing reinforce each other, and it provides children with many opportunities to communicate in writing. This means not only having the children copy letters and words in a workbook, or writing down words the teacher dictates—all of which are valuable practice that should take place regularly—but also occasionally having the children write letters, short stories, captions to pictures, and the like. Of course, kindergartners will often want to say more than they can write correctly, so in these cases the children should be encouraged to use phonetic spelling, that is, "to spell it the way they think it sounds" (so that a child may write, for example, "bot" for "boat"). This occasional practice of phonetic spelling is beneficial for kindergartners because it engages them in actively thinking about the sounds of words and how they are represented, and can make them more interested in writing and more willing to put their thoughts on paper. Of course, children need regular practice with conventional, correct spellings as well.

That, in brief, describes some of what a good kindergarten program will do to help *all* children achieve the goal of beginning to read and write on their own by the end of the kindergarten year. Some children will surpass this goal; others may come close but not quite achieve it. But *every* child should receive appropriate instruction, materials, and support, and should be guided and encouraged to do his or her best to meet the goal.

What Parents Can Do to Help

As parents, you can help your kindergartner take the first steps in learning to read and write. Here are a few suggestions:

- Without question, the single most important and helpful thing you can do is to set aside fifteen or twenty minutes regularly, daily if possible, to *read aloud to your child.* See pages 18–21 in this book for suggested activities to accompany reading aloud.
- Engage your child in "playing" with language. Such play can be spontaneous. Tell "knock-knock" jokes. Ask riddles. Try tongue twisters. If you're old enough to remember the popular song, play the "name game" ("Shirley, Shirley, bo-birley, banana-fanna, fo-firley, me-my-mo-mirley, Shirley!") While driving in the car, you can play rhyming games and memory games, recite (or sing) favorite nursery rhymes, and point to different signs and talk about what they mean. While shopping for gro-

ceries, you can help your child cross items off a list, point to labels and talk about what they mean, and engage in impromptu word games: "Here's a *can* of beans. Let's think of words that rhyme with *can*."

- Help your child make the connection between oral and written language by encouraging her to dictate words for you to write: "You say it and I'll write it." You can start by asking her to dictate something short, such as a title for a drawing she has done. Encourage her to watch as you repeat aloud, word for word, what she has said while you simultaneously print the words. Once you've printed the whole title, reread what you've written while pointing to each word.

- Later, you can encourage your child to dictate something longer, like a story. You can ask him to tell the story of something he has experienced (a birthday party, going to the park or zoo, visiting a relative, baking cookies) or a "made-up" adventure (such as "My Day with a Dragon"). Or you can ask him to retell a favorite story that you have read to him. He may want to look at the book's illustrations to help guide his retelling.

- You can send an important message about the value you place on reading and writing by talking with your child about the schoolwork she brings home. Set aside time to look at her papers with her. Be supportive; praise the effort and don't worry about the errors, such as the inevitable misspelled words. (In school, the teacher should be observing your child's progress and working to correct any consistent pattern of errors.)

Suggested Resources

The resources recommended here are meant to complement, not substitute for, the basal readers and associated materials that schools use to teach reading and writing. Our suggestions are directed to parents, though some teachers may find these additional resources helpful as well, especially if their school has adopted a philosophy or set of materials that neglects the systematic early teaching of decoding skills and the conventions of written language.

The following list is intended to help you get started in locating a few of the many good resources available. There are *many* phonics materials available from many sources; in recommending a few here, we do not mean to exclude others. The recommendations here are for materials that are time-tested and/or readily available, generally at a reasonable cost, and usable by those without special training in the teaching of reading and writing.

Besides the books suggested below, other useful supplies are generally available from teacher supply stores and some toy stores:

- magnetic letters and letter flash cards.
- letter-picture cards (cards with simple pictures and a corresponding letter, for example, the letter "a" with a picture of an apple) and word-picture cards.
- simple bingo or lotto games to practice recognizing letters and words.
- workbooks to practice handwriting.
- alphabet and "first words" activity books.
- computer software for teaching the alphabet, letter sounds, and words. Popular programs, appropriate for children from about three to six years old, include *Alphabet Blocks* and *Beginning Reading* (Sierra On-Line); *Bailey's Book House* (Edmark); *Kid Phonics* (Davidson); and *Reader Rabbit* (Levels 1 and 2) and *Reader Rabbit's Interactive Reading Journey* (The Learning Company).

Alphabet books

(*Note:* Alphabet books are appropriate for *preschool*-age children. We list them here because kindergartners still enjoy them and benefit from them. There are dozens of good alphabet books; here are just a few favorites.)

A Was Once an Apple Pie by Edward Lear, illustrated by Julie Lacome (Candlewick Press, 1992). This favorite alphabet jingle, a delight to read aloud, is accompanied here by colorful illustrations that evoke paper cutouts and patchwork quilts.

Alphabears: An ABC Book by Kathleen Hague, illustrated by Michael Hague (Henry Holt, 1984). Cute, old-fashioned bears—can any child resist?

Chicka Chicka Boom Boom by Bill Martin and John Archambault (Scholastic, 1989). This is a bouncy rhyming book about the alphabet, fun to read aloud, fun to look at, fun to chime in all together with the refrain (identified in the title).

I Spy: An Alphabet in Art by Lucy Micklethwait (Greenwillow, 1992). An unusual alphabet book that asks children to search two-page illustrations for objects that begin with each letter.

On Market Street by Arnold Lobel, illustrated by Anita Lobel (Greenwillow/Mulberry, 1981). A boy goes on a shopping spree through the letters of the alphabet in this elaborate and dazzling alphabet book.

Other resources

Bob Books; More Bob Books; Even More Bob Books by Bobby Lynn Maslen (Bob Books Publications/Scholastic, 1976). These three sets of little books might especially appeal to parents whose children are showing signs of interest in reading on their own.

The books—occasionally whimsical, quirky, and fun—offer cute stories and line drawings that verge on silly but which most children will probably like for that very reason. The books begin with short words and simple consonant sounds, and go on through the three sets to introduce new sounds in a nicely sequenced fashion.

The Cat in the Hat; Green Eggs and Ham; One Fish Two Fish Red Fish Blue Fish by Dr. Seuss (Random House). These are just a few of many beginner books with lots of rhyming words and repetition. Read them aloud over and over. As your child grows familiar with them, he is likely to chime in on such lines as "I do not like them, Sam-I-Am!" If he is ready to read these on his own, that's great—but do not expect it of a kindergartner. Read aloud and enjoy, and check your library for more books designated as "Beginning or Easy Readers."

Dover Publications, 31 East 2nd Street, Mineola, NY 11501. Dover produces many attractive and inexpensive activity books, including many alphabet activity books. Write and request a Children's Book Catalog.

Educators Publishing Service (EPS), 31 Smith Place, Cambridge, MA 02138-1000. This mail-order company has many good teacher-created resources, including such favorites as the *Primary Phonics* series of workbooks and storybooks (described below). Call 800-225-5750 for a catalog.

Primary Phonics Workbooks and Storybooks by Barbara Makar (Educators Publishing Service). These five sets of workbooks and coordinated readers have simple line drawings for many short stories using words with short vowels, long vowels, r-controlled vowels, and other vowel combinations in a carefully controlled sequence. Taken as a whole, they form a fairly comprehensive phonics program, more than most parents are likely to undertake at home (unless, of course, you are homeschooling). For kindergartners, the *Primary Phonics Consonant Lessons Workbook* and the first set of storybooks, which focus on short vowels, might be used at home to complement reading instruction in school. The storybooks have a more traditional look and feel to them than the *Bob Books* (see above). *Primary Phonics* is only one of many sets of phonics materials available from Educators Publishing Service (address above). Call 800-225-5750 for a catalog.

Ladybug Magazine. Colorful, attractive artwork illustrates each issue of this monthly magazine for children about four to six years old, with good read-aloud stories, simple poems, and some simple texts for beginning readers. Many libraries carry the magazine. For subscription information, write to Cricket Magazine Group, 315 Fifth Street, Peru, IL 61354; or call 800-827-0227.

Ready . . . Set . . . Read: The Beginning Reader's Treasury and *Ready . . . Set . . . Read—and Laugh! A Funny Treasury for Beginning Readers*, compiled by Joanna Cole and Stephanie Calmenson (Doubleday, 1990; 1995). Two nicely illustrated collections containing stories, poems, riddles, and word games by well-known writers like Arnold Lobel and Eve Merriam. For most kindergartners, these books will be good to read aloud. But they are also good books to turn to for the child who is growing more confident as a reader and ready for challenges beyond phonetically controlled texts.

Literature

INTRODUCTION: WORLDS OF MEANING

There is one simple practice that can make a world of difference for your kindergartner: *read aloud to your child often*, daily if possible. Reading aloud opens the doors to a world of meaning that most children are curious to explore but cannot enter on their own.

In reading aloud, you can offer your child a rich and varied selection of literature, including poetry, fiction, and nonfiction. Good literature brings language to life and offers children new worlds of adventure, knowledge, and humor.

Kindergartners enjoy traditional rhymes and fairy tales, like those found in the following pages. Even as adults, we find bits and pieces of fairy-tale lore entering our language, as when a sportscaster refers to the triumph of an underdog team as "a Cinderella story," or when a successful businessman is described as having "a Midas touch."

For children, fairy tales can delight and instruct, and provide ways of dealing with the darker human emotions, like jealousy, greed, and fear. As G. K. Chesterton observed, fairy tales "are not responsible for producing in children fear, or any of the shapes of fear. . . . The baby has known the dragon intimately ever since he had an imagination. What the fairy tale provides for him is a St. George to kill the dragon." And, as the celebrated writer of children's tales, Wanda Gag, wrote in 1937, "a fairy story is not just a fluffy puff of nothing . . . nor is it merely a tenuous bit of make believe. . . . Its roots are real and solid, reaching far back into man's past . . . and into the lives and customs of many people and countries." Whatever the geographical origin of the traditional tales we tell here—Africa, Japan, Europe, America, etc.—the stories have universal messages and lasting appeal across cultures and generations.

There are also, of course, many good books for young children by modern and contemporary writers, such as Dr. Seuss, Maurice Sendak, Bill Martin, Jr., Verna Aardema, Shirley Hughes, Richard Scarry, Jack Prelutsky, Rosemary Wells, and many others. Your local library has a treasury of good books, and you might want to consult the lists of recommended works in such guides as:

Books That Build Character by William Kilpatrick et al. (Simon and Schuster/Touchstone, 1994)

Books to Build On: A Grade-by-Grade Resource Guide for Parents and Teachers (Dell, 1996)

The New Read-Aloud Handbook by Jim Trelease (Penguin Books, 1995)
The New York Times Parent's Guide to the Best Books for Children by Eden Ross Lipson
(Times Books, revised and updated 1991)

Beyond stories and poems, you can share appropriate works of nonfiction with your child. Kindergartners are fascinated by illustrated books that explain what things are and how they work, by biographies of famous people when they were children, by books about animals and how they live.

Read-Aloud Activities

Try to set aside a regular time for reading aloud, a time free from other obligations or distractions (including the television, which must be off). When you read aloud, don't feel embarrassed about hamming it up a bit. Be expressive; try giving different characters different voices.

If your child is not used to hearing stories read aloud, you may want to begin by reading some poems or some of the shorter selections in this book. If your child starts to squirm as you read longer stories, take a break from reading and get your child involved: have him look at a picture, or ask him some questions, or ask him to tell you what he thinks about what has happened so far, or have him draw a picture to go with the part of the story you've read.

When you read aloud, most of the time your child will be involved in the simple pleasure of listening. At other times you can involve your child in some additional activities to encourage comprehension and interest. Remember, these activities are not tests. Use them with a gentle touch; relax, have fun together.

- Let your child look through the book before you read it. Let him skim the pages and look at pictures.
- Direct your child's attention to the book's title page. Point to the author's name and read it as written, for example, "Written by Maurice Sendak." If the book is illustrated, also read the illustrator's name, for example, "Illustrated by Trina Schart Hyman." Discuss what the words "author" and "illustrator" mean, and what authors and illustrators do (see also pages 49 and 91 of this book). As you read more and more books, talk with your child about her favorite authors or illustrators. Look in the library for more works by your child's favorite authors and illustrators.
- Sometimes let your child pick the books for reading aloud. If your child has picked a book or books from the library, she may soon learn the lesson that "you can't tell a

book by its cover." If you begin a book that she has chosen and she expresses dislike or lack of interest, don't force her to finish hearing it. Just put the book aside with the understanding that "maybe we'll like this better later."

- As you read, run your finger below the words as you say them. This will help your child associate spoken words with written words, and also expose him to the left-to-right direction of print. In rereading a selection, you can direct your child's attention to individual words as you say them aloud. This helps give your child a sense of words as individual units of speech and thought. Occasionally you can try reading a short sentence aloud, pronouncing each word very distinctly, and then asking your child how many words are in the sentence.

- After reading a story, discuss the *sequence* of events. "Can you tell me what happened first? What did he do next?" You can draw three or four simple pictures representing scenes in the story, then ask your child to arrange the pictures in the proper sequence as she retells the story.

- After reading a poem or a story or a segment of a longer book, help your child *recall details* by asking questions. Keep in mind the five W's: Who? What? When? Where? Why? For example, after reading "Jack and Jill": Who went up the hill? Why? What happened to Jack? To Jill? (Maintain a playful, conversational tone; this is not a test!)

- Engage your child in a discussion of the story by asking questions that go beyond recall of details and take her into interpretation. For example: "Why did all the other ducks make fun of the ugly duckling? How do you think he felt when they made fun of him?"

- Children often have favorite books that they want to hear again and again. Occasionally, when you reread a beloved and familiar story, pause and let your child supply the next word or words from memory. For example, when you say the words of the Big Bad Wolf—"Little pig, little pig, let me come in!"—let him continue: "Not by the hair of my chinny chin chin."

- Help your child memorize a favorite nursery rhyme.

- Act out a story or scenes from a story. Your child doesn't need to memorize a set script; she can use her own language to express a character's thoughts. A few simple props can help: paper bags for masks, old shirts for costumes, a broomstick for a horse—all can be transformed by your child's active imagination.

Familiar and Favorite Poems

PARENTS: Here you will find a selection of traditional Mother Goose rhymes and other favorite poems. Children delight in hearing them read aloud, and they will enjoy and take pride in learning a few of their favorite rhymes by heart.

We also suggest some activities to go along with the poems. By playing with rhyming words, your child can sharpen her awareness of the sounds of spoken words. The activities are for speaking aloud; your child is not expected to read any words.

Activities for Poetry

- Read a rhyming poem aloud to your child. Then reread it and emphasize the rhyming words. Read the poem again and ask your child to "fill in the blank" with the rhyming word. For example:

    "Jack be nimble, Jack be quick.
    Jack jump over the candle _____." ("stick")

- Read a rhyming poem to your child several times. As you talk about the poem, give your child one member of a pair of rhyming words from the poem, then ask what rhymes with it. For example, after many readings of "Twinkle, Twinkle, Little Star," you might ask, "What rhymes with star?" ("are") And, "What rhymes with high?" ("sky") Later you can extend this activity by asking, for example, "Can you think of any other words that rhyme with star?" ("far," "bar," "car," etc.)

- Ask your child to be the "mistake finder." Say a poem that has grown familiar through repetition, but replace a rhyming word with a "wrong" word that doesn't rhyme. Tell your child to clap when she hears a mistake. (Be sure to use a familiar poem so your child can do this activity successfully.) For example:

    "One, two,
    Buckle my shoe;
    Three, four,
    Shut the gate."

At times you can also ask her to correct your "mistake" by supplying the right rhyming word.

- Ask your child to repeat a word you say and then say a rhyming word. For example:

You say: cat
Child says: cat, bat

Here are some words to start with:

cat	bed	map	pig	fan
game	toe	pin	fun	bug
cake	bump	boat	light	ball

You can extend this activity by asking your child to say as many words as he can think of that rhyme with the word you say.

SOME POETRY COLLECTIONS FOR CHILDREN

The Random House Book of Mother Goose, edited and illustrated by Arnold Lobel (Random House, 1986)

The Random House Book of Poetry for Children, edited by Jack Prelutsky (Random House, 1983)

The Rooster Crows: A Book of American Rhymes and Jingles, edited by Maud and Miska Petersham (Macmillan/Aladdin, 1987)

Side by Side: Poems to Read Together, edited by Lee Bennett Hopkins (Simon and Schuster, 1988)

Sing a Song of Popcorn: Every Child's Book of Poems, edited by Beatrice Schenk de Regniers (Scholastic, 1988)

Time to Rise

by Robert Louis Stevenson

A birdie with a yellow bill
Hopped upon the window-sill.
Cocked his shining eye and said:
"Ain't you 'shamed, you sleepy-head?"

Happy Thought

by Robert Louis Stevenson

The world is so full
of a number of things,
I'm sure we should all
be as happy as kings.

Hickory, Dickory, Dock

Hickory, dickory, dock,
The mouse ran up the clock.
The clock struck one,
The mouse ran down,
Hickory, dickory, dock.

Early to Bed

by Benjamin Franklin, from *Poor Richard's Almanac*

Early to bed and early to rise,
Makes a man healthy, wealthy,
and wise.

Diddle, Diddle, Dumpling

Diddle, diddle, dumpling, my son John,
Went to bed with his stockings on;
One shoe off, and one shoe on,
Diddle, diddle, dumpling, my son John.

A Diller, a Dollar

A diller, a dollar,
A ten o'clock scholar
What makes you come so soon?
You used to come at ten o'clock
But now you come at noon!

Hey, Diddle, Diddle

Hey, diddle, diddle,
The cat and the fiddle,
The cow jumped over the moon;
The little dog laughed
To see such sport,
And the dish ran away with the spoon.

Little Bo Peep

Little Bo Peep has lost her sheep,
And can't tell where to find them;
Leave them alone, and they'll come home,
Wagging their tails behind them.

Little Boy Blue

Little Boy Blue,
Come blow your horn,
The sheep's in the meadow,
The cow's in the corn;
But where is the boy
Who looks after the sheep?
He's under a haystack,
Fast asleep.

Baa, Baa, Black Sheep

Baa, baa, black sheep,
Have you any wool?
Yes, sir, yes, sir,
Three bags full.
One for the master,
And one for the dame,
And one for the little boy
Who lives down the lane.

One, Two, Buckle My Shoe

One, two,
Buckle my shoe;
Three, four,
Shut the door;
Five, six,
Pick up sticks;
Seven, eight,
Lay them straight;
Nine, ten,
A big fat hen;
Eleven, twelve,
Dig and delve;
Thirteen, fourteen,
Maids a-courting;
Fifteen, sixteen,
Maids in the kitchen;
Seventeen, eighteen,
Maids in waiting;
Nineteen, twenty,
My plate's empty.

Rain, Rain, Go Away

Rain, rain, go away,
Come again another day.

It's Raining, It's Pouring

It's raining, it's pouring,
The old man is snoring.
He bumped his head
And went to bed,
And he couldn't get up in the morning.

April Rain Song

by Langston Hughes

Let the rain kiss you.

Let the rain beat upon your head with silver
   liquid drops.

Let the rain sing you a lullaby.

The rain makes still pools on the sidewalk.

The rain makes running pools in the gutter.

The rain plays a little sleep-song on our roof
   at night—

And I love the rain.

The More It Snows

by A. A. Milne

The more it

SNOWS-tiddely-pom,

The more it

GOES-tiddely-pom

The more it

GOES-tiddely-pom

On

Snowing.

And nobody

KNOWS-tiddely-pom,

How cold my

TOES-tiddely-pom

How cold my

TOES-tiddely-pom

Are

Growing.

My Nose

by Dorothy Aldis

It doesn't breathe;
It doesn't smell;
It doesn't feel
So very well.

I am discouraged
With my nose:
The only thing it
Does is blows.

Roses Are Red

Roses are red,
Violets are blue,
Sugar is sweet,
And so are you.

Mary, Mary, Quite Contrary

Mary, Mary, quite contrary
How does your garden grow?
With silver bells, and cockle
   shells,
And pretty maids all in a row.

Tommy

by Gwendolyn Brooks

I put a seed into the ground
And said, "I'll watch it grow."
I watered it and cared for it
As well as I could know.

One day I walked in my back yard,
And oh, what did I see!
My seed had popped itself right out,
Without consulting me.

Jack and Jill

Jack and Jill went up the hill
To fetch a pail of water;
Jack fell down and broke his
   crown,
And Jill came tumbling after.

Jack Be Nimble

Jack be nimble,
Jack be quick,
Jack jump over
The candlestick.

There Was a Little Girl

There was a little girl
Who had a little curl
Right in the middle of her forehead;
When she was good, she was very, very good,
And when she was bad, she was horrid.

Little Miss Muffet

Little Miss Muffet
Sat on a tuffet,
Eating her curds and whey;
Along came a spider,
Who sat down beside her
And frightened Miss Muffet away.

Georgie Porgie

Georgie Porgie, pudding and pie,
Kissed the girls and made them cry;
When the boys came out to play,
Georgie Porgie ran away.

Humpty Dumpty

Humpty Dumpty sat
on a wall,
Humpty Dumpty had
a great fall.
All the king's horses,
And all the king's men,
Couldn't put Humpty
together again.

Little Jack Horner

Little Jack Horner
Sat in a corner,
Eating his Christmas pie;
He put in his thumb,
And pulled out a plum,
And said, "What a good boy am I!"

Mary Had a Little Lamb

from the poem by Sarah Josepha Hale

Mary had a little lamb,
    Its fleece was white as snow;
And everywhere that Mary went,
    The lamb was sure to go.

It followed her to school one day,
    That was against the rule;
It made the children laugh and play
    To see a lamb at school.

And so the teacher turned it out,
    But still it lingered near,
And waited patiently about
    Till Mary did appear.

"Why does the lamb love Mary so?"
    The eager children cry.
"Why, Mary loves the lamb, you know,"
    The teacher did reply.

Hot Cross Buns!

Hot cross buns!
Hot cross buns!
One a penny, two a penny,
Hot cross buns!

If you have no daughters,
Give them to your sons;
One a penny, two a penny,
Hot cross buns!

Simple Simon

Simple Simon met a pieman
Going to the fair;
Said Simple Simon to the pieman,
"Let me taste your ware."

Says the pieman to Simple Simon,
"Show me first your penny";
Says Simple Simon to the pieman,
"Indeed, I have not any."

Old Mother Hubbard

Old Mother Hubbard
Went to the cupboard
To get her poor dog a bone,
But when she got there,
The cupboard was bare,
And so her poor dog had none.

Old King Cole

Old King Cole
Was a merry old soul,
And a merry old soul was he;
He called for his pipe,
And he called for his bowl,
And he called for his fiddlers three.

Sing a Song of Sixpence

Sing a song of sixpence,
    A pocket full of rye;
Four and twenty blackbirds
    Baked in a pie.

When the pie was opened,
    The birds began to sing;
Wasn't that a dainty dish
    To set before the king?

The king was in his counting-house
    Counting out his money;
The queen was in the parlor
    Eating bread and honey.

The maid was in the garden
    Hanging out the clothes,
Along came a blackbird
    And pecked off her nose.

Ladybug, Ladybug

Ladybug, ladybug,
Fly away home,
Your house is on fire,
And your children are gone.

Three Blind Mice

Three blind mice,
Three blind mice,
See how they run!
See how they run!
They all ran after the farmer's wife,
Who cut off their tails with a carving
   knife,
Did you ever see such a sight in your life,
As three blind mice?

Jack Sprat

Jack Sprat could eat no fat,
His wife could eat no lean,
And so between the two of them
They licked the platter clean.

Seesaw, Margery Daw

See-Saw, Margery Daw
Jenny shall have a new master;
She shall have but a penny a day,
Because she can't work any faster.

A. RACKHAM

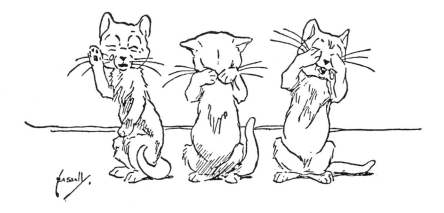

The Three Little Kittens
by Eliza Lee Follen

Three little kittens lost their mittens

And they began to cry,

"Oh, mother dear,

We very much fear

That we have lost our mittens."

"Lost your mittens!

You naughty kittens!

Then you shall have no pie!"

"Mee-ow, mee-ow, mee-ow."

"No, you shall have no pie."

"Mee-ow, mee-ow, mee-ow."

The three little kittens found their mittens

And they began to cry,

"Oh, mother dear,

See here, see here!

See, we have found our mittens!"

"Put on your mittens,

You silly kittens,

And you may have some pie."

"Purr-r, purr-r, purr-r,
Oh, let us have the pie!
Purr-r, purr-r, purr-r."

The three little kittens put on their mittens,
And soon ate up the pie;
"Oh, mother dear,
We greatly fear
That we have soiled our mittens!"
"Soiled your mittens!"
You naughty kittens!"
Then they began to sigh,
"Mee-ow, mee-ow, mee-ow."
Then they began to sigh,
"Mee-ow, mee-ow, mee-ow."

The three little kittens washed their mittens,
And hung them out to dry;
"Oh, mother dear,
Do not you hear
That we have washed our mittens?"
"Washed your mittens!
Oh, you're good kittens!
But I smell a rat close by,
Hush, hush! Mee-ow, mee-ow."
"We smell a rat close by,
Mee-ow, mee-ow, mee-ow."

There Was an Old Woman Who Lived in a Shoe

There was an old woman who lived
    in a shoe,
She had so many children she didn't know
    what to do;
She gave them some broth without
    any bread;
And spanked them all soundly and put them
    to bed.

Star Light, Star Bright

Star light, star bright,
First star I see tonight,
I wish I may, I wish I might,
Have the wish I wish tonight.

Aesop's Fables

A fable is a special kind of story that teaches a lesson. People have been telling some fables over and over for hundreds of years. It is said that many of these fables were told by a man named Aesop (EE-sop), who lived in Greece a very, very long time ago.

Aesop knew bad behavior when he saw it, and he wanted people to be better. But he knew that we don't like to be told when we're bad. That is why many of his fables have animals in them. The animals sometimes talk and act like people. In fact, the animals behave just as well and just as badly as people do. That's because, even when a fable is about animals, it is really about people. Through these stories about animals, Aesop teaches us about how we should act as people.

At the end of the fable, Aesop often tells us a lesson we should learn. The lesson is called the *moral* of the story.

Here are four of Aesop's fables. The first three end by telling you the moral of the story. But the last one does not tell you the moral. When you read the last fable (about "The Grasshopper and the Ants"), talk about what you think the moral of that story is.

The Dog and His Shadow

One day a dog was carrying home a piece of meat, which he held in his mouth. On his way he had to cross a bridge over a stream. As he crossed, he happened to look down into the water. There he saw his shadow, like a reflection in a mirror. He thought his reflection was another dog with a bigger piece of meat than his own. He decided he wanted the other dog's meat, so he opened his mouth and barked. But as he did, the piece of meat in his mouth dropped into the water and was gone forever.

MORAL: If you are greedy, you may lose everything.

The Lion and the Mouse

One day a little mouse was running along when he happened to run across the paws of a big sleeping lion. This woke the lion—and the lion did not like to be waked up before he was ready! The lion was very angry at being disturbed, and he grabbed the mouse in his big paw. He was just about to swallow him when the mouse cried out, "Please, kind sir, I didn't mean to disturb you. If you will let me go, I will be grateful to you forever. And if I can, I will help *you* some day."

The lion laughed a big laugh. How, he thought, could such a little creature as a mouse ever help so great a creature as a lion? All the same, the lion decided to let the mouse go.

Not long after, the mouse was running along when he heard a great roaring nearby. He went closer to see what the trouble was, and there he saw the lion, caught in a hunter's net. The mouse remembered his promise to the lion, and he began gnawing the ropes of the net, and kept gnawing until he had made a hole big enough so that the lion could get free.

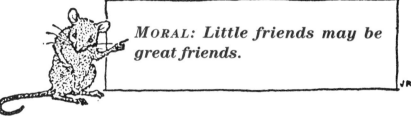

MORAL: **Little friends may be great friends.**

The Hare and the Tortoise

There once was a hare who was always boasting about how fast he could run. One day he said to the other animals, "I'm so fast that no one can beat me. I dare anyone here to a race."

The tortoise said quietly, "I will race you."

"You!" laughed the hare. "That's a joke! Why, I could run circles around you all the way."

"Save your boasting until you've won," said the tortoise. "Shall we race?"

So the race began. The hare darted almost out of sight at once, and very soon he was far ahead of the tortoise, who moved along at a steady, even pace.

The hare knew he was far ahead, so he stopped and said, "I think I'll take a little nap. When I wake up, I can zip ahead of the tortoise without even trying."

So the hare settled into a nice sleep. And he was still asleep when the tortoise passed by. And when the hare finally woke up, he looked ahead, and what did he see? The tortoise was just then crossing the finish line to win the race!

MORAL: Slow and steady wins the race. (Being the most talented doesn't always mean you'll come out on top. Hard, steady work is very important, too.)

The Grasshopper and the Ants

In a field on a fine summer's day, a grasshopper was hopping about, singing and dancing and enjoying himself.

Nearby a group of ants was hard at work. They had built their house underground, and they were filling it with food to last them through the long cold winter ahead.

"Why not come and play with me?" asked the grasshopper. "Why bother about winter? We have plenty of food now. Come, leave your work. Now's the time to dance and sing."

But the ants paid no attention to the grasshopper. They kept working hard, all day and every day.

But not the grasshopper. All summer long, while the ants worked, he jumped about the field, and danced, and sang. Sometimes he'd sit for hours and listen to the humming of the bees, or watch the butterflies flitting about, or take long, lazy naps in the warm sun. And when he woke up he would sing this song:

"The summertime's the time for me,

For then I'm happy as can be.

I watch the butterflies and bees,

I do whatever I may please.

I do no work the livelong day,

I pass the time in fun and play.

Oh, summertime's the time for me,

For I'm as happy as can be!"

Yes, the grasshopper was a happy fellow—but he never thought about the future.

One day the grasshopper woke up and felt a chill in the air. Then he saw the leaves turn red, gold, and brown, and begin to fall from the trees. Then the days kept getting cooler, and soon the grasshopper saw no butterflies or bees, and the fields where he liked to sing and dance turned bare and hard.

Now the cold days of winter were upon him, and the grasshopper was freezing and hungry. He came to the ants' house and knocked on the door.

"What do you want?" asked the ants.

"May I come in and share your food?" asked the grasshopper.

"What did you do all summer?" asked the ants. "Didn't you put away some food to use now?"

"No," said the shivering grasshopper. "I was too busy singing and dancing."

"So," said the ants, "you sang and danced all summer while we worked. Well, now you can sing and dance while we eat!"

And as the hungry grasshopper walked away, he sadly sang this song:

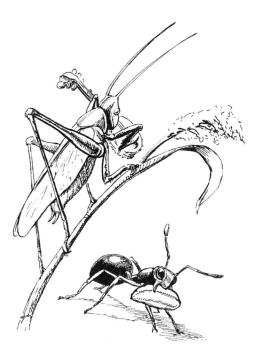

"I did no work all summer long
   And now I know that I was wrong.
   It isn't fair for me to play
   While others work the livelong day.
   Next time I'll work as well as dance,
   Then I'll be ready, like the ants!"

What do you think the moral of this story is?

Stories

The Three Little Pigs

Once upon a time there was an old mother pig with three little pigs. They lived happily together, but then hard times came and there was not enough to go around. So the three little pigs set out to make their own way in the world.

The first little pig met a man with a bundle of straw, and said to him, "Please, sir, give me that straw so that I may build a house."

The man gave him the straw, and the little pig built a house with it.

But soon, along came a big, bad wolf, and he knocked at the door and said, "Little pig, little pig, let me come in."

And the pig answered, "Not by the hair of my chinny chin chin."

So the wolf said, "Then I'll huff, and I'll puff, and I'll blow your house down!" And he huffed, and he puffed, and he blew the house down, and he ate up the little pig.

The second little pig met a man with a bundle of sticks, and said to him, "Please, sir, give me those sticks so that I may build a house."

The man gave him the sticks, and the little pig built a house with them.

Then along came the wolf, and he said, "Little pig, little pig, let me come in."

"Not by the hair of my chinny chin chin."

"Then I'll huff, and I'll puff, and I'll blow your house down!" And he huffed, and he puffed, and he puffed and he huffed, and at last he blew the house down, and he ate up the little pig.

The third little pig met a man with a load of bricks, and said to him, "Please, sir, give me those bricks so that I may build a house."

The man gave him the bricks, and the little pig built a house with them.

Then along came the wolf, and he said, "Little pig, little pig, let me come in."

"Not by the hair of my chinny chin chin."

"Then I'll huff, and I'll puff, and I'll blow your house down!" Well, he huffed, and he puffed, and he huffed and he puffed, and he puffed and he huffed, but he could *not* blow that house down. And when he found that all his huffing and puffing was for nothing, he said, "Little pig, I know where there is a nice apple tree."

"Where?" asked the pig.

"Down at Merry Garden," said the wolf. "If you will be ready tomorrow morning, I will come and get you, and we will go together and pick some apples."

"Very well," said the pig. "I will be ready. What time do you want to go?"

"Oh, at five o'clock," said the wolf.

Well, the next morning the little pig got up at *four* o'clock, an hour before the wolf said he would come. And the little pig picked the apples and came back before the wolf arrived.

This made the wolf very angry indeed, and

he declared that he *would* eat up the little pig, and that he would come down the chimney to get him. When the little pig saw what was happening, he made a blazing fire, and put over it a big pot full of water. The wolf came down the chimney and—*splash!*—fell in the burning hot water, and that was the end of the wolf. And the little pig lived happily ever after.

Goldilocks and the Three Bears

Once upon a time there were three bears who lived in a house in the woods.

Papa Bear was a great big bear. Mama Bear was a middle-sized bear. And Baby Bear was a wee little bear.

Each bear had a bowl for his porridge. Papa Bear had a great big bowl. Mama Bear had a middle-sized bowl. And Baby Bear had a wee little bowl.

One morning Mama Bear made some nice porridge. She put it into the bowls and set them on the table. But the porridge was too hot to eat. So, to give the porridge time to cool, the bears all went out for a walk.

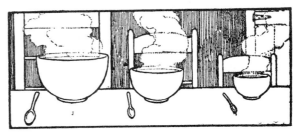

While they were gone, a little girl named Goldilocks came to the house.

First she looked in at the window.

Then she peeped in at the door.

Then she knocked, but no one answered.

Now, you might think that she should turn right around and go home. But no—Goldilocks walked right into the house!

She was very glad when she saw the three bowls of porridge. First she tasted the porridge in the great big bowl, but it was too hot.

Then she tasted the porridge in the middle-sized bowl, but it was too cold.

Then she tasted the porridge in the wee little bowl, and it was just right. She liked it so much that she ate it all up!

Then Goldilocks saw three chairs and decided to sit down to rest. First she sat in Papa Bear's great big chair, but it was too hard.

Then she sat in Mama Bear's middle-sized chair, but it was too soft.

Then she sat in Baby Bear's wee little chair, and it was just right.

She sat and sat till suddenly—*plump!*—the bottom of the chair fell out.

Goldilocks picked herself up and looked for another place to rest. She went upstairs and found three beds.

First she lay down on Papa Bear's great big bed, but it was too high.

Then she lay down on Mama Bear's middle-sized bed, but it was too low.

So she lay down on Baby Bear's wee little bed, and it was just right.

She covered herself up, and then fell fast asleep.

About this time the three bears came back from their walk. They went straight to the table, and suddenly Papa Bear cried out in his great big voice, "SOMEONE HAS BEEN EATING MY PORRIDGE!"

Then Mama Bear looked at her dish, and she said in her middle-sized voice, "SOMEONE HAS BEEN EATING MY PORRIDGE!"

Then Baby Bear looked at his dish, and he said in his wee little voice, "*Someone has been eating my porridge, and has eaten it all up!*"

Then the three bears began to look all around them. Papa Bear said in his great big voice, "SOMEONE HAS BEEN SITTING IN MY CHAIR!"

Then Mama Bear said in her middle-sized voice, "SOMEONE HAS BEEN SITTING IN MY CHAIR!"

Then Baby Bear said in his wee little voice, "*Someone has been sitting in my chair and has broken the bottom out of it!*"

The three bears ran upstairs to their bedroom.

Papa Bear said in his great big voice, "SOMEONE HAS BEEN LYING IN MY BED!"

Then Mama Bear said in her middle-sized voice, "SOMEONE HAS BEEN LYING IN MY BED!"

Then Baby Bear looked at his bed, and he cried out in his wee little voice, "*Someone has been lying in my bed—and here she is!*"

Baby Bear's squeaky little voice startled Goldilocks, and she sat up wide awake.

When she saw the three bears, she gave a cry, and jumped up, and ran away as fast as she could. And to this day, the three bears have never seen her again.

The Three Billy Goats Gruff

Once upon a time there were three billy goats who were all named "Gruff."

The three Billy Goats Gruff longed to go up a hillside covered with thick green grass. They wanted to eat that grass, and so grow nice and fat.

To get to the hillside, they had to cross a brook. Over the brook was a bridge. And under the bridge lived a mean, ugly troll.

Now, the first to cross the bridge was the Little Billy Goat Gruff.

"Trip-trap, trip-trap!" went the bridge.

"WHO'S THAT TRIP-TRAPPING OVER MY BRIDGE?" roared the troll.

And the tiny goat said in a wee small voice, "It is only I, Little Billy Goat Gruff. And I'm going to the hillside to make myself fat."

"Oh-ho!" said the troll. "I am coming to gobble you up."

"Oh, please don't eat me," said the Little Billy Goat Gruff. "I'm too little, yes I am. Wait a bit until my brother comes. He's much bigger."

"Well, be off with you!" said the troll.

Soon the Middle Billy Goat Gruff came to cross the bridge.

"*Trip-trap! Trip-trap! Trip-trap!*" went the bridge.

"WHO'S THAT TRIP-TRAPPING OVER MY BRIDGE?" roared the troll.

And the goat said in a not-so-small voice, "It is only I, Middle Billy Goat Gruff, and I'm going to the hillside to make myself fat."

"Oh-ho!" said the troll. "I am coming to gobble you up."

"Oh no, don't eat me. Wait till my brother comes along. He's *much* bigger."

"Very well; be off with you!" said the troll.

And just then up came the great Big Billy Goat Gruff.

"*TRIP-TRAP! TRIP-TRAP! TRIP-TRAP!*" went the bridge, for the Big Billy Goat Gruff was so heavy that the bridge creaked and groaned under him.

"WHO'S THAT TRIP-TRAPPING OVER MY BRIDGE?" roared the troll.

And a deep, loud voice boomed, "IT IS I, BIG BILLY GOAT GRUFF."

"Oh-ho!" said the troll. "I am coming to gobble you up."

"Well, then, come and try it!" said the Big Billy Goat Gruff.

So the troll climbed up on the bridge.

And the Big Billy Goat Gruff rushed at that troll, and he bumped him and thumped him, and he danced and pranced all over him, till the troll rolled off the bridge into the water, never to be seen again.

After that, the Big Billy Goat Gruff went to the hillside, where he joined his brothers. And they all three got so fat they were scarcely able to walk home again.

> *Snip, snap, snout,*
> *This tale's told out.*

PARENTS: This is a great story to act out. You don't need any props, and with only two children, or a child and an adult, you can do all the parts just by changing your voice a bit. Try it!

Momotaro: Peach Boy

(A folktale from Japan)

Once upon a time, in a small village in the country of Japan, there lived a kind old man and his good, honest wife.

One fine morning the old man went to the hills to cut firewood, while his wife went down to the river to wash clothes. The old woman was scrub, scrub, scrubbing the clothes on a stone when something strange came floating down the river. It was a peach—a very big, round peach! She picked it up— *oof!*—and carried it home with her, thinking to give it to her husband to eat when he returned.

The old man soon came down from the hills, and the good wife set the peach before him. She lifted a knife and brought it close to the big peach when suddenly a little voice cried out, "Stop! Don't hurt me." And as the old man and woman looked on in amazement, the peach split apart and out came a baby boy.

The old man and woman took care of the baby. They were kind to him and raised him as their own son. They called him Momotaro, a fine name, as it means "Peach Boy."

Momotaro grew up to be strong and brave—which was a good thing for the people in the village, because for many years they had been attacked and robbed by the *oni*, who were mean and greedy monsters. Everyone in the village was afraid of the *oni*.

One day, when Momotaro had grown to be a young man, he said to his parents, "I am going to the island of the *oni* monsters who steal from our village. I will bring back what they have stolen, and stop them from harming us ever again. Please make some millet cakes for me to take along on my journey."

The old man and woman were worried, but they made the millet cakes for Momotaro. And so he started on his way.

He had not gone far when he met a dog. "Where are you going, Momotaro?" asked the dog.

"I am going to the island of the *oni* monsters to bring back what they have stolen from my village," said Momotaro.

"And what are you carrying in that sack?" asked the dog.

"I'm carrying the best millet cakes in all Japan," said Momotaro. "Would you like one?"

"Mmm, yes!" said the dog. "And I will come with you to the island of the *oni* monsters. I will help you."

The dog ate the millet cake, then he and Momotaro walked on. They soon met a monkey.

"Where are you going, Momotaro?" asked the monkey.

"I am going to the island of the *oni* monsters to bring back what they have stolen from my village," said Momotaro.

"I will come with you," said the monkey. And Momotaro thanked him and gave him a millet cake.

Now the three of them walked along, when soon they heard a call: "Momotaro, Momotaro! Where are you going?"

Momotaro looked around to see who was calling. A big pheasant flew out of a field and landed at his feet. Momotaro told him that he and his new friends were going to the island of the *oni* monsters. "Then I will come with you and help you," said the pheasant. Momotaro thanked him and gave him a millet cake.

So Momotaro went on his way, with the dog, the monkey, and the pheasant following close behind.

They soon came to the island of the *oni* monsters. The monsters lived in a big stone castle. The pheasant flew over the high castle walls. He swooped down and used his sharp beak to peck, peck, peck at the *oni* monsters. The monsters shouted, and screamed, and ran about in confusion.

Just then Momotaro, with the help of the dog and monkey, broke through the gate of the castle. Oh, what a battle! The dog and monkey scratched and bit the monsters' legs. Momotaro slashed left and right with his sharp sword. Many of the monsters ran away, and soon Momotaro captured their king. When they saw their king held prisoner, the other *oni* monsters bowed down before Momotaro.

Momotaro ordered the monsters to collect all the treasure they had stolen. They brought out beautiful gowns and jewels, and gold and silver, and much more besides.

And so Momotaro took all the riches back to the village. The village was never again bothered by the *oni* monsters. And Momotaro and the old man and the old woman lived in peace and plenty for the rest of their lives.

WHAT IS AN ILLUSTRATOR?

Do you like to draw? Meet Gail McIntosh: she loves to draw. In fact, drawing is her job. She's an artist—a special kind of artist, called an *illustrator*.

An illustrator makes the pictures—the illustrations—that go in a book. Illustrations can be drawings, paintings, even paper cutouts.

Gail drew the pictures for the story "Momotaro: Peach Boy." She also drew and painted many other illustrations in this book (you can see some on these pages: 45, 52, 66, 83, and 89).

Before she draws a picture, Gail begins by imagining, by making pictures in her mind. When someone reads you a story, do you sometimes see pictures of what's happening in your mind? That's what Gail does: she sees pictures in her mind—and then she draws them!

"What I do," says Gail, "is draw, draw, and draw." And even when she's not drawing, she's thinking about drawing. If someone asks her to illustrate a story, she has to think

Gail McIntosh, illustrator.

about what she's going to draw. She has to make choices, such as, "How mean should the troll in 'The Three Billy Goats Gruff' look?"

When you sit down with a book that has pictures, find out who the illustrator is. And the next time you draw or paint, think about those "pictures in your mind" from some of your favorite stories.

The Little Red Hen

Once a hardworking little red hen lived on a farm with a dog, a cat, and a pig. One day she decided to make bread.

"Who will help me cut the wheat to make my bread?" she asked.

"Not I," said the dog.

"Not I," yawned the cat.

"Not I," grunted the pig.

"Then I will do it myself," said the little red hen.

When she had cut the wheat, the little red hen asked, "Who will help me take the wheat to the miller for grinding?"

"Not I," growled the dog.

"Not I," hissed the cat.

"Not I," snorted the pig.

"Then I will do it myself," said the little red hen.

When the wheat had been ground into flour, the little red hen asked, "Who will help me make the flour into bread dough?"

"Not I," sighed the dog.

"Not I," whined the cat.

"Not I," sniffed the pig.

"Then I will do it myself," said the little red hen.

When she had mixed the dough, the little red hen asked, "Who will help me bake the bread?"

"Not I," muttered the dog.

"Not I," murmured the cat.

"Not I," grumbled the pig.

"Then I will do it myself," said the little red hen.

And so, all by herself, she baked a fine loaf of bread. "Now," said the little red hen, "who will help me eat the bread?"

"I will!" barked the dog.

"I will," purred the cat.

"I will!" grunted the pig.

But the little red hen said, "No you won't. I cut the wheat all by myself. I took it to the miller all by myself. I mixed the dough and baked it all by myself. And now I shall eat the bread—all by myself!"

Chicken Little

One fine morning Chicken Little went out to the woods. As she walked along, an acorn fell on her head.

"Oh dear me!" she cried. "The sky is falling. I must go and tell the king!"

On the way she met Henny Penny. "Henny Penny, the sky is falling!" said Chicken Little.

"How do you know?" asked Henny Penny.

"A piece of it fell on my poor head," said Chicken Little.

"Then let us go and tell the king!" said Henny Penny.

So Henny Penny and Chicken Little went along until they met Goosey Loosey.

"Goosey Loosey, the sky is falling!" said Henny Penny.

"How do you know?" said Goosey Loosey.

"A piece of it fell on my poor head," said Chicken Little.

"Then let us go and tell the king!" said Goosey Loosey.

So Goosey Loosey, Henny Penny, and Chicken Little went along until they met Ducky Lucky.

"Ducky Lucky, the sky is falling!" said Goosey Loosey.

"How do you know?" said Ducky Lucky.

"A piece of it fell on my poor head," said Chicken Little.

"Then let us go and tell the king!" said Ducky Lucky.

So Ducky Lucky, Goosey Loosey, Henny Penny, and Chicken Little went along until they met Turkey Lurkey.

"Turkey Lurkey, the sky is falling!" said Ducky Lucky.

"How do you know?" said Turkey Lurkey.

"A piece of it fell on my poor head," said Chicken Little.

"Then let us go and tell the king!" said Turkey Lurkey.

So they went along until they met Foxy Loxy.

"Foxy Loxy, the sky is falling!" said Turkey Lurkey.

"Oh, is that so?" said sly Foxy Loxy. "If the sky is falling, you'd better keep safe in my den, and I will go and tell the king."

So Chicken Little, Henny Penny, Goosey Loosey, Ducky Lucky, and Turkey Lurkey followed Foxy Loxy into his den. And they never came back out again.

Little Red Riding Hood

(A tale from the Brothers Grimm)

There was once a sweet little girl who was loved by all who knew her, but most of all by her grandmother, who could not do enough for her. Once she sent her a cloak with a red velvet hood, and the little girl was so pleased with it that she wanted to wear it always. And so she came to be called Little Red Riding Hood.

One day her mother said to her, "Little Red Riding Hood, I want you to go and see your grandmother, for she is feeling sick. Take her these cakes we baked yesterday; they will do her good. Go quickly, and mind that you stay on the path, and do not stop along the way. When you go into Grandmother's house, don't forget to say 'Good morning' instead of looking all around the house."

"I will do just as you say, Mother," promised Little Red Riding Hood, and she started on her way.

Her grandmother lived in a house in the wood, a half hour's walk from the village. Little Red Riding Hood had only just entered the wood when she came upon a wolf. But she did not know what a wicked animal he was, so she was not afraid of him.

"Good morning, Little Red Riding Hood," said the wolf.

"Good morning, Mr. Wolf," she answered kindly.

"And where are you going so early?" he asked.

"To my grandmother's house."

"And what's that you're carrying?"

"A little basket of cakes, for you see, Grandmother is sick and this will make her feel better."

"And where does your grandmother live?"

"In the wood, a little ways from here, in a cottage under three big oak trees," said Little Red Riding Hood.

"Mmmm," said the wolf as he thought to himself, "What a tender young morsel this little girl is. But she's not enough for a meal. I must manage somehow to eat both her and her grandmother."

He walked along beside Little Red Riding Hood for a while and then said, "Why, look at all the pretty flowers. Why don't you stop to pick some of them? You're hurrying along as if you were late for school, yet the birds are singing and everything is so pleasant here in the wood."

Little Red Riding Hood looked up and saw the sunlight dancing in the leaves of the trees. She saw the lovely flowers around her, and she thought, "I am sure Grandmother would be pleased if I took her a bunch of fresh flowers." So she left the path, and went out of her way into the wood to pick some flowers. Each time she picked one, she saw others even prettier farther on, and so she strayed deeper and deeper into the wood.

As for the wolf, he hurried straight to Grandmother's cottage. He knocked on the door.

"Who's there?" called Grandmother.

"It is I, Little Red Riding Hood," said the wolf in as gentle a voice as he could.

"Oh, lift the latch and come in, dear," said the old woman, "for I am too weak to get out of bed."

So the wolf lifted the latch, swung open the door, pounced upon grandmother, and gobbled her up in one mouthful! Then he dressed himself in one of the old woman's nightgowns and nightcaps. With a wicked grin, he lay down on the bed and pulled up the covers.

Meanwhile, Little Red Riding Hood, having picked all the flowers she could carry, finally found her way back to the path. She walked on quickly until she came to Grandmother's house. She was surprised to find the door open, and as she stepped inside, she felt very strange. "Oh dear," she said to herself, "this morning I was so glad to be going to see my grandmother. Why do I feel so frightened now?"

She took a deep breath and called out, "Good morning." But there was no answer. She went up to the bed. There she saw, as she thought, her grandmother, but she could see only her head, for the wolf had pulled the covers up under his chin and had pulled the nightcap down to his eyes. Little Red Riding Hood thought her grandmother looked strange indeed.

"Oh, Grandmother," she said, "what big ears you have!"

"The better to hear you with, my dear," said the wolf.

"And Grandmother, what big eyes you have!"

"The better to see you with, my dear."

"And Grandmother, what big teeth you have!"

"The better to *eat* you!" cried the wolf as he sprang out of bed and swallowed Little Red Riding Hood in one big gulp.

Now the wolf, feeling stuffed, lay down on the bed and went to sleep, and began to snore *very* loudly. A hunter who was passing by the cottage thought, "My, the old woman sounds terrible! I'd better look inside and check on her." He walked inside and saw the wolf. "Ah, at last I've found you, you wicked beast!" he cried. He was just about to shoot the wolf when he noticed his big belly. So he took a pair of scissors and—*snip, snip*—cut the wolf's belly open.

Out jumped Little Red Riding Hood! "Oh, I've been so afraid!" she said. "It's so dark inside the wolf."

Then out came Grandmother, still alive.

Little Red Riding Hood fetched some large stones, and the hunter filled the wolf's belly with them. When the wolf woke up, he tried to run away, but the stones were so heavy that he sank down and fell dead.

Little Red Riding Hood sat down with her grandmother and the hunter, and together they ate the cakes Little Red Riding Hood had brought. And Little Red Riding Hood said to herself, "After this, I shall always do as my mother tells me, and I shall never leave the path again, not even to pick the pretty flowers."

PARENTS: The Brothers Grimm version of this tale ends with the moral of "never leaving the path." But you might come across other popular versions of this story (based on the retelling by the seventeenth-century French tale-teller Charles Perrault), in which the story ends with the wolf gobbling up Little Red Riding Hood!

The Story of Jumping Mouse

(A Native American legend of the Northern Plains people, retold by John Steptoe)

Once there was a young mouse who lived in the brush near a great river. During the day he and the other mice hunted for food. At night they gathered to hear the old ones tell stories. The young mouse liked to hear about the desert beyond the river, and he got shivers from the stories about the dangerous shadows that lived in the sky. But his favorite was the tale of the far-off land.

The far-off land sounded so wonderful the young mouse began to dream about it. He knew he would never be content until he had been there. The old ones warned that the journey would be long and perilous, but the young mouse would not be swayed. He set off one morning before the sun had risen.

It was evening before he reached the edge of the brush. Before him was the river; on the other side was the desert. The young mouse peered into the deep water. "How will I ever get across?" he said in dismay.

"Don't you know how to swim?" called a gravelly voice.

The young mouse looked around and saw a small green frog.

"Hello," he said. "What is swim?"

"This is swimming," said the frog, and she jumped into the river.

"Oh," said the young mouse, "I don't think I can do that."

"Why do you need to cross the river?" asked the frog, hopping back up the bank.

"I want to go to the far-off land," said the young mouse. "It sounds too beautiful to live a lifetime and not see it."

"In that case, you need my help. I'm Magic Frog. Who are you?"

"I'm a mouse," said the young mouse.

Magic Frog laughed. "That's not a name. I'll give you a name that will help you on your journey. I name you Jumping Mouse."

As soon as Magic Frog said this, the young mouse felt a strange tingling in his hind legs. He hopped a small hop and, to his surprise, jumped twice as high as he'd ever jumped before. "Thank you," he said, admiring his powerful new legs.

"You're welcome," said Magic Frog. "Now step onto this leaf and we'll cross the river together."

When they were safely on the other side, Magic Frog said, "You will encounter hardships on your way, but don't despair. You will reach the far-off land if you keep hope alive within you."

Jumping Mouse set off at once, hopping quickly from bush to bush. The shadows circled above, but he avoided being seen. He ate berries when he could find them and slept only when he was exhausted. Days passed. Though he was able to travel quickly, he began to wonder if he'd ever reach the other side of the desert. He then came upon a stream that coursed through the dry land. Under a large berry bush he met a fat old mouse.

"What strange hind legs you have," said the fat mouse.

"They were a gift from Magic Frog when she named me," said Jumping Mouse proudly.

"Humpf," snorted the fat mouse. "What good are they?"

"They've helped me come this far across the desert, and with luck they'll carry me to the far-off land," said Jumping Mouse. "But now I'm very tired. May I rest here a while?"

"Indeed you may," said the fat mouse. "In fact, you can stay forever."

"Thank you, but I'll stay only until I'm rested. I've seen the far-off land in my dreams and I must be on my way as soon as I'm able."

"Dreams," said the fat mouse scornfully. "I used to have such dreams, but all I ever found was desert. Why go jumping about the desert when everything anyone needs is right here?"

Jumping Mouse tried to explain that it wasn't a question of need, but something he felt he had to do. But the fat mouse only snorted again. Finally Jumping Mouse dug a hole and curled up for the night.

The next day the fat mouse warned him to stay on this side of the stream. "A snake lives on the other side," he said. "But don't worry. He's afraid of water, so he'll never cross the stream."

Life was easy beneath the berry bush, and Jumping Mouse was soon rested and strong. He and the fat mouse ate and slept and then slept and ate. Then one morning, when he went to the stream for a drink, he caught sight of his reflection. He was almost as fat as the fat old mouse!

"It's time for me to go on," thought Jumping Mouse. "I didn't come all this way to settle down under a berry bush."

Just then he noticed that a branch had gotten caught in the narrow of the stream. It spanned the water like a bridge—now the snake could cross! Jumping Mouse hurried back to warn the fat mouse. But the mousehole was empty, and there was a strange smell in the air. Snake. Jumping Mouse was too late. "Poor old friend," he thought as he hurried away. "He lost hope of finding his dream and now his life is over."

Jumping Mouse traveled throughout the night, and the next morning he saw that he had reached a grassy plain. Exhausted, he hopped toward a large boulder where he could rest in safety. But as he got closer, he realized the boulder was an enormous, shaggy bison lying in the grass. Every once in a while it groaned.

Jumping Mouse shivered at the terrible sound. "Hello, great one," he said bravely. "I'm Jumping Mouse and I'm traveling to the far-off land. Why do you lie here as if you were dying?"

"Because I am dying," said the bison. "I drank from a poisoned stream, and it blinded me. I can't see to find tender grass to eat or sweet water to drink. I'll surely die."

Jumping Mouse was sad to see so wondrous a beast so helpless. "When I began my journey," he said, "Magic Frog gave me a name and strong legs to carry me to the far-off land. My magic is not as powerful as hers, but I'll do what I can to help you. I name you Eyes-of-a-Mouse."

As soon as he had spoken Jumping Mouse heard the bison snort with joy. He heard but he could no longer see, for he had given the bison his own sight.

"Thank you," said Eyes-of-a-Mouse. "You are small, but you have done a great thing. If you will hop along beneath me, the shadows of the sky won't see you, and I will guide you to the mountains."

Jumping Mouse did as he was told. He hopped to the rhythm of the bison's hooves, and in this way he reached the foot of the mountains.

"I am an animal of the plains, so I must stop here," said Eyes-of-a-Mouse. "How will you cross the mountains when you can't see?"

"There will be a way," said Jumping Mouse. "Hope is alive within me." He said good-bye to his friend; then he dug a hole and went to sleep.

The next morning Jumping Mouse woke to cool breezes that blew down from the mountain peaks. Cautiously he set out in the direction of the coolness. He had not gone far when he felt fur beneath his paws. He jumped back in alarm and sniffed the air: Wolf! He froze in terror; but when nothing happened he gathered up his courage and said, "Excuse me. I'm Jumping Mouse, and I'm traveling to the far-off land. Can you tell me the way?"

"I would if I could," said the wolf, "but a wolf finds his way with his nose, and mine will no longer smell for me."

"What happened?" asked Jumping Mouse.

"I was once a proud and lazy creature," replied the wolf. "I misused the gift of smell, and so I lost it. I have learned not to be proud, but without my nose to tell me where I am and where I am going, I cannot survive. I am lying here waiting for the end."

Jumping Mouse was saddened by the wolf's story. He told him about Magic Frog and Eyes-of-a-Mouse. "I have a little magic left," he said. "I'll be happy to help you. I name you Nose-of-a-Mouse."

The wolf howled for joy. Jumping Mouse could hear him sniffing the air, taking in the mountain fragrances. But Jumping Mouse could no longer smell the pine-scented breezes. He no longer had the use of his nose or his eyes. "You are but a small creature," said Nose-of-a-Mouse, "but you have given me a great gift. You must let me thank you. Come, hop along beneath where the shadows of the sky won't see you. I will guide you through the mountains to the far-off land."

So Jumping Mouse hopped to the rhythm of the wolf's padding paws, and in this way he reached the far-off land.

"I am an animal of the mountains, so I must stop here," said Nose-of-a-Mouse. "How will you manage if you can no longer see or smell?"

"There will be a way," said Jumping Mouse. He then said good-bye to his friend and dug a hole and went to sleep.

The next morning Jumping Mouse woke up and crawled from his hole. "I am here," he said. "I feel the earth beneath my paws. I hear the wind rustling leaves on the trees. The sun warms my bones. All is not lost, but I'll never be as I was. How will I ever manage?" Then Jumping Mouse began to cry.

"Jumping Mouse," he heard a gravelly voice say.

"Magic Frog, is that you?" Jumping Mouse asked, swallowing his tears.

"Yes," said Magic Frog. "Don't cry, Jumping Mouse. Your unselfish spirit has brought you great hardship, but it is that same spirit of hope and compassion that has brought you to the far-off land. You have nothing to fear, Jumping Mouse. Jump high, Jumping Mouse," commanded Magic Frog. Jumping Mouse did as he was told and jumped as high as he could. Then he felt the air lift-ing him higher still into the sky. He stretched out his paws in the sun and felt strangely powerful. To his joy he began to see the wondrous beauty of the world above and below and to smell the scent of earth and sky and living things.

"Jumping Mouse," he heard Magic Frog call. "I give you a new name. You are now called Eagle, and you will live in the far-off land forever."

The Bremen Town Musicians

(A tale from the Brothers Grimm)

Once upon a time there was a donkey who for many years had carried bags of grain on his back to and from the mill. But at last he grew so old that he could not carry the heavy bags. His master tried to think how he could get rid of his old servant so that he might not have to feed him. The donkey feared what was in his master's mind, so he ran away.

He took the road to Bremen, where he had heard a street band play sweet music, for he thought he could be a musician as well as they.

Soon he came upon an old dog panting for breath, as if he had been running a long way.

"What are you panting for, my friend?" asked the donkey.

"Ah," answered the dog, "now that I am old, and growing weaker every day, I can no longer go to the hunt. My master speaks of getting rid of me, so I have run away."

"Well," said the donkey, "come with me. I am going to be a street musician in Bremen. I can play the flute, and you can play the drum."

The dog was quite willing, and so they both walked on.

Soon they saw a cat sitting in the road with a face as long as three days of rainy weather.

"Now, what's the matter with you, old Tom?" asked the donkey.

"You would be sad," said the cat, "if you were in my place; for now that I am getting old, and my teeth are gone, I cannot catch the mice, and I like to lie behind the stove and purr. They have thrown me out, and, alas, what am I to do?"

"Come with us to Bremen," said the donkey. "I know that you sing well at night, so you can easily be a street musician in the town."

"That is just what I should like to do," said the cat; so she joined the donkey and the dog, and they all walked on together.

By and by, the three musicians came to a farmyard. On the gate stood a rooster, crying "Cock-a-doodle-doo!" with all his might.

"What are you making so much noise for?" asked the donkey.

"Ah," said the rooster, "I heard the cook say that I am to be baked for Sunday dinner. And so I am crowing as hard as I can while my head is still on!"

"Come with us, old Red Comb," said the donkey; "we are going to Bremen to be street musicians. You have a fine voice, and the rest of us are all musical, too."

"I will join you!" said the rooster. And they all four went on together.

They could not reach the town in one day, and as evening came on, they began to look for a place to spend the night.

The donkey and the dog lay down under a large tree. The cat climbed up on one of the branches. The rooster flew to the top of the tree, where he could look all around.

"I see a light from a window," the rooster called to his friends.

"That means there is a house nearby," said the donkey. "Let us ask the people for supper."

"How good a bone would taste!" said the dog.

"Or a nice piece of fish!" said the cat.

"Or some corn!" said the rooster.

So they set out at once and soon reached the house. The donkey, who was the tallest, looked in the window.

"What do you see, old Long Ears?" asked the rooster.

The donkey answered, "I see a table spread with plenty to eat and drink. And robbers are sitting before it having their supper."

"Come down," said the dog, "and we shall think of a way to make the robbers' supper our own."

The four friends talked over what they could do to drive the robbers away. At last they hit upon a plan. This is what they did.

The donkey stood on his hind legs and placed his front feet on the windowsill. The dog stood on the donkey's back. The cat climbed up and stood on the dog's back. And the rooster perched on the cat's head.

Then the donkey gave a signal, and they all began to make their loudest music. The donkey *brayed*, the dog *barked*, the cat *mewed*, and the rooster *crowed*.

The robbers had never before heard such a noise, and thought it must come from witches, or giants, or monsters. They ran as fast as they could to the wood behind the house. Then our four friends rushed in and ate what the robbers had left on the table.

When the four musicians had eaten as much as they could, they were full and ready to sleep. The donkey lay down in the yard; the dog lay behind the door; the cat curled up in front of the fireplace; while the cock flew up to a high shelf. They were all so tired that they soon fell fast asleep.

When all was still and dark, the robber chief sent one of his bravest men back to the house. The man found everything quiet and still, so he went inside. He did not see the cat, and he stepped on her tail. The angry puss flew up, spit at the man, and scratched his face with her sharp claws. It gave the robber so great a fright that he ran for the door, but the dog sprang up and bit him in the leg as he went by.

In the yard the robber ran into the donkey, who gave him a great kick with his hind foot. All this woke the rooster, who cried with all his might, "Cock-a-doodle-doo! Cock-a-doodle-doo!"

The robber ran as fast as his legs could carry him back to his friends.

Gasping for breath, he said, "In that house is a wicked witch, who scratched my face with her long nails. Then by the door stood a man with a knife, who cut me in the leg. Out in the yard was a great giant, who struck me with a huge club. And all the while someone cried out, 'Kill the robber, do! Kill the robber, do!' "

The robbers were filled with fear and ran away as fast as they could. But our four friends liked the little house so well that they stayed there, and as far as I know, they are there to this day.

The Ugly Duckling

(Adapted from the original by Hans Christian Andersen)

It was a lovely summer day in the country. The wheat was yellow, the oats were green, and the hay was stacked in the meadows.

All round the meadows were great forests, and in the middle of the forests lay deep lakes. By the water's edge grew plants with very large leaves, so large that a child could stand under them. Here, a mother duck had chosen to make her nest.

She sat on her eggs, waiting for them to hatch. She was growing tired of waiting. She had been sitting for so long and had so few visitors, because the other ducks preferred to swim around rather than sit among the leaves and quack with her.

At long last the eggs began to crack, one after another. "Cheep! Cheep!" One little head peeped forth, and then another. "Quack! quack!" said the mother duck, and all the little ones stood up as well as they could and peeped about from under the green leaves.

"How big the world is!" cried the little ones—and of course it was big compared to being in an eggshell!

"Do you think this is the whole world?" said their mother. "It reaches far beyond the other side of the garden, to the edge of the wood, where I have never been. Well now, are you all here?" And she looked around and said, "Why, the biggest egg is still in the nest! Oh me, I've been sitting such a long time, and I'm so tired." But, tired as she was, she sat down on the egg.

Just then an old duck swam up and asked, "Well, how are you getting along?"

"This one egg is taking forever!" said the mother duck. "It just won't break. But look at the others! Aren't they the prettiest little ducklings you've ever seen?"

"Let me see the egg that won't break," said the old duck. "Ah yes, believe me, that's a *turkey's* egg. I was tricked by such an egg once myself, and I had such trouble with the little one. I quacked and I scolded, but I just couldn't get him into the water. Yes, that must be a turkey's egg. Just leave it behind and go teach your little ones to swim."

But the mother duck sighed and said, "I've been sitting so long that I may as well stay until the last egg is hatched."

"Do as you please," said the old duck, and away she waddled.

At long last the great egg cracked. "Cheep! Cheep!" said the little one, and out he tumbled—but oh, how big and ugly he was!

"Why, he's not at all like the others," said the mother. "Can it be a young turkey? We shall soon find out. He must go in the water, even if I have to push him in!"

And so the next day—and a beautiful day it was, with the sun shining on the big green leaves—the mother duck took her family down to the water. *Splash!* She went into the water and called to her ducklings, "Quack, quack!" One after another, the little ones jumped right in. The water closed over their heads, but they popped right back up and began swimming. Every one of them floated along pleasantly—even the ugly gray one.

"Why, he's no turkey!" said the mother duck. "See how well he uses his legs, and holds himself so straight. He's my very own duckling, he is. And really, if you look close, he's not so bad-looking after all. Quack, quack! Come, children, I will take you to the farmyard. Stay close to me or someone may step on you. And always look out for the cat!"

As they came to the farmyard, they could hear a horrid noise, a commotion of quacks, honks, hisses, clucks, and gobbles. "Now keep together," said the mother duck, "and bow to the old duck yonder. She is a great lady. Now, bow your necks, children, and say 'Quack.'"

The ducklings did as they were told. But the other ducks looked at them and said, "Just look at that big gray one. How ugly he is! Let's drive him away." And one duck flew at him and bit him on the neck.

"Leave him alone!" cried the mother. "He is doing no harm."

"But he's so big and ugly!" said the other ducks. "We don't like him."

Then the great lady duck spoke up and said, "All of your children are pretty except the one. He has not turned out well. It's a pity you can't hatch him over again."

"Oh," said the mother, "that cannot be, Your Highness. And though he is not handsome, he is a good

child, and a fine swimmer, and I think that, in time, he will grow to look more like the others."

"Well, make yourselves at home, dears," said the old duck.

But the poor ugly duckling, who had come last out of his shell, was bitten, pecked, and teased by the ducks and the hens. Even the turkey puffed himself out like a ship in full sail, and *gobble-gobble-gobbled* till he was red in the face, then charged at the duckling. The poor little thing scarcely knew what to do. He felt so sad, because he looked so ugly, and everyone was laughing at him. Even his brothers and sisters were mean to him, and said unkind things like, "We hope the cat gets you, you ugly thing!"

At last the duckling ran away. He fluttered over the hedges, then on and on he ran, until he came to the marshes where the wild ducks lived. Here he lay the whole night, tired and lonely.

In the morning the wild ducks came to look at the newcomer. "Who are *you?*" they asked. The duckling bowed politely to them, but they rudely responded, "You are really ugly!" The poor duckling—all he wanted was to be left alone to drink a little marsh water.

He lay by the marsh for three days, when he was visited by two wild geese. They were rude as well, and said, "Why, you're so ugly that we like you! Why don't you join us? Not far from here there are some sweet, adorable geese, really lovely maidens. You're so ugly, you'd be a big hit with them!"

Then suddenly—*BANG! BANG!*—shots rang out. The two wild geese lay dead, and the water became red with their blood. *BANG!*—another gun fired, and a whole flock of geese flew up, followed by more and more gunshots from hunters all around the marsh.

Smoke from the guns rose through the trees while the hunters' dogs splashed about in the mud. The little duckling was terrified. He turned his head to hide it under his wing, but then he saw, standing right next to him, a huge dog, with its tongue hanging out of its mouth and its eyes glowing like fire. The dog opened his jaws wide, showing his sharp white teeth, but then—*splash*—he was gone, without touching the duckling at all.

"Well," sighed the duckling, "I should be thankful, I suppose, that I'm so ugly that even the dog won't eat me."

Hours later, when the shooting was over at last, the duckling hurried away from the marsh. He ran over fields and meadows, though the wind was so strong that he had to fight just to move ahead.

In the evening he came to a poor little cottage. The door was crooked, so he could creep inside through an opening. Inside this cottage lived an old woman, with her cat and her hen. The cat could arch its back and purr. The hen laid very good eggs. When

they noticed the duckling, the cat began to purr and the hen cackled and clucked.

Now, the cat and the hen thought they were the most handsome and clever creatures in the world. The duckling did not quite agree, but the hen would not allow him to say so.

"Can you lay eggs? Can you?" the hen asked.

"No," said the duckling.

And the cat spoke up: "Can you arch your back, like this? And can you purr?"

"No."

"Well then, you should just keep quiet when sensible persons are speaking!"

So the duckling sat alone in a corner and felt very sad. But then a thought came to him, a thought of fresh air and sunshine. And he felt such a strong wish to be floating on the water that he couldn't help telling the hen about it.

"What's gotten into you?" clucked the hen. "Where do you get such silly ideas? If you would either lay eggs or purr, you wouldn't have such strange thoughts."

"But it's so glorious to float on the water!" said the duckling. "It's so wonderful to duck your head under, then dive to the bottom."

"You must be crazy!" said the hen. "Do you think I would like to swim? Or ask the cat: he's the most sensible person I know. Do you think he would like to dive down to the bottom of the water? Humph!"

"But you don't understand me," said the duckling.

"Oh, and if we don't understand you, then I would like to know who does," said the hen. "Surely you don't think that you are wiser than we are. If you paid attention, you could learn from us. Now, get busy and lay some eggs or learn to purr!"

"I think," sighed the duckling, "that I shall go back out into the wide world."

"Well then, go!" snapped the hen.

So the duckling went. And he floated on the water, and he plunged under it. But he was lonely, for all the animals would have nothing to do with him because he was so ugly.

Month after month the ugly duckling swam upon the clear water of the great lake. By and by, autumn came. The leaves turned yellow and brown, and the wind caught them and made them dance about. The air was cold, and the clouds were heavy with snow. The poor duckling was cold, lonely, and unhappy.

One evening, just as the sun was setting, a flock of birds rose out of the bushes. Never before had the duckling seen anything so beautiful. Their feathers were white as snow, and they had long, graceful necks. With a strange, wild cry, they spread their splendid wings and soared high, so very high, on their journey away from the cold lake to far-off warmer lands.

The duckling turned round in the water, and stretched his neck to look after them, and let out a cry so loud and strange that he scared himself. He could not stop thinking of these noble, happy birds. They were swans, though the duckling did not know what they were called or where they were going. Still, he loved them as he had never before loved anything. He was not jealous of them, for how could he even wish for such beauty for himself? He would have been happy if the ducks in the farmyard would just put up with him—the poor, ugly duckling.

Winter came on, and it was terribly cold. The duckling had to keep swimming round and round in the water to keep it from freezing. But every night the water froze more and more, till at last the duckling grew so tired that he could only lie still with water freezing around him.

The next morning a farmer passed by and saw the duckling frozen in the lake. He used his wooden shoe to break the ice, then took the duckling home to his wife and children.

The children wanted to play with the duckling, but he feared that they might hurt him, so he flew around and knocked over the milk pail, spilling milk all over the room. The woman screamed and waved her arms, which scared the duckling even more, and he jumped about and flew into a flour tin and a butter tub. The children shrieked and laughed, and tumbled over each other trying to catch him. It was lucky for the duckling that the door stood a little open. He jumped out among the bushes into the snow, and there he lay in a daze.

It would be too sad to tell you about all the hard times the duckling had through the winter.

One day, as he was lying on the marsh, the sun began to shine warm again and the larks began to sing—spring, beautiful spring, had returned!

He stood up and shook his wings. They were stronger than they had ever been, and they lifted him easily. To his great surprise, he found that they carried him quickly to a large garden where the apple trees were in bloom. Then, on a nearby stream, he saw three beautiful swans floating gently on the water. When the duckling saw the lovely birds, he felt a strange sadness.

"I will fly right over to those noble birds," he said. "They may peck me to death because I'm so ugly, but I don't care. It's better to be killed by them than to be bitten by the ducks, pecked by the hens, and have to live through another painful winter."

He flew into the water and swam toward the beautiful creatures. They saw him and swam toward him. He bowed his head low, expecting to be bitten or even killed. But as he looked down, what did he see in the clear water? He saw his own reflection, as though he were looking in a mirror. And he no longer saw an ugly gray bird—for he was himself a swan!

So you see, being born in a duck yard doesn't matter when you've been hatched out of a swan's egg!

Some children came into the garden and threw bread into the water. The smallest child cried out, "Look, there's a new one. He's the nicest of all. He's so young and handsome!" And the old swans bowed their heads before him, which really quite embarrassed the young swan, so that he tucked his head under his wing.

He felt so happy! He remembered how he had been hated and teased, and yet now he heard everyone say that he was the most beautiful of all the beautiful birds. As the sun shone warm and bright, he shook his feathers and stretched his slender neck, and said with all his heart, "Never, ever did I dare even to dream of such happiness, not when I was the ugly duckling!"

Tug-of-War

PARENTS: This is a folktale from Africa. People in different parts of Africa tell it with different small animals—a turtle, a porcupine, a rabbit—as the central character. All versions share a theme (found also in the American Brer Rabbit tales, which have their roots in Africa) of the large, strong characters outwitted by the small, clever ones.

If your child is not familiar with the game of tug-of-war, you may want to describe it before you read this story aloud.

Turtle was small, but he talked big. He loved to boast and brag and say things like, "I'm as powerful as the biggest animals around here, indeed I am. And that includes Elephant and Hippopotamus. That's right: Elephant and Hippopotamus call me 'friend' because I'm as powerful as they are."

One day Elephant and Hippopotamus happened to hear from some of the other animals what Turtle was going around saying. Elephant and Hippopotamus laughed. "So," they said, "Turtle says we call him 'friend'? That's the silliest thing we've ever heard. We don't call him 'friend.' He's so little we don't think of him at all."

And when the animals told Turtle what Elephant and Hippopotamus said, Turtle got mad, very mad. "So, they do not think of me because I'm so small? They do not call me 'friend'?" Well, I'll show them who is really powerful. And they *will* call me 'friend,' just you wait and see!" Then Turtle set off to find Elephant and Hippopotamus.

He found Elephant lying down in the forest. Elephant was big as a mountain; his trunk was long as a river. But Turtle was bold. He walked right up and shouted, "Hey, friend, get up and say hello to your friend."

Elephant looked all around to see where the voice could be coming from. Finally he looked down—*way* down—and spotted Turtle. "Oh, it's you, is it?" said Elephant. "Go away, you small animal of no importance. And watch out who you call 'friend.'"

"I call *you* 'friend' because that's what you are—right, Elephant?"

"Wrong!" rumbled Elephant. "And what is this foolishness I hear, that you claim to be as powerful as I am? Do you dare to think of yourself as equal to me? Don't be stupid, little creature."

"Now, Elephant," said Turtle, "just listen. Yes, I call you 'friend,' and yes, I say we are equal. You think that because you're so much bigger than me, that makes you better. Well, let's have a tug-of-war to find out."

"A tug-of-war?" said Elephant. He laughed so hard the earth shook for miles around. "Why," he said to Turtle, "you haven't got a chance."

"Maybe not, maybe so," said Turtle. "But if you're so sure, what have you got to lose?" Then turtle cut a very long vine and gave one end to Elephant. "Here," said Turtle. "Now, if I pull you down, I am greater. If you pull me down, you are greater. We won't stop tugging until one of us pulls the other over or the vine breaks. And if the vine breaks, we are equal and will call each other 'friend.'"

And Turtle walked off with the other end of the long, long vine until, some time later, he found Hippopotamus bathing in the river.

"Oh, friend, I'm here!" shouted Turtle. "Come out of the water and give your friend a proper greeting, why don't you?"

Hippopotamus could hardly believe his ears. "Don't call *me* 'friend,' you little good-for-nothing!" he bellowed.

"Now hold on, friend Hippo," said Turtle. "You think that because you're so much bigger than me, that makes you better. Well, let's have a tug-of-war to find out. Whoever pulls the other down is greater. We will keep pulling until one of us wins or the vine breaks. And if the vine breaks, we are equal and will call each other 'friend.' "

"You silly turtle, you must have no brain in that little head," said Hippopotamus. "I'll pull you down before you can blink."

"Well, let us see," said Turtle, and he gave Hippopotamus the other end of the long, long vine. "Now I'll go pick up my end," said Turtle, "and when you feel me start tugging, you tug back."

Turtle walked into the forest and picked up the middle of the vine. He gave it a good hard shake. When Hippopotamus felt this, he started to tug. When Elephant felt the tug, he tugged back.

Elephant and Hippopotamus both tugged so mightily that the vine stretched tight. Turtle settled into a comfortable spot and watched for a while as the vine moved just a little bit one way, then just a little the other way. He took out his lunch and munched on his food very slowly, enjoying every bite. Then he yawned and fell asleep.

He woke a couple of hours later, feeling very refreshed from his nap. He looked up to see the vine still stretched tight, and he smiled. Yes, Elephant and Hippopotamus were still pulling with all their might. Neither one could pull the other over.

"I suppose it's about time," said Turtle, and he cut the vine.

When the vine broke, both Elephant and Hippopotamus tumbled down, *WHUMP BUMPITY-BUMP BAM BOOM!*

Turtle went to see Elephant and found him sprawled on the ground, rubbing his head.

"Turtle," said Elephant, "you *are* powerful. You were right, we are equal. I guess that bigger doesn't mean better after all, my, uh, my—*friend.*"

Then Turtle went to see Hippopotamus, who was also sprawled on the ground, rubbing his head.

"So, Turtle," said Hippopotamus, "we are equal after all. You were right, my *friend.*"

From then on, whenever the animals held a meeting, there at the front sat Elephant, Hippopotamus, and Turtle. And they always called each other "friend."

They are friends, yes—but tell me, do you think they are equal?

Cinderella

Once upon a time there was a rich man whose wife lay in bed, very sick. She felt the end of her life drawing near, and she called her only daughter to her bedside. "Dear child," she said, "always be good, and I will look down on you from heaven." Then she closed her eyes and died.

Every day the little girl went to her mother's grave and wept, and she tried always to be good. When the winter came, the snow covered the ground like a white blanket; and when the sun came in the spring and melted it away, the little girl's father married a new wife. And so the little girl had a stepmother—and this was the beginning of a bad time for the little girl.

For you see, the stepmother was the proudest, most disagreeable woman in the land. She had two daughters, who were as proud and hateful as herself. The stepmother could not bear the kind, sweet little girl, who was so unlike her own daughters. She forced her to do the hardest and dirtiest work in the house. The poor girl scoured the dishes, scrubbed the floors, and washed the clothes. When her work was finally done, she would sit, tired and alone, on the hearth by the fireplace, among the ashes and cinders. And so she came to be called "Cinderella."

Cinderella's stepsisters had fine rooms with soft beds and thick carpets and mirrors so large that they might see themselves at full length from head to foot. But poor Cinderella had only a small room in the attic with a wretched straw bed. Yet she bore it all patiently and did not complain to her father, for his new wife ruled him entirely.

Now, it happened one day that the king's son, the prince, announced that he was going to hold a ball. When they heard the announcement, the stepsisters shrieked with excitement. All the young ladies in the kingdom were invited to the palace for a grand evening of dancing and merriment. For days the stepsisters primped in front of their mirrors and talked of nothing but what they would wear.

"For my part," said the older sister, "I shall wear my red velvet dress with lace trimming."

"And I," said the younger sister, "shall have a gold-flowered gown with a diamond belt, quite out of the ordinary!"

And the stepsisters snapped at Cinderella, "You must help us get ready for the ball. Clean our shoes! Comb our hair! Hurry!"

Anyone but Cinderella would have tied their hair in knots, but she helped her stepsisters without complaining. Silently, however, she longed to go to the ball and imagined herself dancing in the arms of the prince.

At last the day came. The stepsisters and their mother left for the palace. Cinderella watched them as long as she could. When she had lost sight of them, she began to cry, so miserable and alone did she feel.

But Cinderella was not alone after all. For she heard a gentle voice ask, "What's the matter, dear?"

She looked up and saw an old woman with a kind face. "I wish—I wish I could—" began Cinderella, but could not finish for all her tears and sobbing.

"You wish to go to the ball—is that it?" said the kind old woman.

"Why, yes!" said Cinderella with surprise.

"Then it shall be so!" said the woman, for she was, you see, Cinderella's fairy godmother. "Now run into the garden," she said to Cinderella, "and bring me a pumpkin."

Cinderella went immediately to the garden, though she could not imagine what a pumpkin had to do with going to the ball. She watched her fairy godmother scoop out the inside of the pumpkin, leaving only the rind, which she then touched with her wand. Instantly the pumpkin turned into a dazzling coach lined with satin!

"Now, dear," said the fairy godmother, "bring me the mousetrap from the house." Cinderella brought the trap, which had six live mice in it. "Open the door of the trap, dear," said the fairy godmother. Then, as each mouse scurried out, she gave it a tap with her wand,

turning them into a fine set of six horses, all a beautiful mouse-colored gray. Next, with a touch of her wand, she turned a big rat into a fat, jolly coachman with long fancy whiskers.

"Well," said the fairy godmother with a smile, "are you pleased? Are you ready to go to the ball?"

"Oh yes!" cried Cinderella. "But . . . must I go in these dirty rags?"

Her godmother laughed and, with a touch of her wand, changed Cinderella's tattered clothes into a glittering gown of gold and silver. And on her feet appeared a pair of glass slippers, the prettiest in the world. Cinderella stepped into the coach. But before she left, her fairy godmother gave her this warning: "Do not stay at the ball after midnight, not even for a moment! When the clock strikes twelve, the coach will once again be a pumpkin; the horses, mice; the coachman, a rat; and your gown, the same old clothes you had on."

Cinderella promised she would leave before midnight. Then, calling out her thanks, away she rode in the coach, feeling happier than she had ever felt before.

At the palace the prince heard that a great princess had arrived, but that nobody knew who she was. So he went to meet her, and gave her his hand, and led her into the great ballroom filled with people. As they entered, a hush fell upon the room. The dancers stopped dancing, the musicians stopped playing: everyone stood still just to look upon the beauty of the unknown newcomer.

The prince asked Cinderella to dance with him. They danced together once, then twice, then again and again. Cinderella's face shone with happiness. Everyone at the ball looked on in admiration—everyone, that is, but the two jealous stepsisters, who glared at the lovely lady, though they had no idea that they were glaring at Cinderella!

Soon a fancy dinner was served, but the prince didn't eat a bit, for he was too busy gazing into Cinderella's eyes. For Cinderella, the music, the dancing, the warm gaze of the prince—all seemed a wonderful dream.

How quickly time slips away when the heart is happy! As Cinderella began to dance again with the prince, she heard the great bell of the palace clock begin to toll: *one . . . two . . . three . . .*

"Oh!" she gasped. "The clock! What time is it?"

The prince answered, "Midnight."

Midnight! Cinderella's cheeks grew pale. She turned and, fast as a deer, ran out of the ballroom, down a long hallway, then down a long staircase. At the foot of the staircase she stumbled: one of her glass slippers fell off! But Cinderella could not stop. Already the clock had sounded its eleventh stroke. As she leapt breathlessly out of the castle into the darkness, she heard the clock sound the last stroke of midnight—and felt her smooth gown turn into the rough cloth of her real clothes.

Her dazzling coach had turned back into a pumpkin, so she ran home alone. When she got there, she was out of breath, but climbed the stairs to her cold attic room. Then she noticed: she was still wearing one glass slipper!

Now, when Cinderella had run from the palace, the prince had raced after her. And though he had not been able to catch her, he did find, at the bottom of the staircase, the glass slipper that had fallen off her foot.

And that is why, the very next morning, the sound of trumpets woke the kingdom, and the prince announced that he would marry the woman whose foot fit the glass slipper. The prince sent men to try the slipper on the foot of every lady in the land.

From house to house they went, trying the slipper on foot after foot. But on one foot the slipper was too long; on another, too short; on another, too wide; on another, too narrow.

And so it went until at last they came to the house of Cinderella and her stepsisters. One by one, the stepsisters squeezed, pinched, and pushed, but the slipper would not fit.

Then, from the shadows, Cinderella stepped forth and said, "Let me see if it will fit me."

"You!" the stepsisters cried. "Go back to the cinders where you belong!"

But one of the prince's men said that he had orders to try the slipper on every maiden in the kingdom. He placed the slipper on Cinderella's foot—and it fit perfectly! The stepsisters' mouths dropped open in astonishment. And they were even more shocked when, from her pocket, Cinderella drew forth the *other* glass slipper.

And now the stepsisters recognized Cinderella as the beautiful lady they had seen at the ball. They threw themselves at her feet and begged her pardon for all of the ways they had treated her so badly. Cinderella was so kindhearted that she forgave them and embraced them.

Later, after Cinderella married the prince, she even invited her stepmother and stepsisters to live at the palace. And there, Cinderella and the prince lived happily ever after.

The Wolf and the Seven Little Kids

(A tale from the Brothers Grimm)

There was once a mother goat who had seven little kids, and she loved them as well as any mother has ever loved her children.

One day she gathered her seven kids around her and said, "Dear children, I must go into the forest to get food for us to eat. While I am away, be on your guard against the wolf. For if he gets inside, he will eat you up, bones and all! The wicked creature often disguises himself. But you can always know him by his rough voice and by the black fur on his paws."

"Don't worry, Mother," said the kids, "we will take good care of ourselves." So the mother goat bleated good-bye and went on her way with a calm mind.

Soon there came a knock at the door, and a voice called out, "Open the door, my dear children. Your mother is back and has brought you each something." But oh, what a rough voice!

"No, we won't open the door!" cried the kids. "Our mother has a sweet, gentle voice, and your voice is rough. You must be the wolf!"

The wolf ran off to a store, where he bought a big lump of a special kind of chalk, which he ate to make his voice soft. Then he came back, and knocked at the door, and called out in a gentle voice, "Open the door, my dear children. Your mother is back and has brought you each something."

But the wolf had put his paws against the window, and the kids could see the black fur.

"No, we won't open the door!" cried the kids. "Our mother's feet do not have black fur. You must be the wolf!"

So the wolf ran to a baker. "Baker," he said, "I have hurt my foot. Spread some dough over it."

And when the baker had coated his paw with dough, the wolf went to the miller. "Miller," he said, "sprinkle some white flour over my paws." The miller said no, for he thought that the wolf must be planning to trick someone. But then the wolf cried, "If you won't do it, I'll eat you up!"

The miller was scared and did as the wolf demanded—which just goes to show how people can be.

For a third time the wolf went to the door, and knocked, and said in a gentle voice, "Open the door, my dear children. Your mother is back and has brought you each something."

"First show us your paws," said the kids. And the wolf put his white, flour-covered paws against the window. "Yes, this must be our dear mother," said the kids, and they opened the door.

In pounced the wolf! The terrified kids tried to hide. The first ran under the table. The second crawled under the bed. The third got into the oven. The fourth ran into the kitchen. The fifth jumped into the cupboard. The sixth ran under a tub. And the seventh climbed inside a big grandfather clock.

But the wolf found them all and gobbled them up—all except the youngest, who was hiding in the grandfather clock.

The wolf, feeling fat and happy, strolled into the forest, lay down under a tree, and fell into a deep sleep.

A short while later the mother goat came home from the woods, and oh! what a sad sight met her eyes. The door stood wide open. Tables and chairs were thrown all about, dishes were broken, quilts and pillows were torn off the beds. She called out for her children, but they were nowhere to be found. She called each one again by name, but no one answered until she called the name of the youngest kid.

"Here I am, Mother," a frightened little voice cried, "here inside the big clock."

And so she helped him out, and heard how the wolf had come and eaten all the other kids. How she cried and cried for her poor children.

Still crying, she wandered outside with her youngest kid, and soon they came to the forest. There they saw the wolf, fast asleep under a tree, snoring so hard that he shook the branches. Then the mother goat saw something moving inside the wolf's body!

"Dear me!" she thought. "Could my poor kids still be alive?" And she sent her youngest kid home to get scissors, needle, and thread. He hurried back, and then the mother goat cut open the wolf. No sooner had she made one snip than out came the head of one of the kids, and then another snip, and another, and one after the other all six of the kids jumped out alive and well—for in his greediness, the wolf had swallowed them whole.

"Now," said the mother to her kids, "fetch some good hard stones, and we will fill his body with them while he's still asleep."

The kids quickly picked up some stones, and they packed them inside the wolf. Then the mother used her needle and thread to sew him up, while he slept and snored all the while.

When the wolf at last awoke, he felt very thirsty. As he walked to the brook, the stones rattled inside him, and he said:

"What is this knocking against my bones?

I thought it was kids but it feels like stones!"

He came to the brook, and he bent over to take a drink. The weight of the stones made him fall—*splash!*—into the water. He sank to the bottom, and was never seen again.

"Hooray, hooray, the wolf is dead!" cried the kids, and they danced around their mother with joy.

King Midas and the Golden Touch

(A myth from ancient Greece, adapted from Nathaniel Hawthorne's *Wonder Book*)

Once upon a time there lived a very rich king whose name was Midas.

Although King Midas lived long ago, he was very like some people today: he was fond of gold. He loved gold more than anything in the world. If he happened to gaze for an instant at the gold-colored clouds of a beautiful sunset, he would wish that the clouds were real gold.

If King Midas loved anything as much or more than he loved gold, it was his little daughter, who was named Marygold. When Marygold would run to meet him with a bunch of buttercups and dandelions, King Midas would say, "Dear child, if these flowers were as golden as they look, then they would be worth picking."

King Midas had once loved flowers. Years before, he had planted a garden full of beautiful, sweet-smelling roses. But now, if he looked at the roses at all, it was only to wonder what they would be worth if each of the rose petals were a thin plate of gold.

Every day King Midas spent many hours locked away in a dark room in the basement of the palace. In this room he stored his treasures. He would go there and carefully lock the door behind him. Then he would take out bags of gold coins, and pour the coins in piles, and run his hands through them. As he did this, he would whisper to himself, "Oh, rich King Midas, what a happy man you are!" But even as he said this, he felt that he was not quite as happy as he might be. For no matter how much he had, he always wanted more.

One day, as Midas was enjoying himself in his treasure room, he looked up and saw a strange young man, who seemed to shine with a golden glow. King Midas knew that he had carefully locked the door so that no one could get into the room, yet here stood this strange young man. And so, King Midas thought, the stranger must have some magic power. But the stranger had a kind smile, so King Midas felt no fear.

Then the stranger spoke to King Midas: "You are a rich man, friend Midas," he said.

"Yes, I have some gold," answered Midas, "but it is not enough."

"What!" cried the stranger. "Then you are not satisfied?"

Midas shook his head.

"What would satisfy you?" asked the stranger.

King Midas imagined one gold mountain heaped on top of another, and another, and another, yet still it seemed not enough. But then a bright idea occurred to him, and he said to the shining stranger, "I wish that everything that I touch may turn to gold."

The stranger smiled and said, "A golden touch! Are you quite sure you would be satisfied then?"

"Yes, I would be perfectly happy, and ask for nothing more," answered Midas.

"Then it shall be as you wish," said the stranger. "Tomorrow, at sunrise, you shall find yourself gifted with the Golden Touch." Then suddenly a great brightness filled the room, causing Midas to squeeze his eyes shut. And when he opened them, the stranger was gone!

The next morning, when the sun had hardly peeped into his room, King Midas jumped out of bed.

He touched a chair. It turned to gold.

He touched the bed and a table, and they were changed to solid, shining gold.

He rushed to put on his shoes, and was amazed to see them turn to gold in his hands.

From his pocket he drew forth a handkerchief, on which his daughter, Marygold, had stitched a design. The cloth had turned to gold, as had his daughter's neat and pretty stitches. And somehow, this change did not quite please King Midas.

But he did not let it trouble him. In great excitement, he opened the door—and was pleased to see the doorknob turn into shining gold—and he ran outside to the garden. He saw many roses in full bloom. He went from bush to bush and touched each one, until every flower, every leaf, and every bud was changed to gold.

Now King Midas was hungry, so he returned to the palace for his breakfast. He lifted his cup of coffee and sipped it, but the instant the liquid touched his lips it turned to gold. He tried to take a bite of a boiled egg, but it, too, turned to gold.

"I don't quite see how I am to get any breakfast!" said King Midas. Then he grabbed a hot potato from his plate and tried to cram it into his mouth and swallow it in a hurry. But the Golden Touch was too quick for him. He found his mouth full, not of soft potato, but of hot metal, which so burned his tongue that he began to dance and stamp around the room.

Just then Midas heard someone crying. He turned to see Marygold enter the room, sobbing as if her heart would break. In her hand she held one of the roses that her father had changed to gold.

"Why, my little lady!" said King Midas. "What is there in this beautiful golden rose to make you cry?"

"Dear father," Marygold answered, "it is not beautiful! It is the ugliest flower that ever grew. As soon as I was dressed this morning, I ran to the garden to gather roses for you. But what do you think has happened? All the beautiful, sweet-smelling roses have been spoiled!"

"My dear little girl," said Midas, who hated to see his daughter sad, "please don't cry." Then he bent down and kissed his child, who he felt was worth a thousand times more than anything he had gained by the Golden Touch.

"My precious Marygold!" he said. But Marygold did not answer.

Alas, what had he done? The moment King Midas's lips touched Marygold's head, her sweet, rosy face turned a glittering yellow color. Little Marygold was a human child no longer, but a golden statue! Yet on her face there remained a questioning look of love and sadness.

King Midas cried out, and wrung his hands, and wished that he were the poorest man in the world if only he could have his daughter back again.

Then he noticed someone standing in the doorway. It was the young stranger, who had appeared the day before in Midas's treasure room. The stranger still shone with a soft glow, and he smiled as he asked the king, "Well, friend Midas, how do you like your Golden Touch?"

"I am very unhappy," said Midas.

"Unhappy?" asked the stranger. "But don't you have everything your heart desired?"

"No," said King Midas. "Gold is not everything. And I have lost all that my heart really cared for."

Then the stranger asked Midas, "Which of these two things do you think is worth the most: the Golden Touch or one cup of clear, cold water?"

"A cup of water!" cried the king.

"Which is worth more?" the stranger asked again. "The Golden Touch or a crust of bread?"

"A crust of bread," said Midas quietly.

"And," the stranger asked again, "the Golden Touch or your own little Marygold?"

"Oh, my child, my dear child!" cried poor Midas. "I would not give one hair of her head even for the power to change this whole big earth into a solid lump of gold!"

"You are wiser than you were, King Midas," said the stranger. "Go, and plunge into the river that runs by your garden. The water will take away the Golden Touch. And fill this pitcher with water, then sprinkle everything you have touched."

King Midas bowed low, and when he lifted his head, the shining stranger was gone. Then the king ran as fast as he could and jumped into the river. He filled the pitcher and ran back to the palace. The first thing he did, as you hardly need to be told, was to sprinkle handfuls of water over the golden figure of little Marygold.

The rosy color came back into her cheeks. She looked in surprise at her father, who was still throwing water on her!

"Father, please stop!" she cried. "See how you have soaked my dress!"

King Midas took Marygold in his arms and kissed her. "Now I am truly happy," he said. "My dear child, you mean more to me than all the gold in the world!"

Snow White

(Adapted from the Brothers Grimm)

It was the middle of winter, and snowflakes were falling like feathers from the sky. A queen sat sewing near a window. The window was framed with a fine black wood called ebony. As the queen sewed, she gazed out the window at the snow. She pricked her finger with the needle, and three drops of blood fell on the snow. And when she saw how bright and red it looked, she said, "Oh, I wish I had a child as white as snow, as red as blood, and as black as the ebony round my window."

It was not long before she had a daughter with skin as white as snow, lips as red as blood, and hair as black as ebony. She was named Snow White, and when she was born, the queen died.

After a year had gone by, the king married again. The new queen was very beautiful, but she was terribly proud. She could not bear to think that anyone might be more beautiful than she. She had a magic mirror, and she would look into it and say:

"Mirror, mirror on the wall,
Who is fairest of us all?"

And the mirror would answer:

"You, Queen, are the fairest of all."

And she was satisfied, for she knew the mirror spoke the truth.

Now, as Snow White grew up, she grew prettier and prettier, and when she was seven years old, she was as beautiful as the day and more beautiful than the queen herself. One day, the queen went to her mirror and said:

"Mirror, mirror on the wall,
Who is fairest of us all?"

And the mirror answered:

"Though you are fair, O Queen, 'tis true,
Snow White is fairer still than you."

When the queen heard this, she turned green with jealousy, and from that moment her heart turned against Snow White. Envy and pride grew in her like weeds, until one day she called for a huntsman and said, "Take the child into the woods so that I may set eyes on her no more. Put her to death, and bring me her heart to prove that you have done it."

The huntsman took the child into the forest. But when he drew his sword, Snow White cried out, "Oh, dear huntsman, let me live. I will go away, far into the woods, and never come back again."

The huntsman took pity on her and said, "Go ahead then, poor child, run away." But he thought that the wild animals of the forest would eat her anyway. A wild boar came running by at just that moment, and the huntsman killed it and took out its heart, which he gave to the queen.

When poor Snow White found herself alone in the woods, she felt afraid and did not know what to do. Even the leaves on the trees seemed to threaten her. She began to run over the sharp stones and through the thorn bushes, and the wild beasts saw her but did not hurt her. She ran as long as her feet would carry her, until at last, as evening fell, she came upon a little house deep in the woods.

She went inside to rest. Inside the house everything was very small, but as neat and clean as possible. By the wall stood seven little beds, side by side, covered with clean white quilts. Nearby there stood a little table, covered with a white cloth and set with seven little plates, seven knives and forks, and seven little drinking cups. Snow White was very hungry, but she didn't want to eat anyone's whole meal, so she took a little porridge and bread from each plate, and a little sip from each cup. After that, she felt so tired that she lay down on one of the beds and fell asleep.

When it was quite dark, the owners of the little house came home. They were seven dwarfs, who worked every day in the mountains, digging with their picks and shovels for gold. When they had lighted their seven candles, they saw that everything in the house was not the same as they had left it.

The first dwarf said, "Who has been sitting in my chair?"

The second said, "Who has been eating from my plate?"

The third said, "Who has taken a bit of my bread?"

The fourth said, "Who has been tasting my porridge?"

The fifth said, "Who has been using my fork?"

The sixth said, "Who has been cutting with my knife?"

And the seventh said, "Who has been drinking from my cup?"

Then the seventh looked around and saw Snow White lying asleep in his bed. He cried out to the others, and they all came running up with their candles, and said, "Oh, goodness gracious! What a beautiful child!" They were so full of joy to see her that they did not wake her.

The next morning Snow White woke and saw the seven dwarfs, and at first she was frightened. But they seemed quite friendly, and asked her what her name was, and she told them. And she told them how her stepmother had wished her to be put to death, and how the huntsman had spared her life, and how she had run the whole day long, until at last she had found their little house.

Then the dwarfs said, "If you will keep house for us, and cook, and wash, and make the beds, and sew, and keep everything tidy, you may stay with us, and we will make sure you have everything you need."

"I'd be happy to," said Snow White. And so she stayed.

Every morning the dwarfs went to the mountain to dig for gold. When the dwarfs were away during the day, Snow White was alone in the house. The dwarfs warned her,

saying, "Don't let anyone in the house! Beware of your stepmother, for she may find out you are here."

And indeed, one day the queen went to her mirror and said:

"Mirror, mirror on the wall,
Who is fairest of us all?"

And the mirror answered:

"O Queen, you are of beauty rare,
But Snow White living in the glen
With the seven little men
Is a thousand times more fair."

The queen gasped. She knew the mirror spoke the truth, and so she knew that the huntsman must have tricked her, and Snow White must be still living. It filled her with rage to think that she was not herself the fairest in the land, so she thought of a plan to get rid of Snow White. She made herself look like an old peddler woman so that no one could tell she was the queen. Then she went across the seven mountains, until she came to the house of the seven dwarfs. She knocked at the door and cried, "Pretty things for sale! Come see my fine silk laces!"

Snow White peeped out the window. "I don't need to be afraid of letting in this good old woman," she thought. So she opened the door and bought the pretty lace.

"Come, child," said the old woman, "and let me lace you up properly." Snow White saw no reason not to trust the woman, so she let her tie the lace around her. But the old woman pulled the lace so tight that it took away Snow White's breath, and she fell down as though she were dead.

"Now," said the queen, "you are no longer the fairest in the land." And she hurried off.

Soon the seven dwarfs came home. They were horrified to see Snow White on the ground, lying so still they thought she must be dead. Then they saw the tight lace around her, and they cut it. She began to breathe again, and little by little she came to life. When she told the dwarfs what had happened, they said, "That peddler woman was the wicked queen! Don't let anyone in when we are away!"

By this time the queen had returned home. She went straight to her mirror and said:

"Mirror, mirror on the wall,
Who is fairest of us all?"

And the mirror answered:

"O Queen, you are of beauty rare,
But Snow White living in the glen
With the seven little men
Is a thousand times more fair."

"Still alive!" cried the queen. "Then I will think of something else to destroy her for sure!" And she used a magic spell to make a poisoned comb. Then she made herself look like a different old woman, and away she went, across the seven mountains, to the home of the seven dwarfs. She knocked at the door and cried, "Pretty things for sale!"

But Snow White said, "Go away. I must not let anybody in."

"Oh," said the old woman, "but surely it's all right for you just to take a look?" And she held up the pretty poisoned comb. And the child liked it so well that without thinking she opened the door.

"Now I shall comb your hair as it *should* be done," said the old woman. As soon as she ran the comb through Snow White's hair, the poison began to work, and the child fell down as though she were dead.

"So, my little beauty, that's the end of you," said the wicked queen as she hurried away.

It was good luck that the seven dwarfs came home soon. They saw the poisoned comb still in her hair, and as soon as they pulled it out, Snow White woke up and told them what had happened. Then they warned her, once again, never to let anyone in the door.

When the queen got home, she went straight to her mirror and said:

"Mirror, mirror on the wall,
Who is fairest of us all?"

And the mirror answered:

"O Queen, you are of beauty rare,
But Snow White living in the glen
With the seven little men
Is a thousand times more fair."

The queen shook with anger. "Snow White shall die," she cried, "even if it costs me my own life!" Then she went to a dark and secret room, and there she made a poisonous apple. It was so big, beautiful, and red that anyone who saw it would long for it, but whoever ate even a piece of it would die. Then the queen made herself look like a poor old woman, and went across the seven mountains to the home of the seven dwarfs. When she knocked at the door, Snow White put her head out the window and said, "I dare not let anybody in. The seven dwarfs told me not to."

"All right, I'll go," said the old woman. "But here, let me give you one of my apples."

"No," said Snow White, "I'm not supposed to take anything."

"Goodness, child, you act like the apples are poisoned!" said the old woman. "Look here, I'll take a bite of this apple myself, all right?"

But the apple had been so cleverly made that all the poison was only in one side—the side that the old woman held out toward Snow White. Snow White looked at the lovely apple, and she wanted it so much that when she saw the old woman take a bite of the other side, she could not resist. She stepped outside, took the apple, and bit it, and fell down dead.

The queen laughed aloud and said, "White as snow, red as blood, black as ebony you may be, but the dwarfs will not be able to help you this time!"

When she went home, she rushed to her mirror and asked:

"Mirror, mirror on the wall,
Who is fairest of us all?"

And the mirror answered:

"You are now the fairest of all."

The dwarfs came home and found Snow White dead. They lifted her up and looked for a lace to cut, or a comb to take out, but they found nothing, and nothing they did helped the child—she was dead. And they sat, all seven of them, around her and wept for three days. And they would have buried her, but still she looked so fresh and alive, with her beautiful red cheeks, that they said, "We cannot hide her away in the ground." So they made a coffin of clear glass, and laid her in it, and wrote her name on it in golden letters, and set it on the mountain, where one of them always kept watch over it. And the birds came and sang sad songs around the coffin of Snow White.

For many years Snow White lay in her coffin, and all the while she never changed, but looked as if she were asleep, with skin as white as snow, lips as red as blood, and hair as black as ebony. Then one day a prince was riding through the woods. He stopped at the dwarfs' cottage. From there he could see the coffin on the mountain, and beautiful Snow White in it. And he said to the dwarfs, "Let me have the coffin, and I will pay you whatever you ask."

But the dwarfs told him they could not part with it, not even for all the gold in the world. Then the prince said, "I beg you to give it to me, for I cannot live without looking upon Snow White." The good dwarfs felt sorry for him and gave him the coffin. The prince called his servants and told them to carry the coffin down from the mountain. As they were carrying it, they stumbled, which gave the coffin, and Snow White in it, a hard shake—and when this happened, the piece of poisoned apple came out of Snow White's throat!

Snow White sat up and cried, "Oh! Where am I?"

The prince, full of joy, said, "You are near me, and I love you more than anything in the world. Come with me to my father's castle and be my bride."

A splendid wedding was held for the prince and Snow White. Snow White's wicked stepmother, the queen, was invited to the wedding. When she had dressed herself in beautiful clothes, she went to her mirror and asked:

> *"Mirror, mirror on the wall,*
> *Who is fairest of us all?"*

And the mirror answered:

> *"Though you are fair, O Queen, 'tis true,*
> *The new bride is fairer still than you."*

And the queen screamed with anger. First she thought she would not go to the wedding. Then she thought she had to go and see the new bride. And when she saw the new bride, she recognized her as Snow White, and she was filled with a terrible rage. In a wild fury, she screamed and stomped her feet and jumped up and down, as though she were wearing red-hot shoes, and then she fell down dead.

Snow White and the prince lived happily ever after.

How Many Spots Does a Leopard Have?

(An African folktale retold by Julius Lester)

One morning Leopard was doing what he enjoyed doing most. He was looking at his reflection in the lake. How handsome he was! How magnificent was his coat! And, ah! The spots on his coat! Was there anything in creation more superb?

Leopard's rapture was broken when the water in the lake began moving. Suddenly Crocodile's ugly head appeared above the surface.

Leopard jumped back. Not that he was afraid. Crocodile would not bother him. But then again, one could never be too sure about Crocodile.

"Good morning, Leopard," Crocodile said. "Looking at yourself again, I see. You are the most vain creature in all of creation."

Leopard was not embarrassed. "If you were as handsome as I am, if you had such beautiful spots, you, too, would be vain."

"Spots! Who needs spots? You're probably so in love with your spots that you spend all your time counting them."

Now there was an idea that had not occurred to Leopard. "What a wonderful idea!" he exclaimed. "I would very much like to know how many spots I have." He stopped. "But there are far too many for me to count myself."

The truth was that Leopard didn't know how to count. "Perhaps you will count them for me, Crocodile?"

"Not on your life!" answered Crocodile. "I have better things to do than count spots." He slapped his tail angrily and dove beneath the water.

Leopard chuckled. "Crocodile doesn't know how to count, either."

Leopard walked along the lakeshore until he met Weasel. "Good morning, Weasel. Would you count my spots for me?"

"Who? Me? Count? Sure. One-two-three-four."

"Great!" exclaimed Leopard. "You can count."

Weasel shook his head. "But I can't. What made you think that I could?"

"But you just did. You said, 'One-two-three-four.' That's counting."

Weasel shook his head again. "Counting is much more difficult than that. There is something that comes after four, but I don't know what it is."

"Oh," said Leopard. "I wonder who knows what comes after four."

"Well, if you ask at the lake when all the animals come to drink, you will find someone who can count."

"You are right, Weasel! And I will give a grand prize to the one who tells me how many spots I have."

"What a great idea!" Weasel agreed.

That afternoon all the animals were gathered at the lake to drink. Leopard announced that he would give a magnificent prize to the one who could count his spots.

Elephant said he should be first since he was the biggest and the oldest.

"One-two-three-four-five-six-seven-eight-nine-ten," Elephant said very loudly and with great speed. He took a deep breath and began again. "One-two-three-four-five-si—"

"No! No! No!" the other animals interrupted. "You've already counted to ten once."

Elephant looked down his long trunk at the other animals. "I beg your pardon. I would appreciate it if you would not interrupt me when I am counting. You made me forget where I was. Now, where was I? I know I was somewhere in the second ten."

"The second ten?" asked Antelope. "What's that?"

"The numbers that come after the first ten, of course. I don't much care for those 'teen' things, thirteen, fourteen, and what have you. It is eminently more sensible to count ten twice and that makes twenty. That is multiplication."

None of the other animals knew what Elephant was talking about.

"Why don't you start over again?" suggested Cow.

Elephant began again and he counted ten twice and stopped. He frowned and looked very confused. Finally he said, "Leopard has more than twenty spots."

"How many more than twenty?" Leopard wanted to know.

Elephant frowned more. "A lot." Then he brightened. "In fact, you have so many more spots than twenty that I simply don't have time to count them now. I have an important engagement I mustn't be late for." Elephant started to walk away.

"Ha! Ha! Ha!" laughed Mule. "I bet Elephant doesn't know how to count higher than twenty."

Mule was right.

"Can you count above twenty?" Leopard asked Mule.

"Who? Me? I can only count to four because that's how many legs I have."

Leopard sighed. "Can anyone count above twenty?" he asked plaintively.

Bear said, "Well, once I counted up to fifty. Is that high enough?"

Leopard shrugged. "I don't know. It might be. Why don't you try and we will see."

Bear agreed. "I'll start at your tail. One-two-three-four-five-six. . . . Hm. Is that one spot or two spots?"

All the animals crowded around to get a close look. They argued for some time and finally agreed that it should only count as one.

"So, where was I?" asked Bear.

"Five," answered Turkey.

"It was six, you turkey," said Chicken.

"Better start again," suggested Crow.

Bear started again and got as far as eleven. "Eleven. That's a beautiful spot right there, Leopard."

"Which one?" Leopard wanted to know.

"Right there. Oh, dear. Or was it that spot there? They're both exquisite. My, my. I don't know where I left off counting. I must start again."

Bear counted as far as twenty-nine this time and then stopped suddenly. "Now, what comes after twenty-nine?"

"I believe thirty does," offered Turtle.

"That's right!" exclaimed Bear. "Now, where did I leave off?"

"You were still on the tail," offered Lion.

"Yes, but was that the twenty-ninth spot, or was it this one here?"

The animals started arguing again.

"You'd better start again," suggested Cow.

"Start what again?" asked Rabbit who had just arrived.

The animals explained to Rabbit about the difficulty they were having in counting Leopard's spots.

"Is that all?" Rabbit said. "I know the answer to that."

"You do?" all the animals, including Leopard, exclaimed at once.

"Certainly. It's really quite simple." Rabbit pointed to one of Leopard's spots. "This one is dark." He pointed to another. "This one is light. Dark, light, dark, light, dark, light." Rabbit continued in this way until he had touched all of Leopard's spots.

"It's simple," he concluded. "Leopard has only two spots—dark ones and light ones."

All the animals remarked on how smart Rabbit was, all of them, that is, except Leopard. He knew something was wrong with how Rabbit counted, but unless he learned to count for himself, he would never know what it was.

Leopard had no choice but to give Rabbit the magnificent prize.

What was it?

What else except a picture of Leopard himself!

WHAT IS AN AUTHOR?

Meet Julius Lester. He's a teacher and he's an *author*. An author is a writer. Authors write books. Many of these books tell stories.

Julius Lester loves to tell stories. He writes them down so he can share them with you. Sometimes he makes up a story out of his own imagination, then writes it down. Sometimes he takes a story that people have been telling each other for many years—like the story called "How Many Spots Does a Leopard Have?"— and he writes it down in the way he likes to tell it.

Julius Lester, author.

Julius Lester is the author of many books. He has won awards for his writing. If you go to a library, you'll find lots of books that say, "By Julius Lester."

When you sit down with a book, find out who the author is. Do you have a favorite author? If you do, then the next time you're at the library, look for more books by that person.

Do you like to tell stories? Someday soon you'll learn to write them down, then you can be an author too!

In Which Pooh Goes Visiting and Gets into a Tight Place

(A selection from *Winnie-the-Pooh* by A. A. Milne)

Edward Bear, known to his friends as Winnie-the-Pooh, or Pooh for short, was walking through the forest one day, humming proudly to himself. He had made up a little hum that very morning, as he was doing his Stoutness Exercises in front of the glass: *Tra-la-la, tra-la-la,* as he stretched up as high as he could go, and then *Tra-la—oh, help!—la,* as he tried to reach his toes. After breakfast he had said it over and over to himself until he had learnt it off by heart, and now he was humming it right through, properly. It went like this:

> *Tra-la-la, tra-la-la,*
> *Tra-la-la, tra-la-la,*
> *Rum-tum-tiddle-um-tum.*
> *Tiddle-iddle, tiddle-iddle,*
> *Tiddle-iddle, tiddle-iddle,*
> *Rum-tum-tum-tiddle-um.*

Well, he was humming this hum to himself, and walking along gaily, wondering what everybody else was doing, and what it felt like, being somebody else, when suddenly he came to a sandy bank, and in the bank was a large hole.

"Aha!" said Pooh. (*Rum-tum-tiddle-um-tum.*) "If I know anything about anything, that hole means Rabbit," he said, "and Rabbit means Company," he said, "and Company means Food and Listening-to Me-Humming and such like. *Rum-tum-tum-tiddle-um.*"

So he bent down, put his head into the hole, and called out:

"Is anybody at home?"

There was a sudden scuffling noise from inside the hole, and then silence.

"What I said was, 'Is anybody at home?'" called out Pooh very loudly.

"No!" said a voice; and then added, "You needn't shout so loud. I heard you quite well the first time."

"Bother!" said Pooh. "Isn't there anybody here at all?"

"Nobody."

Winnie-the-Pooh took his head out of the hole, and thought for a little, and he thought to himself, "There must be somebody there, because somebody must have *said*

'Nobody.' " So he put his head back in the hole, and said:

"Hallo, Rabbit, isn't that you?"

"No," said Rabbit, in a different sort of voice this time.

"But isn't that Rabbit's voice?"

"I don't *think* so," said Rabbit. "It isn't *meant* to be."

"Oh!" said Pooh.

He took his head out of the hole, and had another think, and then he put it back, and said:

"Well, could you very kindly tell me where Rabbit is?"

"He has gone to see his friend Pooh Bear, who is a great friend of his."

"But this *is* Me!" said Bear, very much surprised.

"What sort of Me?"

"Pooh Bear."

"Are you sure?" said Rabbit, still more surprised.

"Quite, quite sure," said Pooh.

"Oh, well, then, come in."

So Pooh pushed and pushed and pushed his way through the hole, and at last he got in.

"You were quite right," said Rabbit, looking at him all over. "It *is* you. Glad to see you."

"Who did you think it was?"

"Well, I wasn't sure. You know how it is in the Forest. One can't have *anybody* coming into one's house. One has to be *careful*. What about a mouthful of something?"

Pooh always liked a little something at eleven o'clock in the morning, and he was very glad to see Rabbit getting out the plates and mugs; and when Rabbit said, "Honey or condensed milk with your bread?" he was so excited that he said, "Both," and then, so as not to seem greedy, he added, "But don't bother about the bread, please." And for a long time after that he said nothing . . . until at last, humming to himself in a rather sticky voice, he got up, shook Rabbit lovingly by the paw, and said that he must be going on.

"Must you?" said Rabbit politely.

"Well," said Pooh, "I could stay a little longer if it—if you—" and he tried very hard to look in the direction of the larder.

"As a matter of fact," said Rabbit, "I was going out myself directly."

"Oh, well, then, I'll be going on. Good-bye."

"Well, good-bye, if you're sure you won't have any more."

"*Is there any more?*" asked Pooh quickly.

Rabbit took the covers off the dishes, and said no, there wasn't.

"I thought not," said Pooh, nodding to himself. "Well, good-bye. I must be going on."

So he started to climb out of the hole. He pulled with his front paws, and pushed with his back paws, and in a little while his nose was out in the open again . . . and then his ears . . . and then his front paws . . . and then his shoulders . . . and then—

"Oh, help!" said Pooh. "I'd better go back."

"Oh, bother!" said Pooh. "I shall have to go on."

"I can't do either!" said Pooh. "Oh, help *and* bother!"

Now by this time Rabbit wanted to go for a walk too, and finding the front door full, he went out by the back door, and came round to Pooh, and looked at him.

"Hallo, are you stuck?" he asked.

"N-no," said Pooh carelessly. "Just resting and thinking and humming to myself."

"Here, give us a paw."

Pooh Bear stretched out a paw, and Rabbit pulled and pulled and pulled. . . .

"*Ow!*" cried Pooh. "You're hurting!"

"The fact is," said Rabbit, "you're stuck."

"It all comes," said Pooh crossly, "of not having front doors big enough."

"It all comes," said Rabbit sternly, "of eating too much. I thought at the time," said Rabbit, "only I didn't like to say anything," said Rabbit, "that one of us was eating too much," said Rabbit, "and I knew it wasn't *me*," he said. "Well, well, I shall go and fetch Christopher Robin."

Christopher Robin lived at the other end of the Forest, and when he came back with Rabbit, and saw the front half of Pooh, he said, "Silly old Bear," in such a loving voice that everybody felt quite hopeful again.

"I was just beginning to think," said Bear, sniffing slightly, "that Rabbit might never be able to use his front door again. And I should *hate* that," he said.

"So should I," said Rabbit.

"Use his front door again?" said Christopher Robin. "Of course he'll use his front door again."

"Good," said Rabbit.

"If we can't pull you out, Pooh, we might push you back."

Rabbit scratched his whiskers thoughtfully, and pointed out that, when once Pooh was pushed back, he was back, and of course nobody was more glad to see Pooh than *he* was, still there it was, some lived in trees and some lived underground, and—

"You mean I'd *never* get out?" said Pooh.

"I mean," said Rabbit, "that having got *so* far, it seems a pity to waste it."

Christopher Robin nodded.

"Then there's only one thing to be done," he said. "We shall have to wait for you to get thin again."

"How long does getting thin take?" asked Pooh anxiously.

"About a week, I should think."

"But I can't stay here for a *week!*"

"You can *stay* here all right, silly old Bear. It's getting you out which is so difficult."

"We'll read to you," said Rabbit cheerfully. "And I hope it won't snow," he added. "And I say, old fellow, you're taking up a good deal of room in my house—*do* you mind if I use your back legs as a towel-horse? Because, I mean, there they are—doing nothing—and it would be very convenient just to hang the towels on them."

"A week!" said Pooh gloomily. *"What about meals?"*

"I'm afraid no meals," said Christopher Robin, "because of getting thin quicker. But we *will* read to you."

Bear began to sigh, and then found he couldn't because he was so tightly stuck; and a tear rolled down his eye, as he said:

"Then would you read a Sustaining Book, such as would help and comfort a Wedged Bear in Great Tightness?"

So for a week Christopher Robin read that sort of book at the North end of Pooh, and Rabbit hung his washing on the South end . . . and in between Bear felt himself getting slenderer and slenderer. And at the end of the week Christopher Robin said, *"Now!"*

So he took hold of Pooh's front paws and Rabbit took hold of Christopher Robin, and all Rabbit's friends and relations took hold of Rabbit, and they pulled together. . . .

And for a long time Pooh only said "Ow!" . . .

And "Oh!" . . .

And then, all of a sudden, he said *"Pop!"* just as if a cork were coming out of a bottle.

And Christopher Robin and Rabbit and all Rabbit's friends and relations went head-over-heels backwards . . . and on the top of them came Winnie-the-Pooh—free!

So, with a nod of thanks to his friends, he went on with his walk through the forest, humming proudly to himself. But, Christopher Robin looked after him lovingly, and said to himself, "Silly old Bear!"

PARENTS: Check out A. A. Milne's *Winnie-the-Pooh* for more stories about Pooh and his friends: Rabbit, Piglet, Eeyore, Kanga and Roo, and Christopher Robin—but not Tigger: that bouncy fellow is introduced in another book, *The House at Pooh Corner*, a selection from which you'll find in *What Your First Grader Needs to Know* (revised edition).

The Velveteen Rabbit; or, How Toys Become Real

(Adapted from the original by Margery Williams)

There was once a velveteen rabbit, and in the beginning he was really splendid. He was fat and bunchy, as a rabbit should be; his coat was spotted brown and white, he had real thread whiskers, and his ears were lined with pink satin. On Christmas morning, when he sat wedged in the top of the Boy's stocking, with a sprig of holly between his paws, the effect was charming.

There were other things in the stocking, nuts and oranges and a toy engine, and chocolate almonds and a clockwork mouse, but the Rabbit was quite the best of all. For at least two hours the Boy loved him, and then there was a great rustling of tissue paper and unwrapping of parcels, and in the excitement of looking at all the new presents, the Velveteen Rabbit was forgotten.

For a long time he lived in the toy cupboard or on the nursery floor, and no one thought very much about him. He was naturally shy, and being only made of velveteen, some of the more expensive toys quite snubbed him. The mechanical toys were very superior and looked down upon everyone else; they were full of modern ideas and pretended they were real. But the Rabbit didn't even know that real rabbits existed; he thought they were all stuffed with sawdust like himself. So the poor little Rabbit was made to feel very insignificant and commonplace, and the only person who was kind to him at all was the Skin Horse.

The Skin Horse had lived longer in the nursery than any of the others. He was so old that his brown coat was bald in patches, and most of the hairs in his tail had been pulled out. He was wise, for he had seen many mechanical toys arrive to boast and swagger, and by and by break their mainsprings and pass away, and he knew that they were only toys and would never turn into anything else. For nursery magic is very

strange and wonderful, and only those playthings that are old and wise and experienced like the Skin Horse understand all about it.

"What is REAL?" asked the Rabbit one day. "Does it mean having things that buzz inside you and a stick-out handle?"

"Real isn't how you are made," said the Skin Horse. "It's a thing that happens to you. When a child loves you for a long, long time, not just to play with, but REALLY loves you, then you become Real."

"Does it hurt?" asked the Rabbit.

"Sometimes," said the Skin Horse, for he was always truthful. "When you are Real, you don't mind being hurt."

"Does it happen all at once, like being wound up," the Rabbit asked, "or bit by bit?"

"It doesn't happen all at once," said the Skin Horse. "It takes a long time. Generally, by the time you are Real, most of your hair has been loved off, and your eyes drop out, and you get very shabby. But these things don't matter at all, because once you are Real, you can't be ugly."

"I suppose you are Real?" said the Rabbit.

"The Boy's Uncle made me Real," the Skin Horse said. "That was a great many years ago; but once you are Real, you can't become unreal again. It lasts for always."

The Rabbit sighed. He longed to become Real, to know what it felt like; and yet the idea of growing shabby and losing his eyes and whiskers was rather sad. He wished that he could become real without these uncomfortable things happening to him.

There was a person called Nana who ruled the nursery. Sometimes she took no notice of the playthings lying about, and sometimes she went swooping about like a great wind and hustled them away in cupboards. She called this "tidying up," and the playthings all hated it. The Rabbit didn't mind it so much, for wherever he was thrown he came down soft.

One evening, when the Boy was going to bed, he couldn't find the china dog that always slept with him. Nana was in a hurry, so she simply looked about her, and seeing that the toy cupboard door stood open, she made a swoop.

"Here," she said, "take your old Bunny!" And she dragged the Rabbit out by one ear and put him into the Boy's arms.

That night, and for many nights after, the Velveteen Rabbit slept in the Boy's bed. At first he found it rather uncomfortable, for the Boy hugged him very tight, and sometimes he rolled over on him, and sometimes he pushed him so far under the pillow that the Rabbit could scarcely breathe. And he missed, too, those long moonlight hours in the nursery, when all the house was silent, and his talks with the Skin Horse. But very soon he grew to like it, for the Boy talked to him and made nice tunnels for him under the bedclothes that he said were like the burrows the real rabbits lived in. And when the Boy dropped off to sleep, the Rabbit would snuggle down close under his little warm chin and dream, with the Boy's hands clasped close round him all night long.

And so time went on, and the little Rabbit was very happy—so happy that he never noticed how his beautiful velveteen fur was getting shabbier and shabbier, and his tail coming unsewn, and all the pink rubbed off his nose where the Boy had kissed him.

Spring came, and they had long days in the garden, for wherever the Boy went the Rabbit went, too. He had rides in the wheelbarrow, and picnics on the grass, and lovely fairy huts built for him under the raspberry canes. And once, when the Boy was called away suddenly, the Rabbit was left out on the lawn until long after dusk, and Nana had to come and look for him with the candle because the Boy couldn't go to sleep unless he was there. He was wet through with the dew, and Nana grumbled as she rubbed him off with a corner of her apron.

"You must have your old Bunny!" she said. "Fancy all that fuss for a toy!"

The Boy sat up in bed and stretched out his hands.

"Give me my Bunny!" he said. "He isn't a toy. He's REAL!"

When the little Rabbit heard that, he was happy, for he knew that what the Skin Horse had said was true at last. The nursery magic had happened to him, and he was a toy no longer. He was Real. The Boy himself had said it.

That night he was almost too happy to sleep. And into his boot-button eyes, which had long ago lost their polish, there came a look of wisdom and beauty.

That was a wonderful summer!

Near the house where they lived there was a wood, and in the long June evenings the Boy liked to go there to play. He took the Velveteen Rabbit with him, and before he wandered off to play, he always made the Rabbit a little nest where he would be quite cozy. One evening, while the Rabbit was lying there alone, he saw two strange beings creep out of the tall grass near him.

They were rabbits like himself, but quite furry and brand-new. They must have been very well made, for their seams didn't show at all, and they changed shape in a queer way when they moved; one minute they were long and thin and the next minute fat and bunchy, instead of always staying the same as he did.

They stared at him, and the little Rabbit stared back. And all the time their noses twitched.

"Why don't you get up and play with us?" one of them asked.

"I don't feel like it," said the Rabbit, for he didn't want to explain that he couldn't get up.

"Can you hop on your hind legs?" asked the furry rabbit.

That was a dreadful question, for the Velveteen Rabbit had no hind legs at all! The back of him was made all in one piece, like a pincushion. He sat still and hoped that the other rabbits wouldn't notice. But wild rabbits have very sharp eyes. And this one stretched out his neck and looked.

"He hasn't got any hind legs!" he called out. And he began to laugh.

"I have!" cried the little Rabbit. "I have got hind legs! I am sitting on them!"

"Then stretch them out and show me, like this!" said the wild rabbit. And he began to whirl around and dance, till the little Rabbit got quite dizzy.

"I don't like dancing," he said. "I'd rather sit still!"

But all the while he was longing to dance, for a new tickly feeling ran through him, and he felt he would give anything to be able to jump about like these rabbits did.

The strange rabbit stopped dancing and came quite close.

"He doesn't smell right!" he exclaimed. "He isn't a rabbit at all! He isn't real!"

"I am Real!" said the little Rabbit. "I am Real! The Boy said so!" And he nearly began to cry.

Just then there was a sound of footsteps, and the Boy ran past near them, and with a flash of white tails the two strange rabbits disappeared.

"Come back and play with me!" called the little Rabbit. "Oh, do come back! I know I am Real!"

But there was no answer. The Velveteen Rabbit was all alone. For a long time he lay very still, hoping that they would come back. But they never returned, and presently the sun sank lower and the little white moths fluttered out, and the Boy came and carried him home.

Weeks passed, and the little Rabbit grew very old and shabby, but the Boy loved him just as much. He loved him so hard that he loved all his whiskers off, and the pink lining to his ears turned gray, and his brown spots faded. He even began to lose his shape, and he scarcely looked like a rabbit anymore, except to the Boy. To him, he was always beautiful, and that was all that the little Rabbit cared about.

And then, one day, the Boy was ill.

His little body was so hot that it burned the Rabbit when he held him close. Strange people came and went in the nursery, and a light burned all night, and through it all the little Velveteen Rabbit lay there, hidden from sight under the bedclothes, and he never stirred, for he was afraid that if they found him, someone might take him away, and he knew that the Boy needed him.

It was a long, weary time, for the Boy was too ill to play. The little Rabbit snuggled down patiently, and looked forward to the time when the Boy would be well again and they would go out in the garden amongst the flowers and the butterflies and play splendid games in the raspberry thicket like they used to.

At last the Boy got better. He was able to sit up in bed and look at picture books while the little Rabbit cuddled close at his side. And one day they let him get up and dress.

It was a bright, sunny morning. They had carried the Boy outside, wrapped in a shawl, and the little Rabbit lay tangled up among the bedclothes, thinking.

The Boy was going to the seaside tomorrow. Now it only remained to carry out the doctor's orders. They talked about it all while the little Rabbit lay under the bedclothes and listened. The room was to be disinfected, and all the books and toys that the Boy had played with in bed must be burnt.

"Hurrah!" thought the little Rabbit. "Tomorrow we shall go to the seaside!" For the Boy had often talked of the seaside, and he wanted very much to see the big waves coming in, and the tiny crabs, and the sand castles.

Just then Nana caught sight of him.

"How about his old Bunny?" she asked.

"That?" said the doctor. "Why, it's a mass of scarlet fever germs! Burn it at once!"

And so the little Rabbit was put into a sack with the old picture books and a lot of rubbish, and carried out to the end of the garden. That was a fine place to make a bonfire, only the gardener was too busy just then to attend to it.

That night the Boy slept in a different bedroom, and he had a new bunny to sleep with him, but he was too excited to care very much about it. For tomorrow he was going to the seaside, and he could think of nothing else.

And while the Boy was asleep, dreaming of the seaside, the little Rabbit lay among the old picture books and rubbish, and he felt very lonely. The sack had been left untied, and so by wriggling a bit he was able to get his head through the opening and look out. Nearby he could see the thicket of raspberry canes in whose shadow he had played with the Boy on bygone mornings. He thought of those long sunlit hours in the garden—how happy they were—and a great sadness came over him. He thought of the Skin Horse, so wise and gentle, and all that he had told him. Of what use was it to be loved and lose one's beauty and become Real if it all ended like this? And a tear, a real tear, trickled down his shabby little velvet nose and fell to the ground.

And then a strange thing happened. For where the tear had fallen, a mysterious flower grew out of the ground. It had slender green leaves the color of emeralds; and in the center of the leaves, a blossom like a golden cup. It was so beautiful that the little Rabbit forgot to cry. And presently the blossom opened, and out of it there stepped the loveliest fairy in the whole world. Her dress was of pearl and dewdrops, and there were flowers round her neck and in her hair. And she came close to the little Rabbit and gathered him up in her arms and kissed him on his velveteen nose that was all damp from crying.

"Little Rabbit," she said, "I am the nursery magic Fairy. I take care of all the playthings that the children have loved. When they are old and worn out and the children don't need them anymore, then I come and take them away with me and turn them into Real."

"Wasn't I Real before?" asked the little Rabbit.

"You were Real to the Boy," the Fairy said, "because he loved you. Now you shall be Real to everyone."

And she held the little Rabbit close in her arms and flew with him into the wood. It was light now, for the moon had risen. All the forest was beautiful. In the open glade between the tree trunks, the wild rabbits danced with their shadows on the velvet grass, but when they saw the Fairy, they all stopped dancing and stood round in a ring to stare at her.

"I've brought you a new playfellow," the Fairy said. "You must be very kind to him and teach him all he needs to know, for he is going to live with you for ever and ever!"

And she kissed the little Rabbit again and put him down on the grass.

"Run and play, little Rabbit!" she said.

But the little Rabbit sat quite still for a moment and never moved. For when he saw all the wild rabbits dancing around him, he suddenly remembered about his hind legs, and he didn't want them to see that he was made all in one piece. He did not know that when the Fairy kissed him that last time, she had changed him altogether. And he might have sat there a long time, too shy to move, if just then something hadn't tickled his nose, and before he thought what he was doing, he lifted his hind toe to scratch it.

And he found that he actually had hind legs! Instead of dingy velveteen he had brown fur, soft and shiny, his ears twitched by themselves, and his whiskers were so long that they brushed the grass. He gave one leap, and the joy of using those hind legs was so great that he went springing about on them, jumping sideways and whirling round as the others did, and he grew so excited that when at last he did stop to look for the Fairy, she had gone.

He was a Real Rabbit at last, at home with the other rabbits.

Autumn passed and winter, and in the spring, when the days grew warm and sunny, the Boy went out to play in the wood behind the house. And while he was playing, two rabbits crept out and peeped at him. One of them was brown all over, but the other had strange markings under his fur, as though long ago he had been spotted, and the spots still showed through. And about his little soft nose and his round black eyes there was something familiar, so that the Boy thought to himself, "Why, he looks just like my old Bunny that was lost when I had scarlet fever!"

But he never knew that it really was his own Bunny, come back to look at the child who had first helped him to be Real.

Two Tall Tales

PARENTS: There's a bit of truth in the two tall tales we tell here: both Johnny Appleseed and Casey Jones were real people. But tall tales aren't known for being truthful, and like all tall tales, these two stories dish up a heaping portion of exaggeration. They present people and deeds bigger than life, but no bigger than the spirit of the people who love to tell tall tales.

Johnny Appleseed

This here is the story of John Chapman, better known as Johnny Appleseed. He lived in this country a long time ago, when America was still growing, and there weren't many towns or cities, but there was a lot of wide-open land.

Now, Johnny was an unusual kind of hero. He didn't lead any soldiers in a war, and he didn't become the President, and he didn't sail ships across the oceans, and he didn't kill dragons or rescue princesses. But still, he was a real hero. And what he did best was—well, you'll see.

People say that when Johnny was a baby, he'd fuss and cry and keep the family awake until they put a twig with apple blossoms in his little hand. Then he wouldn't bang the petals off, or eat them, like other babies would. Instead, he'd just lie there in his crib, looking at those apple blossoms, sniffing at them now and then, as happy as an angel full of ice cream.

When Johnny was a little boy, his mother would wander with him in the woods and show him plants and squirrels and such. He loved the birds and animals almost as much as he loved apples and apple trees. He was never happier than when he was lugging around some little animal or other, even if it was a skunk. And whenever an animal in the neighborhood was sick or had a broken leg, people would say, "Just take it over to Johnny Chapman. He'll fix the little critter right up."

When Johnny grew up, he got an idea in his head, and he couldn't get it out. His idea was that there ought to be more apple trees, *lots* more, and that he was just the fellow to plant them. But he couldn't carry trees all over the country! What he needed was seeds, and plenty of 'em.

Near where Johnny lived there were mills where folks made apple cider. They pressed the juice out of the apples and had no use for the seeds. But Johnny could use them. He took the seeds, washed them off, and let them dry in the sun. When he finished, he had sacks and sacks full of seeds.

So Johnny set off westward, carrying his apple seeds. He carried so many seeds that he couldn't bring along much of anything else. He found a place for his two favorite books, the Bible and *Aesop's Fables*, and he needed a cooking pan, so he wore that on his head.

Johnny walked all over the country, sleeping out in the open, eating whatever was handy, tramping through the mud and snow. He walked and walked, stopping here and there to plant the seeds all along rivers, in meadows, wherever people would let him. Whenever he met a family moving west (which a lot of families were doing in those days), he'd give them a little pouch of seeds so that they could grow their own apple tress. And that's how folks came to know him as "Johnny Appleseed."

Some people thought Johnny was foolish because he gave away his seeds for free—and these people thought that it only made sense to do something if you were going to make money doing it. But Johnny Appleseed would just say, "Money?" And he would snap his fingers. "What do you do with money? Just spend it for clothes or houses or food." Then, without taking a cent from anyone, he'd be on his way.

When anybody brought up the subject of animals, Johnny Appleseed was likely to go through that finger-snapping business again. "Leave animals alone," he'd say, "and they'll do the same by you. They're your brothers and sisters, sort of, only they don't borrow clothes, and they don't argue with you the way human brothers and sisters do."

Once, on a cold winter's day, Johnny was slushing through the snow, and night came. He looked around for some big hollow log to sleep in. He found a dandy log, built a fire nearby, cooked his mush, ate it up, and started to crawl into the hollow log.

When he'd got in about to his hips, he heard a groaning grunt. Peeking in, he saw a big bear lying in there with his paws crossed on his chest, enjoying his winter snooze. Johnny backed out, inch by inch, slow as a snail, being quiet so as not to disturb the bear's sleep. "Beg your pardon, Brother Bear," he whispered. Then he yawned, stretched out, and curled up in the snow.

Johnny Appleseed had something he believed in, and he went to a lot of trouble to

bring it about. He wanted to see a nation of apple orchards, with apple trees in bloom in the spring, and the men and women and children everywhere strong and good and healthy, like Johnny himself.

Johnny lived a long, long time ago, but people say that, even today, if you go to a certain part of Ohio in apple blossom time, and get up before sunrise, and go to a certain old apple tree, you'll see the smoke from Johnny's fire as it dies out. Maybe you'll even catch a glimpse of Johnny's spirit as it moves along westward with the spring, waking up the blossoms and tending the orchards.

Casey Jones

PARENTS: Casey Jones was a real man, born John Luther Jones in 1864. When he began to work for the railroad at age fifteen, everybody called him "Casey" after his hometown, Cayce, Kentucky. His deeds as a railroad engineer have entered the realm of legend and tall tale. The story of the life and dramatic death (in 1900) of Casey Jones lives on mostly in a song, of which there are many different versions. This version of the story of Casey Jones weaves in some lines from the songs about him.

Now gather round, friends, for I want you to hear
The story of a brave engineer.

His name was Casey Jones, and let me tell you, there's never been a man who could drive a train as fast as Casey.

When Casey was a young man, the railroad was about the fastest way of getting 'round. This was back before the time of airplanes or rocket ships, even before fast cars or trucks.

Casey drove a train on the Illinois Central Line. He loved to sit way up in the cabin of the train with his hand on the throttle—that's the handle you use to make the train go slower or, in Casey's case, faster. He loved to see the trees and fields go whizzing by. He loved to make the whistle blow—and there was no other train with a whistle like Casey's: it started out soft, like a whippoorwill, then rose to a howl, like a coyote crying in the night, then faded away into a ghostly whisper.

People always knew when Casey was coming. Even before they could see the train, they could hear the powerful *chugga-chugga, chugga-chugga*, getting louder and louder. Then they'd hear that wild whistle howl. People used to say that when Casey blew his whistle, why, little babies would wake up from their naps, but they wouldn't cry. Instead, they'd make little *chugga-chugga, whoo-whoo* sounds, then fall right back asleep. And people said that when Casey blew his whistle, the cows would give an extra quart of milk, and the chickens lay at least a dozen eggs each. And if you hurried, you could take one of those eggs and crack it into a cold frying pan and put out a piece of plain bread, and just as soon as Casey went blazing by, there in that pan would be a nicely fried egg, over easy, and on the side a plate of hot buttered toast.

Now the reason Casey drove so fast was, he took pride in always being *on time*. He wanted to get that train where it was going when it was supposed to be there, or even a little before. Whenever he started on a trip, the railroad men would wave and yell, "Bring her in on time, Casey!" And they knew he would.

But you can't make a train go fast all by yourself. Casey needed a good fireman to help him, and he had one of the best in Sim Webb. The fireman on a train doesn't put out fires—no, Sim Webb kept the fire going by shoveling coal into it, which got the flames a-roarin', which made a lot of steam, which made the train go fast—and got the train in *on time*.

Once, Casey and Sim almost *didn't* make it on time. They were carrying a load of mail to Memphis, Tennessee, and it was raining cats and dogs. Some people say

The rain had been falling for five or six weeks,
And the railroad track was like the bed of a creek.

At the station in Memphis, the railroad men waited for Casey to arrive. Some said, "There's no way he can make it on time in all this rain. He'll *have* to slow down." But others said, "Just you wait. Casey Jones *always* makes it on time. Running on time is his hobby." And sure enough, just then they saw a light on the tracks up ahead, and heard the lonesome whistle that could only be Casey's, and the train pulled into the station, dripping wet, puffing hard, but *on time*.

Casey and Sim were dog tired and looking forward to a good night's sleep. But they'd hardly settled into bed when a knock came at the door. It seems that the engineer who was supposed to drive the train on the southbound run was sick. Well, they didn't even have to ask Casey if he would take the man's place. Tired as he was, Casey got dressed and headed for the train. And when he got there, he found Sim Webb, already stoking the fire with coal, getting the train ready to carry mail, packages, and some passengers as well.

Now, friends, here's where I have to tell you the sad part of this story, about how Casey met his end.

As Casey mounted to the cabin and took the throttle in his hand, he heard someone shout, "Casey, you're already more than an hour and a half late." But Casey just smiled and thought to himself, "Guess that means I'll have to go a little faster."

He opened up the throttle and the train plunged into the dark, wet night. Sim Webb shoveled the coal as fast as he could, and the train chugged on, faster and faster. "Casey!" Sim yelled. "You're running too fast."

And Casey said, "I believe we'll make it through,
For the engine is a-steamin' better than I ever knew."
And Casey said, "Fireman, don't you fret,
Keep knockin' at the fire door, and don't give up yet.
I'm going to run this train until she leaves the rail
Or we make it on time with the southbound mail."

Casey was "highballing" down the tracks—which means he was pushing that train just as fast as it would go. He was going so fast that it looked like they might even make it on time. But then, as they squealed around a curve, through the darkness Casey saw a light up ahead. But that light wasn't supposed to be there, not on this track. Then Casey knew: there was a train stuck on the track just ahead and *he was speeding straight toward it!*

Casey pulled the brake as hard as he could, and yelled, "Jump, Sim!"

"Casey, you come on!" said Sim.

"Jump!" Casey shouted, and Sim jumped. But Casey stayed on. He knew he couldn't stop the train in time, but he also knew he had to slow it down. He knew if he jumped and let go of the brake, it might mean death for the passengers on the train. So Casey pulled on the brake with all his might, and a terrible screeching, squealing sound ripped through the darkness.

The trains, they met in the middle of a hill
In a head-on tangle that was bound to kill.
He tried to do his duty, the men all said,
But Casey Jones, he ended up dead.

Casey Jones—mounted to the cabin.
Casey Jones—throttle in his hand.
Casey Jones mounted to the cabin
And took his farewell trip to the Promised Land.

Poor Casey. When they found him, he had one hand still tight on the throttle, and one hand tight on the brake. But Casey was the only person who died. The passengers lived because Casey stayed at his post and did his duty.

People say that if you look up in the sky at night and see a light flash across the sky—well, it might be a shooting star, but then again, it might be Casey Jones, high-balling across the heavens, *chugga-chugga, chugga-chuggin'* now and forever, on time till the end of time.

Sayings

PARENTS: Every culture has phrases and proverbs that make no sense when carried over literally into another culture. To say, for example, that someone has "let the cat out of the bag" has nothing to do with setting free a trapped kitty. Nor—thank goodness—does it ever *literally* "rain cats and dogs"!

The sayings and phrases in this section may be familiar to many children, who hear them at home. But the inclusion of these sayings and phrases in the *Core Knowledge Sequence* has been singled out for gratitude by many parents and by teachers who work with children from home cultures that are different from the culture of literate American English.

For kindergartners, we have chosen to introduce a selection of very familiar sayings that are likely to have some connection to the child's world of experience.

April showers bring May flowers.
People use this saying to mean that something unpleasant can cause something pleasant to happen, just as spring rains cause flowers to bloom.

Bob had caught chicken pox and he couldn't go to the fair. "Cheer up, Bob," said his mother. "April showers bring May flowers: you have to stay home, but now we have time to work on that big new puzzle you've been wanting to put together."

Better safe than sorry.
People use this saying to mean it's better not to take a chance than to do something that might be very risky. They say this because you're less likely to be hurt or make a bad mistake when you're careful.

Alex dared Carlos to walk on the railing of the old bridge. "No way, Alex," said Carlos. "It's a long fall into the river. Better safe than sorry."

Do unto others as you would have them do unto you.

This saying is called the Golden Rule. People use it to mean: Treat people as you would like to be treated yourself. It comes from the Bible.

"Molly, stop drawing on Becky's picture," said the babysitter. "Would you like Becky to mess up *your* picture? Remember: Do unto others as you would have them do unto you."

A dog is man's best friend.

Some people think that a dog is more than a pet. They think a dog can also be a really good friend. That's because dogs, like good friends, can be loyal and loving.

Peter had lost his lunch money and torn his favorite shirt. As he walked home, he was feeling sad, but then he heard his dog, Prince, barking. Prince jumped up and licked Peter with his big wet tongue. "Prince," Peter laughed, "it's true: A dog is man's best friend."

The early bird gets the worm.

This saying means that you can usually get ahead of others if you get going before they do. Sometimes people say it to someone who needs a little extra push to do what he is supposed to do.

"Hey, Billy," said Juan, "did you hear? Cary's Card Shop is opening early on Saturday, and the first fifty people in the shop get free baseball cards!"

"That's great!" answered Billy. "Let's find out what time they open and be waiting at the door. The early bird gets the worm, you know."

Great oaks from little acorns grow.

This saying means that, just as a small acorn can grow into a towering oak tree, something that starts out small or not very important can turn out big or very important.

Abraham Lincoln was born in a log cabin and read books by firelight. Even though his family was poor, he became one of the greatest presidents of the United States. His life is true to the saying "Great oaks from little acorns grow."

Look before you leap.

This saying means that you should be careful and think before you rush into doing something.

"Mom!" said Andrew with excitement. "Ben says he'll trade me all his toy cars for my bike? Isn't that great?"

"I don't know, Andrew, is it?" asked his mother. "You ride your bike every day, and a bike costs a lot more than toy cars. Do you really want to trade? You'd better look before you leap."

A place for everything and everything in its place.

This saying means you should put things where they belong. People use this saying when they want people to be neat.

When Andrea came in from playing, she would always kick off her shoes in the hall. Her mother said, "Andrea, your shoes don't belong in the hall. Please put them in the closet. Remember: A place for everything and everything in its place!"

It's raining cats and dogs.

People use this saying to mean that it is raining very, very hard.

"We'd better ride the bus home today. If we walk, we'll get soaked. It's raining cats and dogs!"

Practice makes perfect.

People use this saying to mean that doing something over and over makes you good at it.

Lucy liked taking piano lessons. She practiced every day. Sometimes it was hard, but she felt proud when she learned to play her first song without making any mistakes. She understood now why her teacher always said, "Practice makes perfect."

Where there's a will, there's a way.

This saying means if you want to do something badly enough, you'll find a way to do it.

Lillian had tried and tried to jump rope fifty times in a row, but she always messed up after forty jumps. "Agh!" she said to her friend Betty. "I don't think I'll ever do fifty!"

"Oh yes you will," said Betty. "Keep trying. Where there's a will, there's a way."

II.
History and Geography

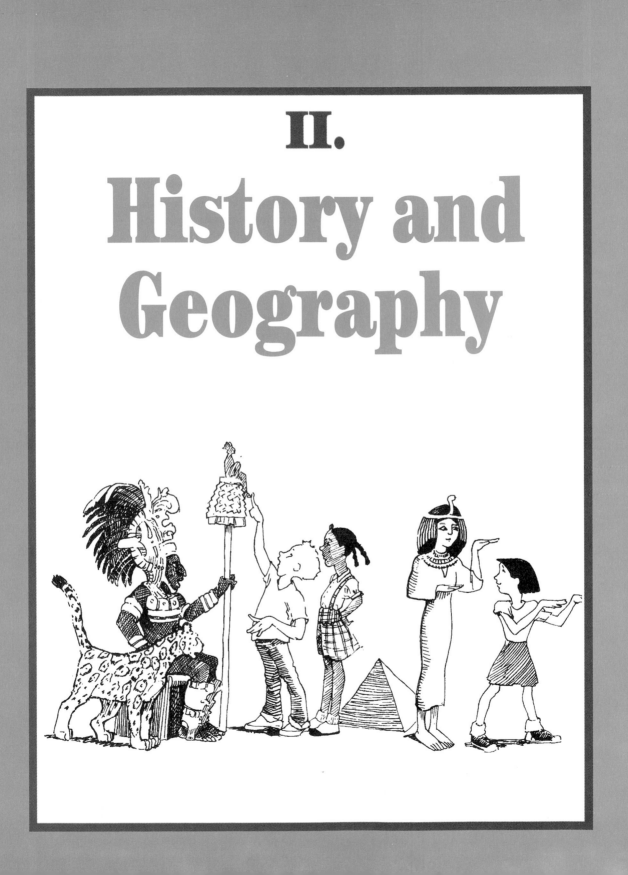

INTRODUCTION

In kindergarten, children often study aspects of their immediate world: the family, the school, the community, etc. While such local studies should be encouraged, we should also take advantage of children's natural curiosity and begin to broaden their horizons. By introducing kindergartners to history and geography, we can foster their curiosity about the larger world and begin to develop their sense of the past and its significance. For young children, we need to emphasize the "story" in history. By appealing to children's naturally active imaginations, we can ask them to "visit" people and places in the past. We encourage you to go beyond these pages to help your child learn about history through art projects, drama, music, and discussions.

In the following pages, we introduce—let us emphasize, *introduce*—a variety of people and events. The children will encounter most of these people and events more fully in their later schooling. For example, we introduce July 4, 1776, as "the birthday of our nation," on the premise that kindergartners can understand the idea of a "birthday." But we do not go into any discussion of the American Revolution (which, by the way, we do introduce in the First Grade book of this series, and explore in some detail in the Fourth Grade book).

In beginning to tell children the story of the past, we have tried to be sensitive about the degree to which, and the manner in which, we expose children to the tragic aspects of history, such as the practice of slavery in the United States. In some cases, we have chosen to leave for later grades some of the darker aspects of history. For example, here we tell the story of Columbus's first journey to the "New World," but we wait until later books in this series to tell about the devastation wrought on Native American peoples by the diseases that came with the European explorers. The goal in kindergarten, then, is less to explore historical events or ideas in depth than to orient the child to the past and plant the seeds of knowledge that will grow in later years.

Suggested Resources

Follow the Dream: The Story of Christopher Columbus by Peter Sis (Knopf, 1991)

Just Like Abraham Lincoln by Bernard Waber (Scholastic, 1964)

My First Presidents' Day Book by Aileen Fisher (Children's Press, 1987)

New True Books series. Children's Press has over thirty books on Native Americans, such as: *The Delaware, The Sioux, The Hopi,* and more.

Samuel Eaton's Day: A Day in the Life of a Pilgrim Boy and *Sarah Morton's Day: A Day in the Life of a Pilgrim Girl* by Kate Waters (Scholastic, 1993; 1991)

World History and Geography

What a Ball! Our World

Step outside and what do you see? Look as far as you can. Do you see houses and backyards? Big apartment buildings? Green fields and mountains? A lake or an ocean?

Whatever you see, it's all part of our world. The world stretches as far as you can see—in fact, a whole lot farther!

Let's imagine that just outside there's a high tower. I mean *really high.* You can climb a ladder to the top, a ladder that's longer than the ladder of the highest slide you've ever climbed. Ready? Start climbing. Keep going—don't stop now. At last you've reached the top. Catch your breath!

Now you're way up high. You can see things you never saw from the ground. You can see how this big world of ours goes on and on and on. Maybe you can see your city or town stretching far, far away. Maybe you can see rows of houses (they look teeny from your perch on the top of the tower), all lined up along streets that look like crisscrossed lines. Maybe you can see the tops of trees and a blue-green line that snakes along through them. What is that wavy line? A river!

Well, we can't stop here. I forgot to tell you: at the top of the tower there's a rocket ship. Yes, it's waiting for you! Climb in! Put on your space suit and strap on the seat belts. Ready for countdown? Five, four, three, two, one—blast off!

You're off to the moon! Here you are, First Kid on the Moon! Step outside your space ship (but keep your space suit on; there's no air to breathe on the moon). Now let's look back to where you came from—our world, the planet Earth. What do you see?

It's a ball! Seen from outer space, our world is a large bluish ball with patches of white swirling around it. What do you think those swirly white patches are? (They're clouds.)

Oceans and Continents

Now, imagine that you have on special space glasses that allow you to peek under all those clouds. If you could, then the Earth would look something like this.

This is how our world, the planet Earth, looks from space.

The planet Earth.

Look at all that blue. It seems to be moving. What do you think it is? That's right—it's water. And what are those big green patches? Did you say, "Land"? Right again.

Do you see that there's a lot more blue than green? Water, water, everywhere! Well, not quite everywhere, but our world is mostly under water. The biggest bodies of water are called *oceans*.

What about those big pieces of land poking through the oceans? They're called *continents*. There are seven of them. Each continent has its own name. The seven continents are:

Asia
Europe
Africa
North America
South America
Australia
Antarctica

As you can see from this map, each continent has a different shape. Run your finger slowly around the outline of each continent. Place a piece of white paper or tracing paper over the map, and with a pencil trace the outline of each continent. (But, since Antarctica is mostly hidden way down at the bottom of this map, you will want to trace it from the map on page 131.)

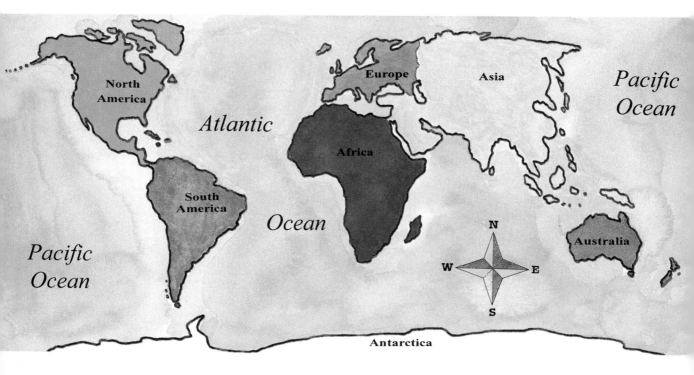

Maps and the Globe

Do you know what you're making when you draw the land shapes on a piece of paper? You're making a *map*. That's what maps are—drawings of the world. Maps give us pictures of the world to study. They help us see the shapes of land and water. Maps can also give us other information. Some maps show where mountains and rivers and lakes are, and give their names. Some show the names of highways and the locations of towns and cities.

These children are using a globe.

There's a special kind of map that isn't flat like paper. Instead, this map is round, like a big balloon. It's called a *globe*. A globe is a little model of our world. Of course, a globe is *much, much* smaller than our planet Earth, just as a Matchbox car is much smaller than a real car or a doll is much smaller than a real person.

At home, school, or the library, look at a globe. Notice how much more water there is than land. Now find each of the seven continents. Use your finger to trace around the outline of each continent.

Which Way Are You Going?

To help you find things on a map or globe, you need to know the four main directions that tell you where things are. Everything on earth is in a certain direction from where you are now. Let's learn the names of the four main directions. They are: **north, south, east,** and **west.**

East is where the sun rises. If you don't know where that is, you can find out early tomorrow morning.

West is where the sun sets. You can find out where that is late today or tomorrow.

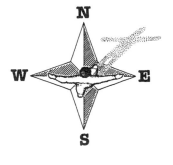

Once you've found out where the sun rises, you can find all the directions from where you are. Here's how. Stick your arms straight out from your sides. Slowly turn yourself until your right arm points to where the sun comes up. Keep your arms straight out! Your right arm is now pointing east and your left arm is now pointing west. Keep those arms straight out just a little longer. Look straight ahead. Your nose is pointing north. The back of your head is facing south.

North, South, East, West

Let's look at the directions on a map. In most maps, the top of a map is north. To go north, move your finger up on the map.

The bottom of a map is south. To go south, move your finger down.

The right of a map is east. To go east, move your finger to the right.

The left of a map is west. ("Left" and "west" sound alike, which can help you remember.) To go west, move your finger to the left.

Have you heard of the North Pole and the South Pole? Those are the special names for the very top of our world, and for the very bottom. Which pole is at the top of our world? Can you find the North Pole on a globe? Can you find the South Pole on a globe?

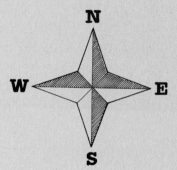

Many maps use a picture like this to show the directions.

Now try this. Here's a picture of a house. There is something near the house on each side. Which direction is each thing from the house?

- The dog is_____ of the house.
- The tree is_____ of the house.
- The cat is _____ of the house.
- The car is _____ of the house.

Around the World in Seven Ways

PARENTS: It is not important that kindergartners be able to define or explain the difference between countries and continents. A complete understanding of the relevant geographical and political concepts requires a level of abstract reasoning that will develop in later years for most children. We provide the basic explanation below because children will hear about both countries and continents, and they can benefit from having at least a working response to their likely question, "What's the difference?"

Let's learn about the seven continents. Do you remember their names? Let's say them aloud: Asia, Europe, Africa, North America, South America, Australia, Antarctica.

As you learn about the seven continents, you'll also hear about some different countries. Countries and continents—what's the difference? Well, countries are usually smaller than continents. For example, let's say you live in the United States of America (do you?). Then that's your country: the United States of America. But your country is only part of a bigger continent. Which continent? North America.

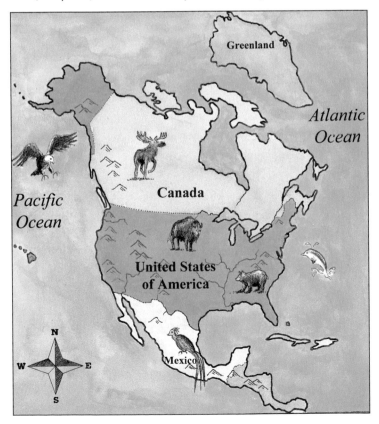

The United States of America is a *country* on the *continent* of North America. There are other countries on the continent of North America. To the north of the United States is the country called Canada. To the south of the United States is the country called Mexico. Each one of these countries has different leaders and different rules. Each country uses a different kind of money. Each country has a different flag. But all three countries are on the same continent: North America.

Now let's learn about the seven continents, and about some of the countries on each continent.

Asia

The largest continent in the world is Asia. Look at Asia on the map.

Put your finger on Asia, but watch out! Asia is home to tigers, elephants, and panda bears, and they might find your finger very interesting.

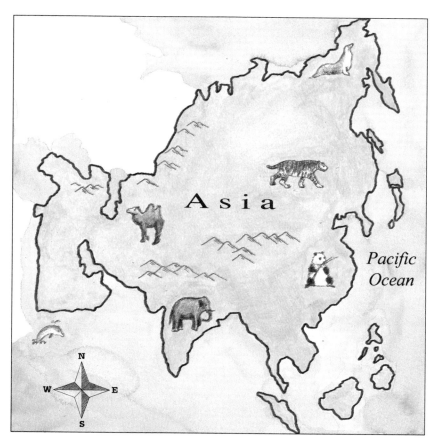

A wall runs for miles and miles across the country of China. This picture shows only a small part of the Great Wall of China. A powerful leader made his people build this wall a long time ago to defend their country from enemies. The wall has watchtowers and walkways. It's so wide that you can ride six horses side by side along its top.

Europe

Look at the map on page 118 and find Asia's neighbor, Europe. Asia and Europe touch each other. Compared to Asia, Europe is a small continent. Europe has beautiful buildings— wonderful palaces, churches, museums, and more!

This is the Eiffel Tower, in the country called France. The Eiffel Tower is made of metal. You can ride to the top of the tower in an elevator and look out over the great city of Paris.

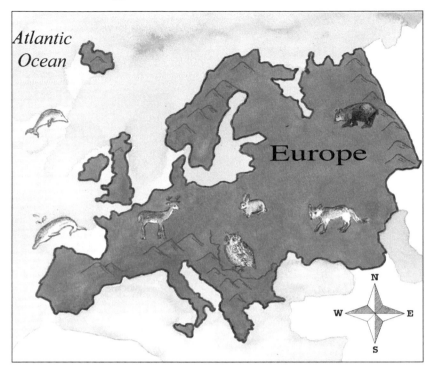

Atlantic Ocean

Europe

N
W   E
S

Here we are in jolly old England, at a place called Buckingham Palace. Who lives in a palace? Why, who else but a king, or a queen, or maybe both? For many, many years, the kings and queens of England have lived in Buckingham Palace. Nowadays, the king or queen doesn't rule England or make the laws anymore, but the English people still like to have a king or queen. Who are those red-coated fellows with fuzzy black hats standing outside the palace? They are the palace guards.

Africa

Look back to the map on page 118. Take your finger and move it down from Europe. You'll soon come to Africa. Use your fingers to measure Africa. See how much bigger Africa is than Europe? Africa is the world's second largest continent. (Do you remember the name of the largest continent?)

Africa spreads over much of the earth. It's a continent of amazing variety. "Variety" means difference. Africa has lots of different kinds of weather and land.

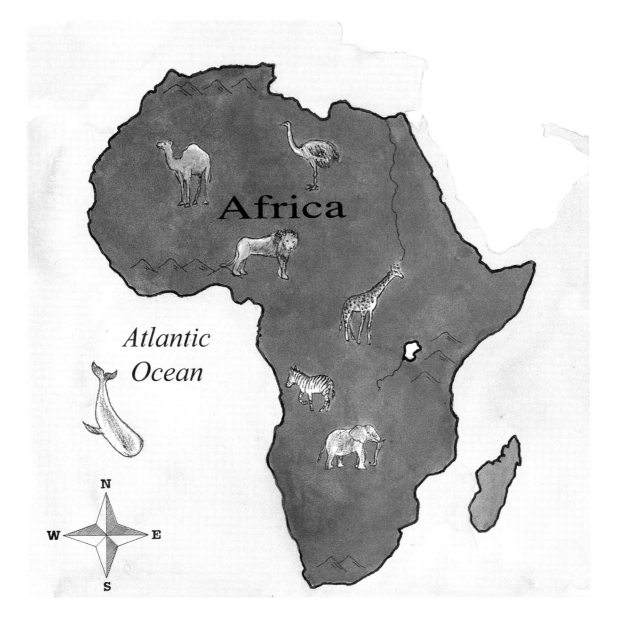

In one part of Africa, there are hot, dry deserts. In another part, there are big stretches of grassland. In another part, there are steamy jungles.

And if you think Africa has lots of different kinds of weather and land, wait till you see the animals. There are hippos and hyenas, leopards and lions, elephants and rhinos, crocodiles and ostriches—and that's just the beginning.

This picture shows a small part of a huge park in East Africa called the Serengeti (sair-in-GET-ee). Here you can find hungry giraffes munching on treetops, lions lounging on rocks, and zebras, antelopes, and cheetahs roaming across the grassland.

This is a picture of a market in Kenya, a country in East Africa. Do you see any fruits or vegetables you recognize?

North America

Look at the map on page 118. Put your finger on Africa. Pretend your finger is a ship. It's time to sail away from Africa. Go west, toward two big connected continents. To get there, you have to cross an ocean first. The name of this big ocean is the Atlantic Ocean.

Let your finger sail over the big waves of the Atlantic Ocean and take you to North America.

You've just crossed one big ocean, the Atlantic, to get to North America. Now, move your finger west across North America. Do you see another ocean on the western side of the continent? This is the Pacific Ocean. A famous song says that the United States of America stretches "from sea to shining sea"—and now you know the names of those two "shining seas"!

Between the Atlantic and the Pacific oceans, on the continent of North America, you'll find deserts, prairies, and forests. You'll find steamy swamps where alligators live, and tall mountains where mountain lions roam. You'll find farms and cities, big and little.

One of the most beautiful places in the United States is the Grand Canyon. A long, long, *long* time ago—millions of years ago—a river ran through here, and the water carved away the land. If you visit the Grand Canyon, there are places where you can go deep down into the canyon. Do you know how you get there? You ride on mules!

These women are doing a popular dance in Mexico. Look at how colorful their special dresses are. (Can you find Mexico on the map on page 121?)

These red-coated fellows from Canada are part of the Royal Canadian Mounted Police, who are known by the nickname "Mounties." The Mounties became famous for tracking down criminals and bad guys on horseback. People say that the Mounties "always get their man," so watch out, bad guys! (Can you find Canada on the map on page 121?)

South America

Look again at the map on page 118. Put your finger on the Pacific Ocean side of North America. Start near the top, then slide your finger down, down, down, following the outline of the land, until you reach another really big piece of land. Do you remember that on most maps north is up and south is down? So, as you slide your finger down, in what direction are you going? When you reach that other big piece of land, you're no longer in North America. You've reached the continent called South America.

Keep sliding your finger down the Pacific Ocean side of South America. You're sliding over the Andes Mountains, the longest mountain range in the world. Do you see the special marks that the map here uses to show these mountains? The marks show you that the Andes Mountains run all the way down the Pacific side of South America. People live in these mountains and some of the people raise helpful furry animals called llamas. Llamas are patient and strong, but don't annoy them. If they get angry, they spit at you!

Atlantic Ocean

Amazon River

South America

Pacific Ocean

N
W   E
S

There's a lot more to South America than mountains. Look on the map on page 128, for a big river. The map uses a blue line to show this river. Of course, the line on the map is small, but this river is *very, very big* and *very, very long*. It's called the Amazon. The Amazon River begins high in the Andes Mountains, then goes on until it runs through a steamy jungle called a rainforest. The Amazon rainforest has anteaters and anacondas (huge snakes), jaguars and sloths, howler monkeys and vampire bats.

Here's a rainforest creature called a sloth. Hey, Mr. Sloth! Don't you have anything better to do than just hang around?

High in the Andes Mountains, there's a very old city called Machu Picchu. Long ago the people called Incas built this stone "city in the clouds." (You'll learn about the Incas in the First Grade book in this series.)

Australia

Australia is the smallest continent. Australia is really a large island. (An island is a piece of land with water all around it.) People in Europe and North America sometimes call Australia the "down under" continent because Australia is "down under" Europe and North America. Australia is the home of some animals that you'll find on no other continent: kangaroos, koalas, and wallabies. And there's one very unusual Australian animal that seems like a mixture of a bunch of animals: it's called a duckbill platypus. (The platypus is pictured on the map. Can you find it?)

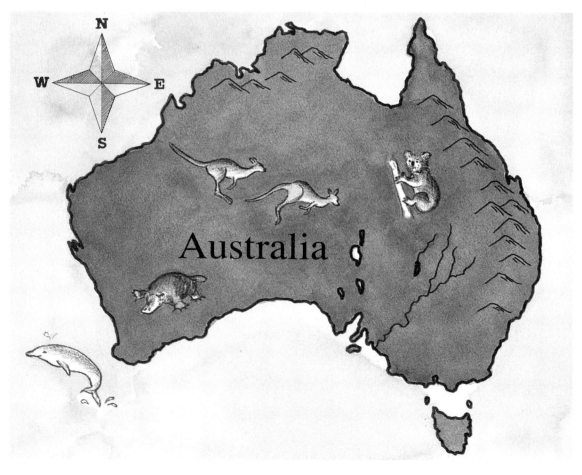

Koalas remind some people of teddy bears, but they're not bears at all. They're actually the same kind of animal as the kangaroo. Both koalas and kangaroos are a kind of animal called marsupials—which means the mothers have their babies in pouches near their belly, and can hop around with them everywhere.

Antarctica

At the very bottom of the world is the continent of Antarctica. Antarctica is the home of—well, almost nothing. It's blanketed by such thick snow and ice that almost no plants grow here and almost no animals can live here. Some animals who live between land and sea call Antarctica home—penguins, for example, and some seals, and whales. But even these animals prefer to stay closer to the warmer islands that are around the continent of Antarctica.

So, if you're planning a vacation, Antarctica is not the place to go.

These giant emperor penguins look like they're dressed for a fancy party!

CAN YOU ANSWER THESE QUESTIONS ABOUT THE CONTINENTS?

1. Which is the biggest continent?

2. On which continent will you find the Andes, the longest mountain range in the world?

3. If you wanted to see a giraffe or zebra living in the wild (not in a zoo), which continent would you visit?

4. On which continent will you find these three countries: Canada, the United States, and Mexico?

5. Koalas and kangaroos live on which continent?

After you've answered the questions, go to a globe or map. Point to and name each of the seven continents.

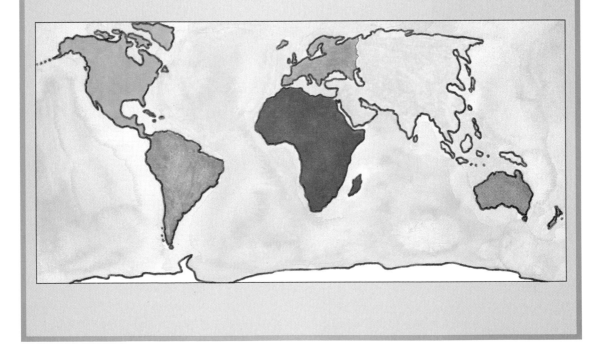

American History and Geography

PARENTS: Please read the World History and Geography section of this book with your child first, as the following section assumes some familiarity with terms introduced in World History and Geography.

Your Country

Do you live in the United States of America? Then that's your country. Sometimes people use shorter names for the United States of America, such as America, the United States, or the U.S.A.

You know that your country, the United States, is part of a bigger piece of land, called a continent. Do you remember which continent the United States is part of? It's the continent called North America.

Parents: Help your child point to the approximate location where you live in the United States. Does your child know the name of where he or she lives?

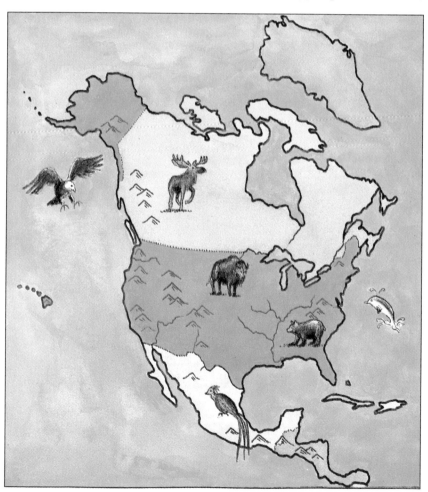

Most of the United States is clumped together in the middle of the continent of North America. But you have to look elsewhere for two parts of the United States. The map on page 133 shows you these two parts. One is very big, and parts of it are very cold: it's called Alaska. The other is a small group of islands, called Hawaii, in the Pacific Ocean. In warm Hawaii, there are many beautiful beaches.

The American Flag

Almost every country has a flag. A country's flag has a special design on it. From this picture, you can see why the American flag has been nicknamed "the stars and stripes" and "the red, white, and blue."

Have you ever seen the American flag waving in the breeze? It's a glorious sight! Which brings to mind another nickname for our flag: "Old Glory."

Looking Back

If you travel around your country now, you'll come to lots of big towns and cities, with many houses and tall buildings and thousands and thousands of people. But a long time ago, there were no big towns and cities. And there were not nearly as many people as you see today.

Let's go way back, to the time before big towns and cities. Let's go back hundreds of years. You know all those homes and buildings you see today? All the school buildings, churches, banks, shopping centers, gas stations, skyscrapers—well, imagine them all fading away. As they disappear, you see something taking their place: thick forests and wide-open grasslands.

Now, let's follow a path through an imaginary forest. It winds into the cool shade of the trees. Let's pretend that this path is taking us back, back to the time of the first Americans. And let's meet some of the first Americans.

The First Americans: Many Peoples and Many Places

Trees everywhere: thick maples, skinny birches, and giant oaks surround you. What's that moving? It's a deer. It sees you and runs like a flash. You try to follow. Where did that deer go?

You follow a path to the edge of a clear space between the trees. But stop: there's somebody there. You see a tall young man with long, shining black hair. He's carrying something across his strong shoulders. It's the deer!

You follow the young man, who walks steadily to his home. He lives in a village, with homes that look like long wooden tunnels. They're made of bent wooden poles and the bark of birch trees. You notice men building a new house. The young man you followed places his deer on the ground. You want to know more about him and his people—if only you could talk to him. Wait! Is he signaling you? You approach quietly. He motions for you to sit down.

The young man speaks. His language is not English, but magically, you understand

"We are the People of the Longhouse."

him. "You are welcome among us," he says as he offers you a drink of cool water. "We are the People of the Longhouse." Now that you've seen their homes, you can tell why.

Nearby a woman is grinding ripe, dry kernels of corn and talking with an older woman, who's in charge of the home. The women are talking about choosing the new leader of the tribe. "The women here always choose the leader," the young man explains, "but the leader is a man." With a proud glance at the deer that he has carried back, the young man tells you that the men hunt deer, bears, turkeys, and other animals with their bows, arrows, and spears. He tells you that his father is at the river's edge building a canoe from a birch tree.

You ask the young man if all of America's first people live this way. "No," he replies. He stands and extends his arm, and points into the distance. "Far away from here," he says, "beyond the mountains, there are few forests but the grass grows high on the plains. There the people speak a different language, and they do not hunt for bears or deer. Instead, the people of the plains hunt a big shaggy animal called the buffalo. They do not live in longhouses. They make their homes, called tipis [TEE-pees], from buffalo hide. They also use the buffalo hide to make warm robes and to make the soles of their shoes, called moccasins. They roast buffalo meat for food. The people of the plains tell stories by painting designs on—can you guess? Buffalo hide!"

The Plains Indians hunted the buffalo.

The young man takes a breath and is about to go on, but just then someone calls his name. The young man's father is calling out to him that the canoe is finished and it's time to go fishing! You wave good-bye to the young man, who runs off to meet his father.

Would you like to hear a story from the Northern Plains people? Then turn in this book to "The Story of Jumping Mouse" on page 56.

Homes in the Desert, Homes by the Ocean

You've learned something important: you've learned that the first Americans were *not* one group of people who all lived in the same way. They were many different people who lived in different ways. There were the people of the longhouse, who lived, hunted, and farmed in the eastern woodland forests. There were the plains people, who hunted the buffalo. And far from them, there

Cliff houses in the desert.

were other people who lived in a place with no tall trees or rich brown earth. They lived in the desert, where the land is dry and rocky.

The people of the desert cut their homes in hard rock cliffs, and they used a special kind of mud, called adobe. Hundreds of people made their homes in these cliffs! Their land was dry, and they had little water. But still, the people of the desert learned to grow corn, beans, and squash. They became very skilled at using the earth to make strong, beautiful clay pots.

It's amazing that people could live where there was so little water. But now let's find out about some other people, whose lives were very different because they had so *much* water. They lived far to the north of the people of the desert. They lived by the Pacific Ocean. The people by the Pacific caught and ate many fish, like the strong-swimming salmon. They cut down trees and carved them into canoes. And some of the people carved trees into totem poles. With their tools they turned the wood into amazing faces and figures, and often painted them in bright colors. The figures on the poles helped them remember stories of the great deeds of their families and their people.

A totem pole.

The first Americans are also called Native Americans. ("Native" is a word that means "born here.") Many Native American people still live today in many places across the United States. Native Americans are also called American Indians. How did that name come about? To find out, we have to learn about some other people who came to America.

These children in Pryor Elementary School are members of the Crow tribe in Montana.

Christopher Columbus

For a long time, only the Native American people lived on the continent of North America. But then other people came here. These people came from Europe, all the way across the Atlantic Ocean.

One of the first Europeans to come here was a man named Christopher Columbus. Columbus was a sailor. He was also a dreamer, who dreamed about making a great voyage across the ocean.

In Columbus's time, you had to be daring to make a long ocean voyage. Back then, people could not travel as we do today. Today, you can get in a fast airplane and fly from one continent to another in less than a day. But back then, a trip could take months, even years. Back then, people had to walk or ride on animals. Or they had to board sailing ships and rely on the wind to blow them where they wanted to go. (Those old ships didn't have powerful engines to push them the way big ships do now.)

Where did the Europeans want to go? Most of all, to Asia. Travelers who had been to Asia told stories of palaces covered with gold and valuable jewels. And in Asia there were things that European people liked but could not get at home. The Europeans liked delicious spices, such as pepper. And they liked fine cloth, such as silk. But the Europeans could only get spices and silk from people in faraway Asian countries like China, Japan, and India.

The Europeans called all those Asian countries "the Indies." They spent a lot of time trying to figure out the quickest way to get from Europe to the Indies. In the time of Columbus, it was very hard to get to Asia from Europe. The voyage by sea was long, slow, and dangerous. You had to sail a long way south, *way, way* down to the very bottom of the continent of Africa, then *way, way* back up to Asia.

Now, Christopher Columbus had an unusual idea. He thought, "I don't want to follow the path that others have taken. It takes too long to get to Asia by sailing around Africa. Some people say the world is flat. But I know the world is round, and I think it's not too big. So, I should be able to get to Asia by sailing across the Atlantic Ocean instead. That way I'll bump into Asia from the other side."

Do you see what Columbus was thinking? If you look at a globe or a world map (like the one on page 118), you can see he had a good idea—except for two things. First, the earth is *a lot* bigger than he thought. And second, he didn't know about the big continent of North America lying right in his path! But don't think Columbus was stupid: in his time, hundreds of years ago, people in Europe just didn't know that the continent of North America existed.

When Columbus told people of his plan, lots of them laughed at him and said he would never make it. But not the king and queen of a country called Spain. When Columbus told King Ferdinand and Queen Isabella his plan, they thought about it for a long time, and at first they thought it wouldn't work. But finally they said, "All right, Christopher Columbus. We will help you make your voyage."

King Ferdinand and Queen Isabella helped by paying for Columbus's voyage. He needed ships and sailors. And he needed lots of supplies, including food and water. When you're on a long voyage across the ocean, you can't just stop at a grocery store to pick up a few things!

The Voyage to the "New World"

In the year 1492 three small ships set off across the Atlantic Ocean. These ships were named the *Niña*, the *Pinta*, and the *Santa María*.

You might think the sailors on these ships would be excited about their voyage. But they weren't. Columbus had planned a voyage that would take them across an unknown ocean, far out of sight of land—and in those days, sailors did not like to sail where they couldn't see land in the distance.

In the *Niña*, the *Pinta*, and the *Santa María*, Columbus and his crew set off for the Indies. They sailed and sailed for many days. After a few weeks the sailors started to grumble: "Shouldn't we be seeing land by now? Does our captain really know what he's

Columbus's ships, the *Niña*, the *Pinta*, and the *Santa María*.

doing?" Some began to get angry: "Show us the Indies, Columbus!" they shouted. Others grew scared: "How do we know that the sea ahead isn't filled with monsters?" they whispered. Others demanded, "Turn back, Columbus, before it's too late!"

Even Columbus was beginning to worry. "We really should be in the Indies by now," he thought. But he didn't want his men to worry. So he called out to them, "Not much farther, men! Take heart: we'll be there soon!" The men grumbled—but at least they didn't throw Columbus overboard!

After more than a month at sea, a sailor cried out the words that everyone had been longing to hear: "Land ho!" They had done it! With weary legs but happy hearts, they stepped from their ships onto a sandy beach. Very soon they met the native people, who were friendly to Columbus and his crew. Columbus was so sure he had reached the Indies that he called the native people "Indians"—and the name has been around ever since.

When Columbus landed, he didn't find what he expected. There weren't many spices, and there was no silk to be found. It took years for people to realize that Columbus and his men had not landed in the Indies at all. They had not reached Asia. Instead, they had landed off the shore of two continents that the Europeans back then didn't know about: North America and South America.

For the Europeans, this was a whole new world! For many years after Columbus's voyage in 1492, Europeans called North and South America "the New World," because for them it was a new place to explore and settle.

"Turn back, Columbus, before it's too late."

When did Columbus first sail to the New World? You'll always remember if you learn this little rhyme:

In fourteen hundred and ninety-two
Columbus sailed the ocean blue.

Pilgrims in the New World

Many years after Columbus, people in another European country began to think about coming to North America. These people were English—from the country called England.

A long time ago, on a windy day in September, a group of English people boarded a small ship called the *Mayflower*. Who boarded the *Mayflower?* Well, some sailors, of course, and lots of passengers—almost too many for the small ship! There were mothers and fathers, some young men, and thirty-four children—not to mention two dogs, a big hungry cat, and some chickens, cows, and pigs.

We call the passengers on the *Mayflower* the Pilgrims. Why did the Pilgrims want to travel to America? They knew the ocean voyage would be hard and dangerous. They knew they were leaving their homes in England, and they had no homes waiting for them in America.

The Pilgrims made the hard trip to America because they wanted to pray and worship in a way that was not allowed in England. The Pilgrims were very religious people. Because they wanted to pray and live in the way they believed was right, they were willing to sail off to the New World.

The Pilgrims, gathered on the deck of the *Mayflower*, pray before their long trip to America.

What was their trip like? Let's imagine that you could talk to one of the children who made the trip. Here's the story she tells you.

A Hard Journey

Our minds were made up to go— to leave England and build a new life in the New World.

I was scared and sad about leaving, but also a little excited. When we got to the harbor, there was our ship, the *Mayflower,* waiting for us. My mother said the *Mayflower* was a bonny ship—"bonny" means "beautiful." But it looked so *small* to me.

The ship was so small, and the ocean so very big! Many times the waves rose up as though they wanted to crush us. Storm after storm, week after week!

Oh, how we longed to feel the sun on our faces, or feel the breeze in our hair. But the sailors wanted none of us on deck during a storm. They said we were a nuisance.

So mostly we had to stay below. We sat on our hard bedding and hugged each other and prayed and sang. The waves tossed our little boat as though it weighed no more than a feather. We had to hold on tight to keep from sliding across the floor.

We had little to eat but hard biscuits and moldy cheese. There was no place to wash. Sometimes it smelled so bad I could hardly breathe. We got wet, dirty, and sick. One man died. I cried and wondered if the journey would ever end.

But it was not all sadness. On one of those stormy days, as we were tossed about, there in our ship, a baby was born! And he was named—what else?— "Oceanus," which means "from the ocean"!

At last we came to land, bonny land! It mattered not to us that the land was rocky, or that it was cold. We bowed our heads and gave thanks, for at last our hard journey was over!

A Thanksgiving Feast

When the Pilgrims came ashore, they named their new home Plymouth, after the town in England they had left behind. They anchored the *Mayflower* near a boulder, which has ever since been known as Plymouth Rock.

You might think that after all their troubles on the ocean, the Pilgrims' hard times would be over. But now they faced new troubles. It was winter, and the air was damp and cold. They had to build new homes. They had to find fresh water. It was too late in the year to grow crops for food. They started to run out of the supplies they had brought over on the *Mayflower*.

The Pilgrims might not have made it without the help they got from the woodland Indian people called the Wampanoag (WAHM-puh-nog). They shared their food with the Pilgrims and helped them hunt for more. Still, it was a very hard winter, and when it was finally over, only half of the brave Pilgrims were still alive.

But they didn't give up. When the warm spring breezes came, they worked hard to build new homes and grow crops for food. The Wampanoag Indians showed the Pilgrims how to plant new crops, like corn. They also taught the Pilgrims a lot about catching fish, and about hunting for food.

What a joy it was for the Pilgrims to see their crops growing through the summer months: wild rice, pumpkins, cranberries, and rows and rows of corn! When fall came, the Pilgrims felt so thankful for the harvest, and for their lives in the New World, that they held a celebration. Some of their woodland Indian friends joined them for a great

The first Thanksgiving.

feast—a feast that you might know as Thanksgiving. They prepared platters heaped with corn and other vegetables. They cooked fish, deer, and turkeys. Their Thanksgiving feast lasted for three days!

Happy Birthday, America!

The Pilgrims came to America from England. Many, many other people came to America, too. They came from other European countries, such as France and Spain. But in the early years of our country, most came from England.

England, as you know, is far from America (as you can see on a world map or globe). There's a whole ocean between England and America. (Do you remember the name of this ocean? In case you forgot, it's called the Atlantic Ocean.)

Back in England, the people were ruled by a king. You've seen pictures of kings, right? A king wears a crown and fancy robes. He gives orders and everyone is supposed to do what he says.

The people who came to America from England were supposed to obey the king of England. And for a long time they did. But sometimes they disagreed with the English king. Sometimes they said, "The king is so far away, in a place that's very different from America. How does he know what's best for us? Should we always be ruled by a faraway king? Should we always let someone else make the rules that we have to obey? Well, maybe we should think about ruling ourselves!"

And that's what the people in America did. On July 4, 1776, we Americans decided to be free from England and rule ourselves. We decided to become a new country, our own country, called the United States of America. That's why July 4, 1776, is the birthday of our nation.

The Fourth of July is also called Independence Day

The Statue of Liberty was a birthday present to the United States. For our country's one hundredth birthday, the people of France gave us this tall and beautiful statue of a lady, sometimes called "Miss Liberty." "Liberty" means "freedom." The Statue of Liberty stands in New York's harbor. She holds the torch of freedom in her hand, and shines a light for all the world to see.

because it's the day we said we would no longer be part of England: instead, we announced that America was now "independent," which meant free to make our own rules and choose our own leaders. On July 4, 1776, some of our leaders signed a very important paper—in fact, it's one of the most important pieces of writing in our country's history. It's called the Declaration of Independence, and it explained why our country should be free of England. (Before we could be free, we had to fight a war. You'll learn about that war, called the American Revolution, in the First Grade book in this series.)

Americans still celebrate Independence Day every year on the Fourth of July. Sometimes you'll see fireworks, or go on a picnic, or watch a parade. On Independence Day, the Fourth of July, we celebrate our country and our freedom and our democracy.

Fireworks on the Fourth of July.

"Democracy"—What's That?

It's a big word, and a very important word to Americans. "Democracy" means "rule of the people."

Now, why is that so important? Because when the United States of America was a new country, most people in most parts of the world did not rule themselves. Most people were ruled by kings or queens who decided just about everything. But when our country began, we decided to do things differently. In America, we decided to let ordinary people rule themselves.

That's what we mean when we say America is a democracy: it's a place where ordinary people rule. In a democracy, there is no king or queen to decide things. People talk about what they think is best for the country. Then they make their own decisions about what to do.

Not Completely Free

You've learned that on July 4, 1776, the United States of America became a free country. But not everyone in America was free.

The slaves were not free.

In the southern part of the United States, black people were not free. By sunrise on July 4, 1776, black men and women were hard at work. They cut tobacco and picked cotton in the hot sun. They pulled vegetables and hoed the dirt. If they grew tired, they could not stop to rest, because nearby there was a man—a white man— who might use the whip in his hand to beat them if they stopped working.

Away from the fields, up at the big house, a black man hitched the horses to a carriage and prepared to drive a white man wherever he wanted to go—even though the driver could not go where *he* wanted. Black women cooked big meals over hot stoves— not for themselves but for the people who owned the house.

The people who owned the house were the "masters." They didn't own just the house: they also owned the black people. What's that? How can you *own* a person? A person is not a thing! You can't buy or sell a person, as you can buy or sell a house, or a wagon, or a cow, can you?

Well, you can't now, but you could back then. In the southern part of America, the black people were not free: they were slaves. Slaves could be bought and sold. The white people were their masters. The slaves had to do what the masters said.

The slaves were brought to America from Africa. They didn't come here because they wanted to. They were forced to come. And when they got here, they were forced to work, and all their hard work was for their masters. They were not free.

Many, many years later, after a terrible war, slavery was ended in America. It took a long time for people to realize that in the United States, freedom is not just for some people, but for *everyone*, no matter what color you are.

Presidents: Leaders in a Democracy

In the United States we don't have a king or queen, but we do have leaders. We choose the people we want to lead us. In the United States we call our most important leader the President.

George Washington, our first President.

George Washington: The Father of Our Country

Our first President was George Washington. You can see his picture on a quarter and on a dollar bill.

George Washington is known as "the father of our country." Americans trusted George Washington. People said he was "first in war, first in peace, and first in the hearts of his countrymen."

Why did the people love Washington so much? Because he worked hard to help the country. And because he was an honest man, and people respected that.

There's a famous story about George Washington. It's a legend, meaning that it probably didn't really happen, but people keep telling the story because it has something real at the heart of it. The legend of "George Washington and the Cherry Tree" tells us about Washington's honesty. Here's the story.

George Washington and the Cherry Tree

When George was a small boy, his father gave him a fine new hatchet. George was delighted. He tried his new hatchet on logs from the woodpile: *chop, chop, chop!*

Then a thought came to him: wouldn't it be exciting to cut down a real tree?

So he went into the nearby orchard. He saw a fine young tree and set to work: *chop, chop, chop!* The tree fell—*bang!*—to the ground. George was pleased: how well his hatchet chopped! But then he looked at the tree. It was a special cherry tree that had been sent to his father from England. George began to feel uneasy.

Soon his father came home. When he went into the orchard, he saw the cherry tree lying on the ground. He was angry: he had hoped soon to pick some large, juicy cherries from this tree, but now look at it! He asked one person after another who had done this deed. No one knew. Finally he came to young George.

By this time George knew that he had done something wrong and thoughtless. He felt ashamed, and also scared, for his father was very angry.

"George," said his father sternly, "do you know who cut down my cherry tree?"

What should George do? He looked up and saw his father's angry eyes. But George did not turn away. He said, "Father, I cannot tell a lie. I cut down the tree. I did it without thinking, and I am sorry."

"I am sorry, too, my boy," said George's father. "But I would rather lose all my trees than have you tell a lie or be afraid of telling the truth."

Thomas Jefferson: The Idea Man

Thomas Jefferson was the third President of the United States. You can see his picture on a nickel.

Thomas Jefferson.

When Thomas Jefferson was a boy, people noticed his red hair and freckles, his bright green eyes, and his huge appetite for—what do you think? No, not candy or ice cream, but books! Which of course does not mean he *ate* books. But he read as many as he could get his hands on, and he wanted to understand everything in them.

On days when his friends would play games or go hunting, Tom would sneak a book from his father's library and settle down to read. There were so many questions he wanted to answer! Who were the great heroes and what did they do? Why do violets grow in the woods? How do you play the violin? Jefferson taught himself to play the violin by reading a book!

But don't get the idea that Thomas Jefferson was no fun. He liked horseback riding and dancing and exploring the woods near his home. But most of all he liked books. He even said, "I cannot live without books!"

From so much reading, and so much thinking about what he read, Jefferson got many ideas. He wrote down many of his ideas in books of his own. He also wrote (with a little help from some friends) something that's shorter than a book, but is one of the most important pieces of writing in our country's history. You've heard of it: it's the Declaration of Independence.

In the Declaration of Independence, Thomas Jefferson said, "All men are created equal." No one had ever started a country with that idea before.

Honest Abe Lincoln

Look at a penny. Do you know the face on this coin? That's Abraham Lincoln, the sixteenth President of the United States.

Young Abe grew up on the frontier, where there weren't many people, though there were, as Abe once said, "many bears and other wild animals." His family was not rich. Their home was a small log cabin with only one window.

Every day Abe helped his father with the farmwork. He was a strong boy—so strong that by the time he was only eight years old, he could swing an axe and chop trees almost as well as a fullgrown man.

Young Abe Lincoln reads by firelight.

Abe helped clear the woods and plow the fields. At night, even though he was very tired, he worked hard at something else: he taught himself to read.

Now, this was in the days before electricity, so Abe couldn't just switch on a light. At night in the dark log cabin, the only light came from the fireplace. In the glow of the firelight, Abe read as many books as he could. Books were scarce in those days: there were no libraries on the frontier! Many families did not own any books except a Bible. Abe would sometimes walk for miles just to borrow a book to read. One of his favorite books told about the life of George Washington.

President Lincoln with his son Tad.

There's a story people tell about young Abe Lincoln and that book he liked so much, the book about George Washington. The book did not belong to Abe; he had borrowed it. He would read it at night until it was time to go to sleep. To keep the book safe, he stuck it between two logs in the cabin. But one night it rained, and the book got soaked. The very next morning Abe took the book to its owner. He said that he had ruined the book, and he offered to pay for it. The man who owned the book was not angry with Abe, because he told the truth.

As a young man, Abraham Lincoln split wood into fence rails for his neighbors. He worked on a boat, and as a postman, and as a storekeeper. Once, when he was minding the store, a customer paid him six cents too much. When Abe Lincoln realized the mistake, he walked six miles to return the money to her.

For much of his life, Lincoln was known as "Honest Abe." It's good that hardworking, honest Abraham Lincoln became our country's President when he did, for he led our country through some of its most difficult times.

Theodore Roosevelt.

Theodore Roosevelt: The Teddy Bear President

Meet Theodore Roosevelt, the twenty-sixth President of the United States. He didn't like the nickname "Teddy," though many people called him that.

When he was a little boy, Theodore was not very healthy. He had trouble breathing and he could not see well. He was determined to do something important with his life, but his sick body stood in his way. His father said, "Theodore, you have the mind but not the body . . . you will have to make your body."

Theodore worked on making both his mind and body stronger. He read many books. He wanted to learn everything he could about nature. He collected bugs, mice, birds, and other creatures for his own little museum. His father built a gymnasium in their home, and Theodore exercised every day. He worked hard and his weak body became strong. When Theodore grew up, he became a boxer, a hunter, a cowboy, a crime fighter, a writer—and a President of the United States!

"TR," as he was sometimes called, loved to be outdoors, and he enjoyed hunting. He also believed in playing by the rules and being fair. Once, on a hunting trip, someone who was with President Roosevelt fired at a little bear and missed. The President had a perfect shot at the bear, but he refused to shoot. The first shot had surprised the little bear, and now he was too dizzy and confused to escape. Teddy Roosevelt said it wasn't fair to shoot a bear in that condition.

Well, the next thing you know, newspapers around the country were printing drawings of Teddy Roosevelt with his arm around a little bear. The newspaper reporters wrote about TR's sense of fair play. Then toy companies got the idea to make little stuffed bears and call them Teddy Bears, after our "Fair Play President," Teddy Roosevelt!

Mount Rushmore

For a long time people have thought that these four presidents—Washington, Jefferson, Lincoln, and Roosevelt—are special. About seventy years ago, a man had a big idea—in fact, a *very* big idea. He thought, "Why not carve the faces of these great Presidents in rock, and make them so big that everyone can see them for miles around?" That's just what he did, on a mountainside in the state of South Dakota, with a lot of help. It took many workers fourteen years to carry out the sculptor's design of

Mount Rushmore. What kinds of tools do you think they used? Would you believe they used huge drills, dynamite, and jackhammers to shape the hard granite rock? What a tremendous job to turn a mountain into a monument!

Other Presidents

There have been many other Presidents of the United States. You'll learn about them later (in school and in the other books of this series). The important things to know now are, first, that the President is the leader of our country; and, second, that *we choose* the people we want to lead us. They don't get the job just because, like kings or queens, they're born into a certain family. Instead, every four years, grown-ups in the United States get to choose the person they want to be their President. That's called voting. We vote to choose our President.

Who is President now? Do you know? See if you can find out, because that person may change our country and your life!

The President lives in a special home called the White House. The President's home is a place that all Americans can visit. If you go to the city of Washington, D.C., try to see this beautiful place.

III.
Visual Arts

INTRODUCTION

For the kindergartner, art should mostly take the form of *doing*: drawing, painting, cutting and pasting, working with clay and other materials. In this section, we suggest many activities your child can do, sometimes with your help. You can also find good art activities in some of the books recommended below.

By reading this section aloud with your child, you can also help him or her learn some of the ways that we talk about art, and introduce some wonderful works of art. In this way, your child will come to understand that, while art is *doing*, it is also *seeing and thinking*. By looking closely at art, and talking about it, your child will begin to develop a love of art and a habit of enjoying it in thoughtful, active ways.

But let us repeat: Beyond looking at art and talking about it, do try to provide your child with materials and opportunities to be a practicing artist!

Suggested Resources
Art activity books:
Kids Create! Art and Craft Experiences for 3- to 9-Year-Olds by Laurie Carlson (Williamson Publishing, 1990)

Scribble Cookies and Other Independent Creative Art Experiences for Children and *Mudworks: Creative Clay, Dough, and Modeling Experiences* by MaryAnn F. Krohl (Bright Ring Publishing, 1985 and 1989)

Something to Do (When There's Nothing to Do): A Coloring and Activity Book by Mary Englebreit (Andrews and McMeel, 1995)

Books that reprint artworks for children:
Colors, Lines, Shapes, Stories, four books by Philip Yenawine (Museum of Modern Art and Delacorte Press, 1991)

The *Come Look with Me* series by Gladys Blizzard (Thomasson-Grant); titles include *Come Look with Me: Enjoying Art with Children* (1990); *Come Look with Me: Animals in Art* (1992); *Come Look with Me: World of Play* (1993), *Come Look with Me: Exploring Landscape Art with Children* (1992).

The *I Spy* series by Lucy Micklethwait (Greenwillow Books); titles include *I Spy* (1992), *I Spy Two Eyes* (1993), and *I Spy a Lion* (1994).

Coloring books:
Masterpieces by Mary Martin and Steven Zorn (Running Press, 1990)

Various coloring books from Dover Publications, 31 East 2nd Street, Mineola, NY 11501

What Do Artists Do?

Do you like to play with clay, draw pictures, and build with blocks? When you do these things, you're making art! People have been making art since the earliest times. In fact, making art is one thing that makes people different from animals. Can a cat draw? No, but you can!

People who create art are called artists. Some artists draw with pencil on paper. Some artists paint pictures. Maybe you've used brushes and watercolors to paint on paper. Many painters use oil paints to paint pictures on a thick, tough material called canvas. Other artists cut paper or other ma-

terials, such as cloth, into pieces, then they glue the pieces onto a surface to produce what's called a collage. Other artists make statues; these artists are called sculptors. One thing that all artists need is imagination, which is something you probably have plenty of!

Here is a child's collage. You can make a collage, too. The only things you need are paper, scissors, and glue.

Color, Color Everywhere

What color are your eyes? What colors are the clothes you're wearing? What color is a school bus? What color is the sky today?

The world is alive with color. How many colors can you name? Red, blue—what else?

When we think of some things, we think of their colors. When we think of the sky, we think of blue. What color does grass make you think of? How about ketchup? Color can make a big difference in the way we see some things. Would you like to dip french fries in *green* ketchup? Wouldn't it be funny to drink *blue* milk? You can put a few drops of blue food coloring in a glass of milk and try it. It tastes the same, but does it look right?

Some colors are "warm," like reds and oranges. This doesn't mean that a red page is actually warm to the touch. But it does mean that such colors can give us a warm kind of feeling. Warm colors, like red, orange, and yellow, might make us think of a fire engine, or flames, or the sun, or sandy beaches.

Some colors are "cool," like blues and greens. They make us think of the cool ocean or a shady lawn. While warm colors seem to jump forward, cool colors seem to be farther away. Paintings made up of mostly cool colors usually have a different feeling than those with mostly warm colors.

Activity: Separate your crayons, markers, colored pencils, or oil pastels into warm and cool piles. Then draw a picture of a tree using only warm colors. Next draw the same thing using only cool colors. When you look at your pictures, what thoughts do each of them bring to mind? Which is your favorite?

Activity: You can make your own color paintings with a sponge, some paper, and tempera or poster paints. Take a sponge, wet but not dripping, and run it over the paper. Then dip your brush in the paint and let the paint drip onto the paper. Do this with several colors. What happens? The paint drops spread out and mix together. Now, what will you call your color painting?

Here are two paintings, one done with mostly cool colors and the other with mostly warm colors. In Pieter Bruegel (BROY-ghel) the Elder's *Hunters in the Snow*, what season is shown? Have you ever noticed how there are fewer bright colors in winter than in spring? The artist used mainly white, black, and brown to suggest the cold winter weather. The trees are bare, and the icy gray-green of the frozen pond is matched by the dull color of the sky. Brrr!

Bruegel lived in the north of Europe, where the winters are long and very cold. Many years after Bruegel, and far, away from Europe, there lived an artist by the name of Paul Gauguin (go-GAN). He spent part of his life on an island in the South Pacific Ocean called Tahiti, where it never gets cold. In his painting called *Tahitian Landscape*, Gauguin used warm colors to make us feel the hot sun and see the bright, clear skies. Red, yellow, and orange are warm colors. Look at Gaugin's painting and point to all the warm colors you can find.

Some artists use color in their paintings, but they don't include people or things. Helen Frankenthaler's *Blue Atmosphere* is a painting made up of colors. The colors seem to float in the air because of the special way the artist put the paint on the canvas. Though the artist called this painting *Blue Atmosphere,* there's a lot of red in it. The fiery red seems to be pushing back the cool, deep blue. What name would *you* give this painting?

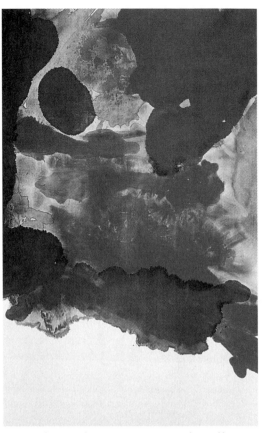

Follow That Line!

You may not notice it unless you're looking for it, but you're surrounded by lines. Lines are all around us in nature and in art. You make lines every time you write your name or draw a picture. Lines on the street tell cars what side to stay on. Sidewalks are filled with lines and cracks. Zebras are striped with lines. Bare tree branches make lines against the sky. Look at your hands: they're covered with thin lines.

Lines come in all kinds: straight, curved, zigzag, and wavy.

straight   curved   zigzag   wavy

Each kind of line has its own personality. Straight lines point us in a direction, like an arrow. Curved lines make us think of motion, like a ball rolling. Zigzag lines are full of energy, like a bolt of lightning. Wavy lines can be calm, like waves lapping on a beach.

Activity: Hunt for lines where you live. Do you see straight lines around windows and doors? Curved lines around a clock face? Can you find any wavy lines (perhaps in curtains) or zigzags? Now, make a "line book." You'll need

paper and crayons. Using as many colors as you want, on one page draw straight lines. (You can draw two pages of straight lines if you want: one page up and down, the other page across.) On another page, draw zigzag lines. On another page, draw wavy lines. On another page, draw curved lines. On a final page, draw each kind of line, just once or as many times as you want.

Artists use lines in different ways. Here's a painting by Joan Miró (ZHU-ahn mih-ROW) in which the lines are easy to see. But what is it a painting of? The title will help you. Miró called his painting *People and Dog in the Sun*. Miró believed in painting what he saw in his dreams, and as you know, dreams can be a little strange. Let's look at the lines in Miró's painting. Can you find some straight lines? How about some curving lines? Miro has lines come together to make shapes. What do you think the round red shape is supposed to be? (Think of the title.) Where is the dog? Use your finger to trace along the lines that the artist has used to draw the people and the dog. If you turn the picture upside down, only then does the big boy stand on his feet!

Now let's look at a painting by Henri Matisse (ma-TEECE). The first thing you might notice about *The Purple Robe* is the bright, joyful colors, but for now let's look at the lines in the painting. Matisse painted many bold, thick lines. (See how different they are from the sharp, thin lines used by Miró in *People and Dog in the Sun*.) In *The Purple Robe,* look for lines that are like each other. These repeating lines are called *patterns*. Do you see the different patterns on the wallpaper behind the woman? One side has a pattern of straight lines,

while the other side has a curvy pattern. Take your finger and trace the different lines. Look for other patterns: don't forget the robe, or the vase on the table. Can you find some patterns where you live?

Look at this picture by the Japanese artist Hokusai (HOE-coo-sye). It's made up completely of lines. What did Hokusai draw? You may not know exactly, but you probably recognize a person holding a musical instrument that looks a little like a banjo. Hokusai named this drawing *Tuning the Samisen*. It's a picture of a musician

getting her instrument ready to play. Can you find some thin lines in the drawing? How about some thick ones? Do some things in the drawing look soft to touch? Does anything look hard and smooth?

Activity: Find one of your favorite toys and put it on the table in front of you. You can use a teddy bear, a fire truck, a doll, a boat—whatever you like. Look at your toy to see if it has any straight lines. Does it have any curved or zigzag lines? Using a pencil, draw the outline of your toy. Keep making lines that show what your toy looks like. When you finish your drawing, you can color it with crayons or paint it if you want to.

A child used lines to draw this doll.

Looking at Pictures—Really Looking!

PARENTS: Art is first and foremost making and doing. Children need lots of time and materials to draw, paint, cut, paste, work with clay, etc. But the love of art also develops through seeing. Looking at works of art and talking about them can be a rewarding and enjoyable experience.

This section is meant to provide ways for you and your child to look at and talk about works of art. As your child looks, it will be helpful for him to touch the pictures, tracing lines or pointing out colors. We suggest some specific questions to direct your child's attention. Be positive in responding to your child's reactions and questions, and feel free to go beyond the questions provided or to follow the path of your child's curiosity.

Snap the Whip.

An American artist, Winslow Homer, painted this picture more than one hundred years ago. It shows boys playing a game at recess: do you see the little red schoolhouse in the background? (Does it look like your school?) In the game of Snap the Whip, children hold hands in a line, then they run behind a leader, who runs fast and turns quickly—so quickly that you can get thrown out of the line! Have you ever played this game?

- How can you tell the boys are moving?
- Name some of the colors in the painting. Do the colors seem mostly "cool" or "warm" to you?
- If you were going to be one of the children in the painting, which one would you be? Why?
- If you were to paint a picture of children playing a game, what would you paint? What would your picture look like?

Children's Games. Pieter Bruegel painted this picture more than four hundred years ago. But many of the games it shows are still played by children today. Bruegel painted more than ninety different games in this single painting!

- Do you see any games you recognize or have played yourself? Can you find children playing marbles? Tug-of-war? Leapfrog? Do you see the children walking on stilts and rolling hoops? (If you have a magnifying glass, it may help you see the tiny figures. Of course, what you're looking at in this book is just a small copy of the painting. The real painting is a whole lot bigger. How big? About four feet high by five feet long. An adult can help you measure off those dimensions.)
- To see all of these games going on at once, where would you have to be standing?
- What colors did Bruegel use for the children's clothes? Do the children in the painting dress differently from the way you dress today?

Le Gourmet.

This painting is by Pablo Picasso. A "gourmet" (gore-MAY) is someone who knows a lot about good food.

- What is the little girl doing?
- What might be in her bowl? Does she like it?
- What colors has Picasso used in this painting? What color did he use most?
- If you were going to make a painting using a lot of one color, what color would you use?

The Banjo Lesson. This painting is by the African-American artist Henry O. Tanner. (Can you see where he painted his name in the lower-left corner?)

- Who do you think these two people might be? What are they doing?
- How do you think the man feels about the boy?
- What part of the painting has the most light? Where do you think this light might be coming from? Do you see how Tanner has made the two people stand out by shining the light around them?

The Bath. The woman who painted this, Mary Cassatt (ka-SAHT), was an American, though she lived most of her life in Paris (a big city in France). She loved to paint pictures of women and children together. When she painted this picture, about one hundred years ago, many people did not have running water and big bathtubs. Children were sometimes washed with water in a small basin.

- How do you think the basin got filled with water? Is there something in the picture that someone used to fill the basin?
- Who do you think these two people might be? How does the woman seem to feel about the child?
- Use your finger to trace some of the different lines you see in the painting.
- *The Bath* might remind you of the painting you just looked at, *The Banjo Lesson.* Can you think of some ways in which these paintings are alike?

Mother's Helper.
This painting is by the Mexican artist Diego Rivera (dee-AY-go ri-VAIR-a).

- Think about the title of the picture, _Mother's Helper_. What do you think the girl is helping her mother do?
- Look at the expressions on the faces. How do you think the girl and her mother feel? If they were to speak, who would speak first, and what do you think she might say?
- Look away from the picture and then quickly look back at it. What do your eyes see first? Are they drawn to the bright yellow-orange bouquet near the center? Where else is this color repeated? What other colors did Rivera use?

It's fun to look at and talk about art. Whether you see a painting in a museum, a store, a house, or reproduced in a book, here are some things you can talk about that will help you _really look_ at the picture:

- Does the painting have one color that seems to stand out most?
- Pick out three colors and see how many places the artist has repeated them.
- Describe some of the lines in the painting. Are they straight, curved, zigzag, or wavy? Are they thick or thin, clear or blurry? Do any of the lines make a pattern?
- If there are people in the painting, what do their expressions tell you about them? What might they be thinking or saying?
- Can you imagine a story about this painting? Would it be happy, scary, funny, serious, mysterious, or something else?

Sculpture: Statues, Monuments, and More

Look at these pictures. The first one shows a statue of one of our Presidents, Abraham Lincoln. The second one shows a totem pole that was made by Native Americans who live near the Pacific Ocean.

The statue and the totem pole are also called sculptures. A sculpture isn't flat like a painting. You can walk around a sculpture and look at it from all sides. Or, if it's a small sculpture, like this blue hippopotamus, you can pick it up and examine it. An artist who creates a sculpture is called a sculptor.

Have you ever made your own sculpture out of clay? Sculptures are usually made of clay, wood, metal, stone, or plastic. Have you seen any sculptures in your town or city?

Sculptures come in all sizes, from figures as small as your thumb to works bigger than a full-grown tree.

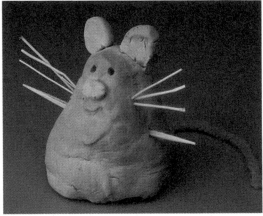

You can make a mouse like this one out of some clay, a few toothpicks and broom straws, and a little yarn.

A very big statue is probably the most famous sculpture in the United States: the Statue of Liberty. "Miss Liberty" was designed as a lighthouse. Can you find her torch? Did you know that the Statue of Liberty is so big that people can walk around inside it and climb up to its head? The statue is made up of hundreds of sheets of a metal called copper, over a strong framework of iron. It is one of the largest sculptures in the world.

Activity: Make a turtle sculpture. You will need: modeling clay or play dough, a plastic knife or a pencil. Divide your clay into two parts. One part should be twice as big as the other one. Make two balls out of your clay. The big ball is going to be your turtle's body, the little ball will be the head. Stand on your tiptoes and drop the big ball on a smooth floor. Now the ball of clay should have a flattened side. Pick up the clay and turn it over. Make legs by pressing the flattened ball at four corners. Turn the clay over and stick the smaller ball to the front of the larger ball,

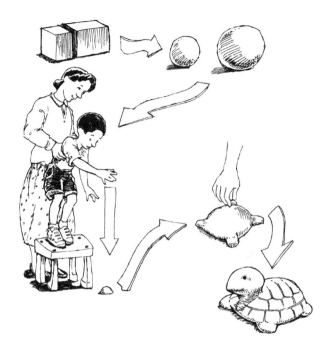

smoothing them together with your thumbs. Then you can make a design on the turtle's back with a plastic knife or a pencil. To sign your sculpture, you can put your name or initials on the turtle's stomach if you like.

Lobster Trap and Fish Tail.

Mobiles

Did you know that some sculptures can actually move? The American artist Alexander Calder invented the mobile. Most sculptures stand still, but a mobile moves! Look at *Lobster Trap and Fish Tail.* Which part do you think is meant to be the trap, and which the fish tail? Do the dark shapes at the bottom remind you of plants swaying under water? Calder carefully balanced all the sections of this mobile so that even the slightest breeze would push its shapes in one direction or the other. He also had to arrange the arms so that none of the parts would hit each other when they moved. Mobiles are fun to watch!

Activity: With an adult's help, you can make a mobile. You'll need two plastic drinking straws, about four feet of string or fishing line, some cardboard (or heavy construction paper), and scissors. Use a small piece of the string to tie the two straws together to form an "X." Then use about a foot of string to hang the mobile from. Draw four shapes or objects on the cardboard. You could make the moon and some stars, or some of your favorite animals, or some shapes like triangles, circles, and squares. Whatever shapes you decide on, make them about the same size. Cut out the shapes and decorate them on both sides. Now ask an adult to help you punch a hole in the top of each shape. Cut four pieces of string, each about 10 inches long. Tie one end through the hole in each shape, and the other end to one of the ends of the crossed straws. Hang your mobile where there's a breeze and watch it move!

IV.
Music

INTRODUCTION

We encourage you to give your child a wide range of musical experiences—singing songs, listening to all kinds of music, dancing around at home, attending local musical performances.

One of the best and easiest activities is *singing with your child*. We suggest some favorite songs in this section (see pages 184–91). If you don't feel confident about your own singing voice, remember that in your own home, you're the star! It's fine to play tapes and compact discs for your child (see the Suggested Resources, below), but the more you sing with your child, the more comfortable you'll feel, and the more you'll both enjoy music together.

Some families will choose to provide their children with lessons that will take the children to a level of musical competence beyond what we describe in the following pages. Of course, different children will develop musical appreciation and skills at different rates and to different degrees. What's important is for you and your child to enjoy music and have fun with it.

You can help develop your child's knowledge and appreciation of music through the activities suggested in this section. Some of the activities ask your child to play with the basic elements of music, such as rhythm, pitch, and tempo. Others involve moving and listening to music. Repetition is fine: children love to hear, sing, or dance to the same song over and over again.

Have fun and enjoy these activities and songs with your child.

Suggested Resources
Books:
Kids Make Music! by Avery Hart and Paul Mantell (Williamson Publishing, 1993)
My First Music Book by Helen Drews (Dorling Kindersley, 1993)

Recordings that collect favorite songs for children:
Disney's Children's Favorites, vols. 1–4 (Disney Songtapes)
Family Folk Festival: A Multi-cultural Sing-Along (Music for Little People)
Shake It to the One That You Love the Best: Play Songs and Lullabies from Black Musical Traditions by Cheryl Warren Mattox (Warren-Mattox Productions, 1989)
Wee Sing Sing-Alongs series (Price Stern Sloan)

Do You Like Music?

Do you like music? Do you like to sing and dance? Do you have a favorite song or a favorite kind of music?

You can make music by drumming on a pot, or humming through a paper-towel tube, or shaking a plastic container half-full of dry beans, or plucking rubber bands stretched over a small open box. With a little imagination, you can be a one-man band, with all sorts of homemade instruments!

Would you like to play an instrument someday? With practice, maybe you'll learn to play one of the instruments pictured here.

PARENTS: If you have recordings that feature the instruments pictured here, play them and point out the sound of the specific instruments to your child. If you and your child get a chance to see, hear, and touch the actual instruments, that's even better!

flute

drum

trumpet

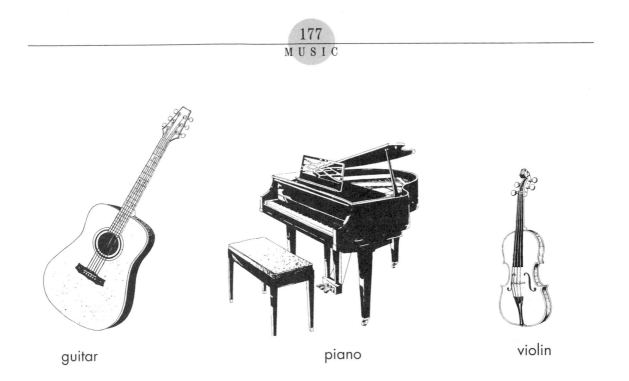

guitar   piano   violin

What instrument are these children playing?

Musical Activities for Parents and Children

Activity 1: MOVING RESPONSIVELY TO MUSIC

You and your child can have fun moving to music. When you play music, talk about how the music makes you feel, and encourage your child to be comfortable and creative: there is no right or wrong way to move to the music. At times, get up and move with your child; it's fun!

Get Ready: Go to a room in which you can move around comfortably. There, you'll need to have the equipment necessary to play a recording of one of the following selections or some other music that encourages steady, rhythmic movement.

SUGGESTED MUSIC: recordings of Tchaikovsky's *Nutcracker* ballet; or "The March of the Siamese Children" from the Rodgers and Hammerstein musical *The King and I*; or "The March of the Toys" from Victor Herbert's *Babes in Toyland*.

Go: Play the music and talk with your child about the way the music makes him feel. Ask him, "How does this part of the music make you feel like moving?"

For *The Nutcracker,* you can play music from different scenes, and move in different ways as suggested by the music. Some contrasting scenes you might want to try include, from Act I, "March"; and, from Act II, "Tea (Chinese Dance)," "Trepak (Russian Dance)," and "Dance of the Sugar Plum Fairy."

Go a Little Further: Listen with your child to Camille Saint-Saëns's *Carnival of the Animals,* which uses different instruments of the orchestra to paint musical portraits of animals. (Many recordings of this work are available; some include a narrator reading amusing poems written by Ogden Nash to go along with the music.) You and your child can "act out" the animals by using different movements while listening to the music, such as hopping, skipping, bucking, short steps, or high steps.

Activity 2: "BEAT IT!"

Get Ready: Talk with your child about steady sounds, that is, sounds that you hear over and over again, such as the ticking of a clock, or the sound made by windshield wipers or a washing machine.

Tell your child that a steady sound has a steady *beat,* like her own heartbeat. Have her place her hand over her heart and ask her, "Do you feel the steady beat?" (If she can't feel it, have her run around or jump up and down, then try to feel it.)

Now tell your child that you're going to say a rhyme with a steady beat. Tell her to listen to the following rhyme:

> Clap your hands
> On the beat.
> Steady sounds
> Are so neat!

After you repeat the rhyme a few times, begin clapping your hands to its steady beat, and ask your child to join you in "clapping to the beat," as follows:

> **Clap** your **hands**
> **On** the **beat.**
> **Stead**-y **sounds**
> **Are** so **neat!**

Go: Tell your child that you're going to play a game called Beat It! You're going to use your hands and feet to make different steady beats. Ask her to watch and listen as you do the following:

> *clap, clap, stomp*
> *clap, clap, stomp*
> *clap, clap, stomp*

Ask your child to join in with the beat. Then let her continue clapping and stomping the beat on her own a few more times.

Continue the game with other steady beats. Follow the pattern: you clap and stomp, she joins in, then she finishes on her own. You can make up your own steady beat, but keep it simple at first, such as:

- *clap, stomp, clap, stomp*
- *clap, clap, clap, stomp*
- *stomp, stomp, clap*

You can also ask your child to make up a steady beat for you to follow.

Go a Little Further: You and your child can clap to the beat in poems with strong cadences, including many Mother Goose rhymes (see pages 22–36), such as:

Pat-a-cake, **pat**-a-cake, **bake**r's **man!**
Bake me a **cake** as **fast** as you **can.**

You can also clap to the beat in many children's songs. For example:

Old MacDonald **had** a **farm,**
E-I-E-I-O.

Activity 3: LOUD AND QUIET

This activity has several parts. It begins with everyday sounds, then uses a familiar song, then drumming, and finally recorded music.

Which baby is loud? Which baby is quiet?

Get Ready: Ask your child to talk with you about loud sounds and quiet sounds (you can raise your voice on "LOUD" and whisper the word *"quiet"*). A baby crying is LOUD; a baby sleeping is *quiet.* Ask your child to point to various objects in the room that make a sound: a telephone, a squeaky door, a fan, a smoke alarm, a refrigerator. Ask if the sound they make is loud or quiet. Then talk about sounds your child is familiar with (not necessarily in the room but anywhere) that are usually loud (for example, a siren or a bus engine) or usually quiet (for example, a whisper or a cat's purr).

Now ask your child to sing with you a song that has some LOUD parts and some *quiet* parts. One such song is an old favorite, "John Jacob Jingleheimer Schmidt." Here are the words:

> John Jacob Jingleheimer Schmidt,
> His name is my name too.
> Whenever we go out,
> The people always shout,
> JOHN JACOB JINGLEHEIMER SCHMIDT!

Repeat it three times. Sing the first four lines more quietly each time, until on the third time you are just whispering the lines; but in all verses end with a loud shout!

Go: Now you need a toy drum—or if you don't have a drum, you can use an upside-down kitchen pot or bucket or an empty oatmeal container. You also need something to use as a drumstick, such as a pencil or wooden spoon.

Say the following lines with your child several times, making your voice sound LOUD on the first two lines and *quiet* on the second two lines. Then ask him to say the lines with you and play the drums as the words direct. (You can show him how to use his fingertips to rub the drum for a quiet sound.)

> MY DRUM CAN SOUND LOUD,
> WITH A LOUD SOUND, A LOUD SOUND.

> *My drum can sound quiet,*
> *With a quiet sound, a quiet sound.*

Talk with your child about what he does differently to make the drum sound loud or quiet.

Go a Little Further: Listen to music with dramatic contrasts between loud and quiet passages. Talk with your child about how the loud and quiet sounds change the way the music feels, and what kind of different movements he could do to go along with the loud and quiet parts. For example, a favorite work that builds dramatically from quiet to loud is Grieg's "In the Hall of the Mountain King" from *Peer Gynt*. Have your child tiptoe during the quiet parts, and jump up and down during the loud parts.

Activity 4: FAST AND SLOW

Get Ready: Talk with your child about animals that usually move slowly, such as turtles and cows. Then talk about animals that can move very quickly, such as birds and mice. Ask your child to think of other animals that we think of as usually moving slowly or quickly.

Go: Sing "Old MacDonald" with your child, then choose one of the animals you discussed earlier that moves slowly. Sing a verse of "Old MacDonald" in which you name this slow animal, and sing at a slow tempo (you'll have to use your imagination when you sing the sound the animal makes). Encourage your child to choose another slow-moving animal and sing the next verse by herself, again singing at a slow tempo. For example:

Old . . . Mac . . . Don . . . ald . . . had . . . a . . . farm. . .
   E . . . I . . . E . . . I . . . O.
And . . . on . . . this . . . farm . . . he . . . had . . . a . . . turtle . . .
   E . . . I . . . E . . . I . . . O.
With . . . a . . . ho . . . hum . . . here
   and . . . a . . . ho . . . hum . . . there, etc.

Then ask:
- "What animal can move fast?"
- "At what speed should we sing the verse for this animal?"

For example, you could sing at a brisk tempo:

Old MacDonald had a farm, E-I-E-I-O.
And on this farm he had a rabbit, E-I-E-I-O.
With a zip-zip here and a zip-zip there, etc.

Go a Little Further: Listen to music that is sometimes slow and sometimes fast. For example, "In the Hall of the Mountain King" from Grieg's *Peer Gynt* starts out moderately slow and turns furiously fast by the end. Then ask your child:
- "What movement would you like to do when the music is slow?"
- "What movement would you like to do when the music is fast?"
Play the music again and have your child move to the music. If you're feeling up to it, join in!

Activity 5: HIGH AND LOW

Get Ready: You'll need a simple xylophone for this activity. If your child has never played a xylophone before, begin by letting him play freely with the instrument. (Although this activity assumes the use of a xylophone, you can adapt the suggestions to a keyboard instrument, such as a piano, toy or real, or a small electronic keyboard.)

Tell your child that you're going to play a game with *high* and **low** sounds (change the pitch of your voice to illustrate *high* and **low**). Help him think of high and low sounds in nature. For example, you could say:

- "A bird high in the sky makes a *high* sound: *tweet, tweet.*"
- "A bullfrog down in a swamp makes a **low** sound: **croak, croak.**"

Go: Use a book or similar object to prop up the end of the xylophone with the shortest key (this can help visually reinforce the concept of high and low). Tap the longest bar on the xylophone. Then tap the shortest bar. Repeat this a couple of times, then tell your child which sound is high and which is low (remember to change the pitch of your own voice to illustrate *high* and **low**):

Here's how to arrange the xylophone.

- [*as you tap the shortest bar*] "This is like the bird: *tweet, tweet.* This is a *high* sound."
- [*as you tap the longest bar*] "This is like the bullfrog: **croak, croak.** This is a **low** sound."

Now, tap the longest bar, then tap the shortest bar and ask your child:

- "Which sound was *higher*—the first or the second?"

Again, tap the longest bar, then tap the shortest bar and ask your child:

- "Which sound was **lower**—the first or the second?"

Continue by asking your child to identify which sound is higher or lower as you tap two more bars near the ends of the xylophone. Now switch roles: have your child tap two bars and ask you which sound is higher or lower

If they are available, bells of different sizes also provide a good way to illustrate high and low. With two bells, one big and one small, you can show that big things make low sounds, and little things make high sounds.

Favorite Songs

PARENTS: At home, in the car, in the bathtub, walking along: there are many good times and places for singing, and many wonderful songs to sing. Here are some to share with your child. (See also page 175 for some suggested song recordings.)

Bingo

There was a farmer had a dog,
And Bingo was his name-o.
B-I-N-G-O, B-I-N-G-O, B-I-N-G-O,
And Bingo was his name-o.

Go in and out the Window

Go in and out the window,
Go in and out the window,
Go in and out the window
As we have done before.
[*You may also hear the last line as "As fast as you can go."*]

Hush, Little Baby

Hush, little baby, don't say a word,
Papa's gonna buy you a mocking bird.
And if that mocking bird won't sing,
Papa's gonna buy you a diamond ring.
And if that diamond ring turns brass,
Papa's gonna buy you a looking glass.
And if that looking glass gets broke,
Papa's gonna buy you a billy goat.
And if that billy goat won't pull,
Papa's gonna buy you a cart and bull.
And if that cart and bull turn over,
Papa's gonna buy you a dog named Rover.
And if that dog named Rover won't bark,
Papa's gonna buy you a horse and cart.
And if that horse and cart fall down,
You'll still be the sweetest little baby in town.

London Bridge Is Falling Down

London Bridge is falling down,
Falling down, falling down,
London Bridge is falling down,
My fair lady.

How shall we build it up again,
Up again, up again,
How shall we build it up again,
My fair lady?

Build it up with iron bars,
Iron bars, iron bars,
Build it up with iron bars,
My fair lady.

Iron bars will bend and bow,
Bend and bow, bend and bow,
Iron bars will bend and bow,
My fair lady.

Build it up with wood and clay . . .
Wood and clay will wash away . . .

Build it up with silver and gold . . .
Silver and gold will be stolen away . . .

[Repeat first verse.]

Here We Go Round the Mulberry Bush

Here we go round the mulberry bush,
The mulberry bush, the mulberry bush,
Here we go round the mulberry bush,
So early in the morning.

This is the way we wash our face . . .

This is the way we brush our teeth . . .

This is the way we put on our clothes . . .

This is the way we clap our hands . . .

[Sing other verses about other things you do.]

My Bonnie Lies over the Ocean

My bonnie lies over the ocean,
My bonnie lies over the sea,
My bonnie lies over the ocean,
Please bring back my bonnie to me.

Bring back, bring back,
Oh, bring back my bonnie to me, to me.
Bring back, bring back,
Oh, bring back my bonnie to me.

Old MacDonald

Old MacDonald had a farm, E-I-E-I-O.
And on this farm he had some chicks, E-I-E-I-O.
With a chick-chick here and a chick-chick there,
Here a chick, there a chick, everywhere a chick-
   chick,

Old MacDonald had a farm, E-I-E-I-O.
And on this farm he had some ducks, E-I-E-I-O.
With a quack-quack here and a quack-quack there,
Here a quack, there a quack, everywhere a quack-
   quack . . .

[*Continue in the same manner with:*
   cow: moo-moo
   sheep: baa-baa
   pig: oink-oink, etc.]

Twinkle, Twinkle, Little Star

Twinkle, twinkle, little star,
How I wonder what you are.
Up above the world so high
Like a diamond in the sky.
Twinkle, twinkle, little star,
How I wonder what you are!

Pop! Goes the Weasel

All around the cobbler's bench,
The monkey chased the weasel,
The monkey thought 'twas all in fun,
Pop! goes the weasel.

A penny for a spool of thread,
A penny for a needle,
That's the way the money goes,
Pop! goes the weasel!

I've no time to sit and sigh,
No patience to wait till bye and bye,
Kiss me quick, I'm off, good-bye,
Pop! goes the weasel.

Go Tell Aunt Rhody

Go tell Aunt Rhody,
Go tell Aunt Rhody,
Go tell Aunt Rhody,
The old gray goose is dead.

The one she's been saving
The one she's been saving
The one she's been saving
To make a feather bed.

She died in the mill pond
She died in the mill pond
She died in the mill pond
Standing on her head.

[*Repeat first verse*]

The Bear Went over the Mountain

The bear went over the mountain,
The bear went over the mountain,
The bear went over the mountain,
To see what he could see.
And all that he could see,
And all that he could see,
Was the other side of the mountain,
The other side of the mountain,
The other side of the mountain,
Was all that he could see!

Jingle Bells

Dashing through the snow,
In a one-horse open sleigh,
O'er the fields we go,
Laughing all the way.
Bells on Bobtail ring,
Making spirits bright,
What fun it is to ride and sing a sleighing song tonight!

Jingle bells, jingle bells, jingle all the way,
Oh, what fun it is to ride in a one-horse open sleigh!
Jingle bells, jingle bells, jingle all the way,
Oh, what fun it is to ride in a one-horse open sleigh!

The Farmer in the Dell

The farmer in the dell,
The farmer in the dell,
Heigh-ho, the derry-o,
The farmer in the dell.

The farmer takes a wife . . .

The wife takes a child . . .

The child takes a nurse . . .

The nurse takes a dog . . .

The dog takes a cat . . .

The cat takes a rat . . .

The rat takes the cheese . . .

The cheese stands alone . . .

The Hokey Pokey

You put your right foot in,
You put your right foot out,
You put you right foot in,
And you shake it all about,
You do the Hokey Pokey,
And you turn yourself around,
That's what it's all about.
You put your left foot in . . .
You put your right hand in . . .
You put your left hand in . . .
You put your head in . . .
You put your whole self in . . .

If You're Happy and You Know It

If you're happy and you know it, clap your hands. [*clap, clap*]
If you're happy and you know it, clap your hands. [*clap, clap*]
If you're happy and you know it,
And you really want to show it,
If you're happy and you know it, clap your hands. [*clap, clap*]

If you're happy and you know it, stomp your feet. [*stomp, stomp*] . . .

If you're happy and you know it, shout hooray. [*hooray!*] . . .

If you're happy and you know it, do all three. [*clap, clap; stomp, stomp; hooray!*] . . .

Kookaburra

Kookaburra sits in the old gum tree,
Merry, merry king of the bush is he;
Laugh, Kookaburra, laugh, Kookaburra,
Gay your life must be.

Kum Ba Yah

Chorus:
Kum ba yah, my lord, kum ba yah,
Kum ba yah, my lord, kum ba yah,
Kum ba yah, my lord, kum ba yah,
O, lord, kum ba yah

Verse:
Someone's sleeping, lord, kum ba yah,
Someone's sleeping, lord, kum ba yah,
Someone's sleeping, lord, kum ba yah,
O lord, kum ba yah.

[*Sing other verses with "laughing," "dreaming," "crying," "singing"; then repeat chorus.*]

Row, Row, Row Your Boat

Row, row, row your boat
Gently down the stream,
Merrily, merrily, merrily, merrily,
Life is but a dream.

The Wheels on the Bus

The wheels on the bus go round and round,
Round and round, round and round,
The wheels on the bus go round and round,
All through the town.
The wipers on the bus go swish, swish, swish . . .
The doors on the bus go open and close . . .
The driver on the bus says, "Move on back!" . . .
The babies on the bus say, "Waa, waa, waa" . . .
The mommies on the bus say, "Shhh, shhh, shhh" . . .
The kids on the bus go up and down . . .

[*Repeat first verse*]

This Old Man

This old man, he played one,
He played knick-knack on my thumb,
With a knick-knack, paddy-wack, give a
    dog a bone,
This old man came rolling home.

This old man, he played two,
He played knick-knack on my shoe . . .

This old man, he played three,
He played knick-knack on my knee . . .

This old man, he played four,
He played knick-knack on my door . . .

This old man, he played five,
He played knick-knack on my hive . . .

This old man, he played six,
He played knick-knack on my sticks . . .

This old man, he played seven,
He played knick-knack up in
    heaven . . .

This old man, he played eight,
He played knick-knack on my gate . . .

This old man, he played nine,
He played knick-knack on my spine . . .

This old man, he played ten,
He played knick-knack over again . . .

V.
MATHEMATICS

INTRODUCTION

We hope that parents will place a special emphasis on the activities in this section. The most effective kindergarten programs in the world provide youngsters with lively and almost daily exposure to age-appropriate math concepts and operations, thus giving the children a comfortable familiarity with the elements of math, as well as a firm foundation for later mastery.

Among grown-ups, mastery of math has been shown to be a reliable road to getting a good job in the modern world. Yet the greatest barrier to mastery—"math anxiety"— usually arises in the early grades, because children have not been made to feel at home with the conventions and procedures of math. The only good way for them to gain the needed familiarity, and avoid the widespread symptoms of math anxiety, is to provide them with a lot of lively exposure and practice at an early age.

Practice does not mean mindless repetition but, rather, varied practice, including the use of countable objects (often called "manipulatives" in schools) and also some paper-and-pencil work. Regular practice and review in the early grades will make the basic ideas and operations of math interesting and familiar, and eventually lead children to the effortless, automatic performance of basic operations upon which later problem solving depends.

If we adults have "math anxiety" ourselves, our duty is to avoid conveying to our children the idea that we "don't like math" or "aren't good at math." By engaging our children in the kinds of activities suggested in this section, we can let them know that math is important and interesting to us. Keep in mind, however, that *the activities suggested here are supplemental ways for parents to reinforce their children's learning at home. They are not sufficient for teaching math in school,* where children need more extensive opportunities for practice and review.

Suggested Resources
Books:
Chicken Soup With Rice: A Book of Months and *One Was Johnny* by Maurice Sendak (HarperCollins, 1962, 1962)
Today Is Monday by Eric Carle (Scholastic, 1993)
Too Many Balloons by Catherine Matthias (Children's Press, 1982)

Software:
James Discovers Math (Broderbund)   *Math Rabbit* (The Learning Company)
Millie's Math House (Edmark)

Patterns and Classifications

PARENTS: When you recall your earliest experiences with math, you may think of counting on your fingers, or perhaps adding and subtracting: $2 + 2 = 4$, $3 - 1 = 2$. Besides such familiar operations, early math also involves some fundamental concepts and ways of thinking.

Children need to learn how to sort and classify, and many start to learn these skills well before kindergarten. By their kindergarten years, they are ready to recognize likeness and difference, to see patterns, and to sort objects according to specific attributes, such as size, color, or function. You can help your child reinforce these concepts through some activities.

Activity 1: COLLECTING THINGS BY LIKENESS

Get Ready: Tell your child you're going on a "likeness hunt." Get a paper bag and tell your child that you're going to collect objects that are alike in some way and put them in the bag. Talk about what sorts of things you will collect and how they will be alike. You may want to collect things that are all one color or things that are all used in the same way (things to eat with, things to draw with, etc.).

Go: With your child, label the bag with the attribute or characteristic you've selected, such as "red things" or "things used to eat with." Now it's time to collect. Together look for objects in and around where you live. If necessary, you can model the selection of the first object or two by finding an object and saying, "Look, here's a red crayon. We can put it in our bag because it's red."

Think and Talk: Guide your child to comment on each object as it goes in the bag, by asking:

- "Why does this one go in the bag?" (If he says, "It's red," you can reinforce the idea of likeness by saying, "Yes, like all the other things.")
- "What else can you find that's red [or used for eating, etc.]?"

On another day, repeat this activity with a new bag and a new quality that makes the things alike. This is, by the way, a good activity to begin in the morning because you'll find that as you go through your day, you and your child will find objects for your collection even when you aren't thinking about the game.

Activity 2: SORTING EVERYDAY OBJECTS

Get Ready: You will need an assortment of familiar items from around the house. Choose items that can be sorted into two groups according to a specific attribute, such as size, color, or function. For example, collect a bunch of socks, some white and some with designs. Or gather some books, some big and some small.

Go: With the pile of mixed-up items in front of you, tell your child you're going to separate the objects into two groups. Ask her to guess the rule you're using to separate the objects. Then start to put items into two groups: for example, the white socks in one pile, the socks with designs in another.

Talk and Think: To help your child focus on the concepts of likeness and difference, ask:

- "How are all the items in each group alike?"
- "How are the items in these two groups different?"
- "Here's one more item. Where would you put it? Why?"
- "What do you think is the rule for sorting these items?"

Go a Little Further: Give your child an item that doesn't belong in either group; for example, if you're sorting big and small books, give her a spoon. Then talk about why the item is different and why it can't be sorted into either group.

Activity 3: ALIKE AND DIFFERENT

Get Ready: Put a variety of different objects in a bag. Choose items that can be grouped in different ways—by color, shape, texture, or function: for example, crayons, buttons, or blocks in different colors and shapes. Be sure to include at least one set of items that share the same function, such as three different drinking cups.

It's easier to see some qualities of things than others, so it may help to examine some of the objects with your child in order to help him see both the obvious characteristics of an object, such as color, and the less obvious qualities, such as function. For example, if you examine a common pencil, you can ask such questions as: "What color is it?" (Yellow.) "What do we use it for?" (To write with.)

Go: Dump the objects on the floor and spread them around if necessary. To model the activity for your child, pick up two items that are alike in some way and tell your child how they are alike and how they are different. For example: "Here are two cups. They are alike in the way that we use them; we use them both to drink with. They are different in their color: one is red, but the other is blue." Then tell your child to pick two other items that are alike in some way. Discuss the items by asking:

- "How are the items alike?"
- "How are they different?"
- "Can you find another item that belongs with these?"
- "How is it like the other items?"

As your child answers the questions, occasionally give him words that help him categorize. For example, if your child picks two red blocks and says that they are alike because "they're both red," you might say, "Yes, they're both red; the way they're alike is their *color.*" With two writing implements—for example, a pen and a pencil—if your child says they're alike because "they're both long," you might add, "Yes, and another way they're alike is the way we *use* them: we use them both to write with."

Activity 4: SHAPE SORT

Get Ready: To do this activity, your child needs to be familiar with the four basic shapes pictured here and with their names. If she is not yet familiar with these shapes and their names, we suggest that first you do Activities 1–2 in the Geometry section of this chapter (see pages 236–37).

You will need:
sturdy paper such as poster board
crayons
scissors

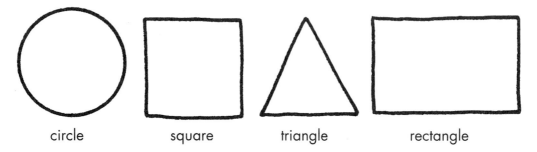

circle   square   triangle   rectangle

Review with your child the shapes pictured here and tell her their names several times. You might want to have her touch each shape and say or sing its name. You can point out that a square and a rectangle are alike: they both have four sides. But in a square, the sides are all the same.

Draw some circles, squares, triangles, and rectangles of different sizes on sturdy paper. As you draw, talk with your child about the shape names. Let her join in the preparation by coloring the shapes before you cut them.

Go: Spread the cutouts on a flat surface. Ask your child to pick one and help her examine the shape by asking:
- "How many sides does this shape have?"
- "Are the sides straight or round?"
- "Does the shape look the same if I turn it this way? How does it change?"
- "Can you tell me the name of this shape?" (If your child correctly names the shape, you can reinforce the name by repeating it: "That's right, it's a [name of shape].")

Talk and Think: Pick another shape that's different from the first one. To help your child focus on the differences, put the shapes side by side and ask:
- "How are the shapes different from each other?"

- "Do both shapes have sides?"
- "Does each shape have the same number of sides?"
- "If we turn the shapes this way, do they still look different?"

Then ask her to sort the rest of the shapes and tell which shapes belong together and why.

Go a Little Further: Have a scavenger hunt for shapes. For example, your child may compare a rectangle and a tabletop; an ice-cream cone and a triangle; or a tire and a circle. The hunt can take place at home, in the park, in the car, or anywhere else that shapes exist—that's everywhere!

Activity 5: SHAPE TRAIN

Get Ready: This activity will help your child learn how to identify and describe patterns of alternating shapes.

You will need a bunch of blocks. Make sure there are at least eight blocks of two different shapes, such as four blocks with square faces and four blocks with triangular faces.

After you collect the blocks, discuss the names of the block faces with your child and give him some time to examine and touch the two kinds of shapes.

Go: Tell your child that you're going to build a "shape train." To get started, lay six blocks in a row, alternating the shapes. To help your child understand the pattern, point to each block face and ask:

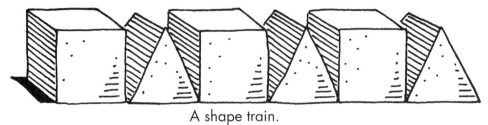

A shape train.

- "What shape is the first car? And the next? And the next?"

Talk about the pattern with your child; for example: "Do you see the pattern? There is a triangle car, then a square car, then a triangle car, then a square car." Then tell your child that you want to continue the pattern, and ask him to add another car. Ask:

- "What shape should the next car be? Why?"

Talk and Think: To help your child focus on different patterns, use the same blocks to form a different pattern, such as two squares and two triangles. Ask:
* "How many squares are there?"
* "How many triangles?"
* "What pattern can you see in this shape train?"

Ask your child to add more blocks to the train and describe the pattern.

Go a Little Further: Introduce another shape, such as a rectangle. Work with your child to make and describe other shape trains. Encourage him to name the shapes he uses to build the train and then describe the pattern he has made.

Activity 6: POTATO PRINTS
Get Ready:

You will need:
2 large potatoes
a paring knife
newspaper
tempera paint in several colors
some big sheets of paper
paper towels

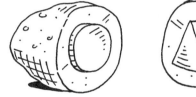

Warning: The adult must do all the cutting in this activity. Explain that *you* are going to cut the potatoes so that they can be used to print shapes: a square, a rectangle, a circle, and a triangle. First, cut the potatoes in half and draw an outline of one shape on each half. Next, cut down around each outline, which will leave a raised shape that you can use to print with.

Cover your work surface with newspaper; this activity can get messy! Put about two tablespoons of tempera paint on a small plate or in a shallow plastic lid. Show your child how to dip the potato stamp into the paint to coat only the raised shape. Then show your child how to make a print by pushing the potato stamp firmly and evenly on a piece of paper.

Go: To get started, let your child make any prints he wants on a big sheet of paper. Children love to print and will enjoy just printing before you begin to work on patterns. (You'll need to rinse the potato stamp and dry it on a paper towel if your child wants to dip the same potato stamp into different colors.)

When your child is ready, get a new piece of paper and stamp out a pattern on it. Begin with a pattern of two shapes, for example, a triangle and a circle. Alternate the shapes but use only one color. Repeat the pattern three times. Ask your child to copy the pattern. It's okay if your child makes mistakes doing this—it's all part of learning. While your child is stamping the pattern, ask:

- "What are the names of the two shapes we're using?"
- "Which shape comes first?"
- "Which shape comes next?"
- "Which shape comes after that?"
- "What pattern do you see?"

Ask your child to continue the pattern.

Go a Little Further: Add another shape to the pattern so that you're using three different shapes: for example, a triangle, a circle, and a square.

Activity 7: MORE PLAY WITH PATTERNS
Get Ready:

You will need:
colored construction paper
scissors

   Using three different colors of paper, cut out 18 of each shape (circle, triangle, rectangle, square), each about three by three inches. In other words, when you're finished you'll have, for example, 18 triangles: 6 blue, 6 yellow, and 6 red.

Go: To help your child focus on color patterns, choose one shape and create a color pattern, such as blue triangle/red triangle/yellow triangle. Repeat the pattern several times. Then point to the pattern and ask:
• "What is the name of this shape?"
• "What is the color of this shape?"
• "Are the colors of the shapes alike or different?"
• "What pattern do you see?"
Ask your child to continue the pattern. Then have him explain his choices.

Go a Little Further: Ask your child to make up his own pattern. To make the activity more challenging, guide him in creating a pattern that repeats both shape and color, such as blue square/yellow triangle/blue square/yellow triangle.

Numbers and Number Sense

PARENTS: We encourage you to read this introduction, which is addressed to you, before proceeding with the activities for your child that begin on page 206.

You may already have shared with your child some familiar counting rhymes, such as "One, two, buckle my shoe" (page 25) or:

> One, two, three, four, five,
> I caught a fish alive;
> Six, seven, eight, nine, ten,
> I let it go again.

Through such counting rhymes and games, many children, even before kindergarten, learn to recite numbers aloud ("one, two, three, four, five . . .") in the same way they sometimes recite the alphabet song, without really understanding what the numbers (or letters) represent, except that they are said in a certain order. Reciting the numbers aloud in order, quickly and without missing a number, is an important first step toward using numbers in a meaningful way.

Next, children can begin to combine their recitation of the number sequence with the act of counting objects. Counting aloud a group of objects then becomes the foundation for learning addition, subtraction, and place value in first grade.

Children also need to become aware that written numerals (1, 2, 3 . . .) correspond to what they have been saying when they recite the number sequence aloud. They need to learn to put these written numerals in order, to match the written numerals to groups of objects having the same quantity, and to write the numerals themselves.

With practice, kindergartners can learn to write the numerals. You can help at home by having your child practice writing one numeral at a time. You can use workbooks available at bookstores and toy stores, or you can provide paper with broadly spaced lines, on which (as illustrated below) you lightly write the numeral a few times for your child to trace over, to be followed by writing the numeral several times without tracing it.

Your child should write the numerals as directed by the arrows in the following chart. Early in the kindergarten year, your child should practice until he can write all of the numerals from 1 through 10 without help. Later, as your child works with

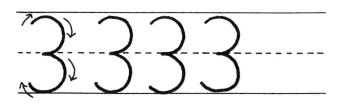

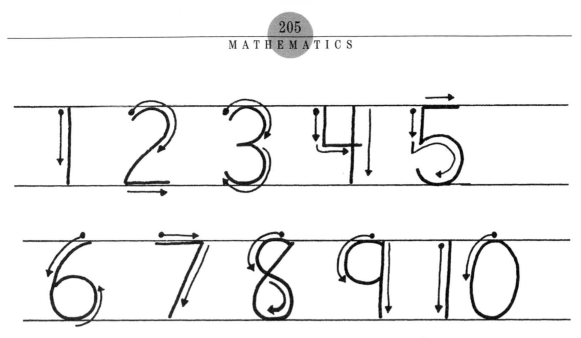

Handwriting chart for numerals. Start at the dot.

quantities greater than 10, he can practice writing the numerals for those quantities. You might want to pay special attention to the differences between potentially confusing numerals, such as: 6 and 9; 1 and 7; 12 and 21; 13 and 31; etc.

To summarize, early in the kindergarten year, your child should learn to count from 1 to 10 fast without making any mistakes, and to write the numbers up to 10. He may need to review the numbers many times in order to learn them. By the end of the kindergarten year, your child should be comfortable counting to higher numbers (a reasonable goal is counting by ones up to 31, and counting by fives and tens up to 50), as well as writing the corresponding numerals.

Here are some excellent counting books that can make learning about numbers enjoyable for both you and your child:

Anno's Counting Book by Mitsumasa Anno (Harper, 1975)
Numbears: A Counting Book by Kathleen Hague (Scholastic, 1986)
One Bear at Bedtime by Mick Inkpen (Little Brown, 1987)
One Hungry Monster: A Counting Book in Rhyme by Susan Heyboer O'Keefe (Joy Street Books, 1989)
Seven Blind Mice by Ed Young (Scholastic, 1992)

Activity 1: NUMBERS FROM 1 TO 10

PARENTS: Read the following aloud with your child:

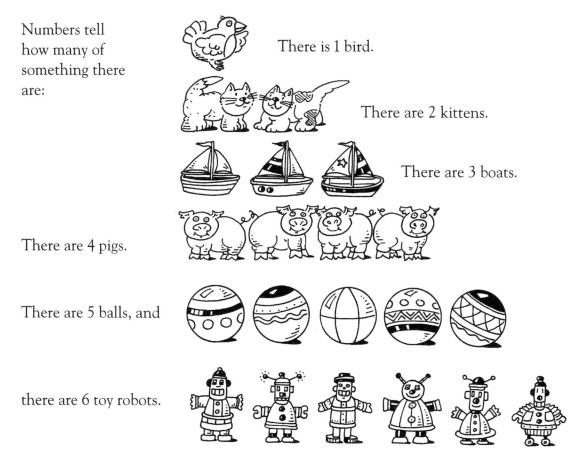

Numbers tell how many of something there are:

There is 1 bird.

There are 2 kittens.

There are 3 boats.

There are 4 pigs.

There are 5 balls, and

there are 6 toy robots.

Here are the numbers from 1 to 10. Let's point to each number as we say it aloud in order:

1 2 3 4 5 6 7 8 9 10

Can you put your finger on the number that shows
- how many years old you are?
- how many feet you have?
- how many fingers you have?
- how many noses you have?

Activity 2: LOADING THE TRAIN: COUNTING OBJECTS TO 10

Get Ready: In this activity your child will count objects while picking them up and moving them from one pile to another. When children start counting the number of things in a group, it helps if they can touch and manipulate the things they are counting.

You will need:
at least 55 dried beans (or buttons or other small objects for counting)
a bowl
an egg carton
scissors

Go: Put 55 beans in a bowl. Set this aside as you prepare the egg carton as follows: cut the top off the egg carton and set it aside. Now cut the bottom of the carton in half down the middle of the long dimension. Then tape these two sections together, end to end, so that you have a single line of little cups. Cut the line so that you end up with ten cups. This is the "train," and now it's time to load the "cars."

Tell your child that you're going to play a counting game in which you "load the railroad cars," but that each car must have a different amount put in it. Point to the cup on the left and say, "The first car gets one bean." (If you want to pretend that the beans are lumps of coal, or gold, or whatever, that's fine.) Model the activity for him so that he sees how to say the number "one" as he picks up one bean and puts it in the first cup. Model the activity again for the next cup: as you pick up the first bean, say "one" and put it in the cup; as you pick up a second bean, say "two" and put it in the cup.

Have your child start from the beginning. Tell him he is to put 1 bean in the first car, 2 in the next car, 3 in the next car, and so on up to 10 beans in the last car. Remind him to continue saying the number as he picks up each bean, each time. Your child may need some coaching in order to time the action of picking up a bean with saying a number: the picking up and the counting aloud need to be simultaneous (some children will tend to say the numbers aloud faster than they pick up the objects).

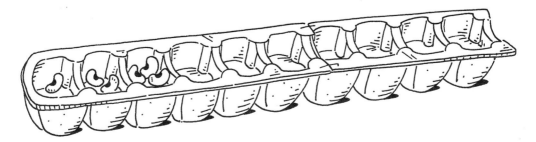

Activity 3: THE SIZE OF 10
Get Ready:

You will need:
15 small objects like buttons, raisins, macaronis,
    or pieces of O-shaped cereal
2 small clear plastic bags

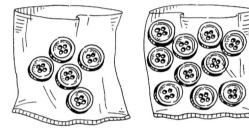

Go: Put 5 of the small objects you have selected in one of the plastic bags and 10 in the other. Put the bag with 5 items on a table in front of your child. Ask her to guess, without counting, if the bag has 5 or 10 items. Then ask:
- "How can you tell?"
- "How can you find out if there are that many in the bag?"

Have her count to find out how many are in the bag.

Talk and Think: To help your child think about the size of 10, put the bag with 10 items in front of her and ask:

- "What about this bag? Do you think there are five buttons or ten buttons?"
- "How can you tell?"

Then have your child count to find out how many are in the bag.

Go a Little Further: Later, when your child is comfortable with counting larger quantities, you can put 20 buttons in a clear plastic bag. Ask her to guess if there are 20 or 50 buttons in the bag. Then she can count to find how many are in the bag.

Activity 4: COUNTING GAME

Get Ready:

You will need:

paper

markers, pencils, or crayons

small objects to be used as markers, like buttons or pebbles

Tell your child you're going to play a number game. Make up a game board like the one below, with a path of squares numbered in order. Have your child help you write the numbers in the squares.

Go: Tell your child to put a button (or pebble) on square 1. Then tell her to say each number as she moves the button from one space to the next. When she gets to the last number on the board, have her turn around and move the button back to number 1, saying the numbers backward. Then ask:

- "What is the first number on the board?"
- "What is the last?"
- "Can you say every number that you put your button on?"
- "Can you say the numbers backward?"

Talk and Think: To help your child focus on counting numbers, place her button on a number on the board. Then ask:

- "Which number is the button on?"
- "Which number comes before it? After it?"
- "Can you count forward from where the button is to ten?"
- "Can you count backward from where the button is to one?"

You can have fun counting backward by singing this favorite song with your child:

TEN LITTLE MONKEYS

Ten little monkeys jumping on the bed,
One fell off and bumped his head.
Mama called the doctor, and the doctor said,
"No more monkeys jumping on the bed."

Nine little monkeys jumping on the bed,
One fell off and bumped his head.
Mama called the doctor, and the doctor said,
"No more monkeys jumping on the bed."

Eight little monkeys jumping on the bed,
One fell off and bumped his head. . . .

Go a Little Further: You can challenge your child by extending the game board to higher numbers. A reasonable goal for kindergartners is gradually to build up to counting by ones to 31. As for when to introduce the higher numbers, you may want to ask your child's kindergarten teacher when the class will begin working with numbers greater than 10, so that you can reinforce the classroom learning at home.

Your child may need a little extra help when he first works with numbers greater than 10, since the English names for numbers do not always give a clue to the actual quantity. That is, in some languages, the numbers after 10 are logically called "ten-one," "ten-two," and "ten-three," but in English we say "eleven," "twelve," and "thirteen." This may cause some initial confusion for your child, but encouragement and gentle review will lead to understanding.

Activity 5: HOW MANY?

Get Ready: This activity helps children develop number sense. You will need at least 30 pennies.

Go: Arrange 6 pennies in a row and another 6 pennies in a cluster. Ask your child which group has more pennies. Then take the cluster of pennies and line them up coin-for-coin under the row of pennies. Have your child count along with you as you point to the pennies in each line. Ask:

- "How many pennies are in this group?"
- "How many are in the other group?"
- "Are there the same number of pennies? How do you know?"

Talk and Think: For more practice with number sense, arrange 5 pennies in a row and 5 in a stack. Point to the stack and ask:

- "Do you think this group has more pennies?"
- "How can you find out?"

Go a Little Further: Make three groups of pennies of equal amounts up to 10. Arrange one group in a row. Put the second group in a cluster, and stack the third group. Talk with your kindergartner about which group she thinks has the most pennies. Then ask her to arrange the other two groups coin-for-coin under the row of pennies.

Activity 6: NUMBER MATCH

Get Ready:

You will need:
a pack of three-by-five-inch unlined index cards
crayons, markers, or pencils

Tell your child that you are going to prepare some cards so you can play a kind of matching game.

On ten of the index cards, draw large dots for the numbers from 1 to 10. Your child can color in the dots. Next, have your child count the dots on each card and draw a numeral on a blank card to match the number of dots. When he's finished, you'll have one set of ten dot cards and one set of ten numeral cards.

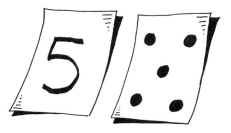

Go: Tell your child to mix up each pile of cards and place the piles face down on a table. Then take turns turning up a card in each pile until someone finds a dot card and a numeral card that match. Keep playing by reshuffling the unmatched cards and putting them back into two piles until you've matched all the pairs.

Talk and Think: As you play, ask:
- "How many dots are on this card? What number does the other card show?"
- "Do they match? How can you tell?"

Go a Little Further: Ask your child to put the number cards in order, laying them out flat on a table from left to right. You might need to help by putting the first two or three cards on the table to show him what you mean. Then ask him to put the matching dot cards in order under the number cards.

Activity 7: ONE MORE, ONE LESS

Get Ready: To give your child practice with the concepts of more and less, you will need:

at least 10 blocks or 10 large beads
a string or a shoelace

Tell him that you're going to play a game in which you say a number and he shows that number by lining up that many blocks or putting that many beads on the string or the shoelace.

Go: Say any number between 1 and 10, such as 5, and ask your child to show that number of blocks. To focus on the concept of one more, say:

- "Now show me one more than five."
- "How many is that?"

Then start over and have your child show a different number. This time, ask him to show one less and to tell how many that is.

Talk and Think: Continue choosing new numbers for your child to show. For the fourth or fifth number that you choose, have him predict without counting what will be one more and one less. Then have him make one more or one less and count to be sure. Ask:

- "How can you tell what is one more [or one less]?"
- "Can you tell without counting the blocks?"

Activity 8: MOST AND FEWEST

Get Ready: Tell your child that you're going to play a counting game together using the names of family members. If your family is small, include the names of family friends or pets.

You will need:
a sheet of paper
a marker or a pencil

Go: Ask your child to name four or five family members. As she names each person, use the marker to write the names in big letters on a sheet of paper. When you complete each name, point to the name and read it with your child. Then ask:

- "Which name has the most letters?"
- "Why do you think this name has the most letters?"
- "How can you tell?"
- "How many letters does it have?"

Then ask your child to count to find out how many letters there are.

Talk and Think: To focus on the concept of fewest, ask her which name has the fewest letters:

- "How can you tell this name has the fewest letters?"
- "How many letters does it have?"

Have your child count to find out.

Activity 9: COUNTING MORE THAN 10 OBJECTS

Get Ready: Children find it easier to count objects when they can touch objects that are lined up in an organized way. With practice, your kindergartner will find it easier to keep track of items that aren't organized or touchable. To start out, let your child help you gather between 10 and 31 small items, such as paper clips, macaronis, or small toys.

Go: Arrange the items in a row and ask your child to count them. Ask:

- "How many [paper clips, macaronis, etc.] are there?"

Then spread the items around and ask your child to count them. Ask:

- "How many did you count this time?"
- "Which way that you counted is easier?"
- "Is there a way you can organize these to make them easier to count?"

Go a Little Further: Go outside and ask your child to count something that cannot be touched, such as a row of windows. Again, ask how many he counted to be sure he understands that the last number counted is how many there are.

Activity 10: THINGS THAT COME IN PAIRS

Get Ready: To get started, have your child look at a stuffed animal or doll. Ask her to name parts of the stuffed animal or doll that come in twos:
- "What do you see that your animal [or doll] has two of?"
Then tell your child that "a pair is two of something that go together," and that the animal (or doll) has a pair of eyes, and a pair of arms, etc.

Go: Arrange several groups of like objects, including some pairs of objects, such as a pair of shoes, a pair of forks or spoons, etc. Other groups should contain three objects. Say:

- "Here is a pair of shoes; there are two shoes, and they go together. Can you show me some other pairs of things here?"
- "How do you know this is a pair?"
- "Why isn't this group a pair?"

Activity 11: COUNTING BY TWOS

Get Ready: Tell your child that you're going on a shoe hunt. Try to find at least five pairs of shoes and line them up in pairs next to each other. Then tell your child that you're going to find out how many shoes there are by counting them two ways.

Go: First, ask your child to count the shoes one by one. Tell him he is "counting by ones." Then, tell him there is another way to count the shoes called "counting by twos." Ask him to listen as you point and count the shoes. Put the emphasis on every second number. For example, you could whisper the numbers 1, 3, 5, 7, 9 and say the numbers 2, 4, 6, 8, 10 in a loud voice. After this, count the shoes by twos: 2, 4, 6, 8, 10. Repeat and then ask your child to follow along. Then give him an opportunity to count the shoes by twos on his own. Ask:

- "How many shoes are there? Can you count them by twos?"

Go a Little Further: Use other items, such as spoons or crayons, and gradually use more than ten items. Start with a review of counting by twos up to 10, then ask:

- "What number comes next if we keep counting by twos?"

Activity 12: COUNTING BY FIVES AND TENS

Get Ready:
You will need:
a big sheet of sturdy paper
finger paints

Tell your child that you are going to make a handprint poster. You're using finger paints, so do this where it's okay to make a mess! (*Note:* Your child should already have practiced counting by ones to 30 before you do this activity.)

Go: Use the finger paints to make colorful handprints all over the paper. If possible, have family members or friends make handprints, too. At first, start with six handprints; later, you can work up to ten handprints. When the poster is finished, point to it and ask:

- "How many fingers are there?"
- "How could you find out?"

Point to one hand print, and ask:

- "How many fingers are on this one hand?"

Point to the next handprint and ask your child to continue to count. Continue until your child has counted all the fingers on the poster. Ask:

- "How many fingers are there in all?"

Talk and Think: Explain to your child that there is a faster way to count. This fast way is called "skip counting," and explain that you're going to "skip-count by fives." Say:
- "We're going to count five fingers at a time, like this: five, ten, fifteen, twenty . . ." (As you count, move your finger from one hand on the poster to another.)

Have your child listen as you skip-count by fives. After repeating the pattern, ask her to join in. Repeat the same procedure as you skip-count by tens. Then ask:

- "Did you end up with the same number when you counted by ones? How about fives?"
- "Which way is faster?"

Go a Little Further: The next time the family is having dinner, ask how many toes are under the table.

Activity 13: HALF AND HALF

Get Ready:

You will need:

10 items of one kind that are of particular interest to your child,
   such as stickers, cookies, or small toy cars
8 pennies
a slice of bread

Go: Spread the 10 items out on a table. Ask your child to show a fair way to share the items between the two of you.

When your child has made two equal shares of the 10 items, explain that each share is *half* of the whole group of items: you have one half, and he has the other half.

Now, show your child the 8 pennies; allow him to count them. Then put all 8 pennies in a pile between you. Give 2 pennies to your child. Ask:

• "Do you have half?"
• "Can you show me how to share them fairly, half for you and half for me?"

Talk and Think: Many kindergartners don't yet understand that halves are equal in size. To focus on the concept of halves as equal shares, ask:

• "Do we each have the same number of toy cars [or other items]?"
• "How could you find out?"

Go a Little Further: Put the piece of bread on the table, and ask your child to show a fair way to break it into 2 pieces to share, half for you and half for him. After he has broken it (in roughly two equal pieces), ask:

• "Is my half of the bread the same size as yours, or is it a different size?"

Reinforce what he has done by saying, "You have *half* of the *whole* piece of bread, and I have *half* of the *whole* piece of bread, and both halves are equal."

Activity 14: A GOOD-JOB GRAPH

Get Ready:
You will need:
a sheet of paper
crayons or markers

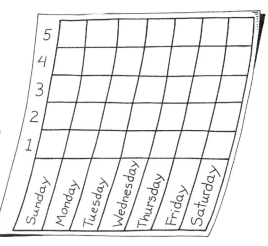

Tell your child that the two of you are going to make a Good-Job Graph, which will show some of the good things she does in a week. You can talk together about what sort of jobs to include: picking up toys, brushing teeth, washing hands before dinner, helping Mom or Dad, etc.

Write the days of the week along the bottom of a sheet of paper and numbers up to 5 along the side edge. Post this chart in an easy-to-reach spot and explain that every day she can color a square on the graph for each of the "good jobs" she does. Try to help her record from 1 to 5 "good jobs" a day.

Go: At the end of the first day, look at the graph with your child. Point to the name of the day and ask:

• "How many 'good jobs' did you do today?"
• "How do you know?"

At the end of each day, look at the graph together and make some comparisons by asking:

• "How many squares did you color today?"
• "Was that more or less than yesterday?"

Talk and Think: To help your child think about graphs, at the end of the week, ask:
• "On which day did you color the most squares? How many did you color?"

Go a Little Further: Ask your child:
• "How many good jobs did you do in all this week?"
To help her answer this question, ask her how she could find the answer to that question. You might need to coach her that one way to find out would be to count all the squares on the graph. Then ask her to count all the squares.

Activity 15: BLOCK TRAIN

Get Ready: This activity provides practice with order words—"first," "second," "third," etc. Let your child help you gather:

6 blocks
6 different small objects (such as a button,
a piece of macaroni, a pebble, etc.)

Go: Tell your child to build a block train by arranging the blocks in a row. Then have her put one of the small objects on top of each block. Identify one car for your child by using an order word such as "first" or "second" in a sentence, like this: "The button is on the *second* block." Then have your child identify the other cars, using an order word. Ask:

• "Which block is carrying the macaroni?"
• "Which block is carrying the pebble?"

Continue until you and your child have identified all the blocks by their order words.

If your child has trouble using these words, say them all aloud in order as you point to each car. Have her repeat them as you point to blocks first in order and then at random. Then repeat the questioning activity.

Money

PARENTS: Even before children know what money is for, they are fascinated by the shape and appearance of coins and bills. By kindergarten, your child probably also realizes that money is important.

Kindergartners need to know that money is used to buy things, and that different kinds of coins and bills have different values. The following activities will help children start to recognize coins and the $1 bill and to understand what each is worth. At this point, don't expect your child to be able to trade coins for other coin combinations of the same value. Exchanging money is a skill that will come later.

Activity 1: IDENTIFYING MONEY

Get Ready:

You will need:

4 small containers such as margarine tubs

a way to label your containers (masking tape and pen or marker)

coins: at least 2 of each type of coin

Label the containers "1¢," "5¢," "10¢," and "25¢." Pile the coins in front of the containers. Tell your child that together you are going to separate the coins into different groups.

Go: Spread out the coins. To get started, pick up one of each kind of coin and tell your child what it is: penny, nickel, dime, or quarter. Give him an opportunity to look at the coins and say their names to you. Ask him to watch as you put one coin of each type in a container. Then ask him to sort the rest of the coins. Depending on your child's experience with money, you can explain what each coin is worth as you sort, or simply have him tell you in which container to put the coins.

Talk and Think: To help your child become familiar with coins and their values, have him look over the coins pictured below in order of their value. Read through the text about what each coin is worth and what the cent sign means.

quarter   penny   nickel   dime

- "The sign ¢ means cent or cents."
- "A penny is worth 1¢."
- "A nickel is worth 5¢."
- "A dime is worth 10¢."
- "A quarter is worth 25¢."

Explain that the pictures show both sides of each coin. Tell him that the side with a head on it is called the *heads* side of the coin. Point out that the faces on the heads sides of the coins are all the faces of famous presidents (you can learn about some of them in the American History and Geography section of this book). And tell him that the other side is called the *tails* side. Then have him look again at real coins and ask him to show you their heads and tails sides. Ask:

- "Are all the kinds of coins the same shape? Are they all the same size and color?"
- "How is the penny different from all the other coins?"
- "Which coin looks smallest? Is this coin worth less than a penny? Less than a nickel?"
- "Which coin looks largest? Is this coin worth more than the other coins?"

Go a Little Further: The next time you go shopping, give your child a change purse with some coins. Ask for his help in picking out coins to give the cashier. For example, you can ask for three pennies, one dime, or other coins, and your child can supply them. (But don't expect him to know which coins add up to a certain amount. That skill comes later.)

Activity 2: MONEY BINGO

Get Ready: Tell your child that you are going to play Money Bingo. Before you begin, remind your child of what a penny, a nickel, a dime, and a quarter are worth. Also be sure she knows that a dollar is worth 100 cents. Show her the cents sign and the dollar sign, and show how these denominations are written: 1¢, 5¢, 10¢, 25¢, $1.00. You will need:

stiff paper or poster board
scissors
a ruler
crayons or markers
buttons or other small items for markers
a supply of coins and $1 bills
a box or hat

Make at least two bingo cards. Each card should have five squares across and five squares down. Instead of numbers, use these labels: 1¢, 5¢, 10¢, 25¢, $1.00 in the squares. Let your child help you write the numbers and dollars and cents signs on each card.

If your child has never played bingo, explain that you are going to cover the rows on the cards with markers and that the first person to cover a whole row—across, up and down, or diagonally—calls out "Bingo!"

Go: Put the coins and dollar bills in the box or hat, then give each player a bingo card and about a dozen markers. To play the game, choose a coin or bill and hold it up. As you hold up each denomination of money, ask these questions:
• "What am I holding up?"
• "How much is it worth?"
Then each player puts a marker in every box on the card that says the amount just held up. When one of you calls out "Bingo!" ask your child to remove each marker and read out the money values underneath. Now you're ready to play again.

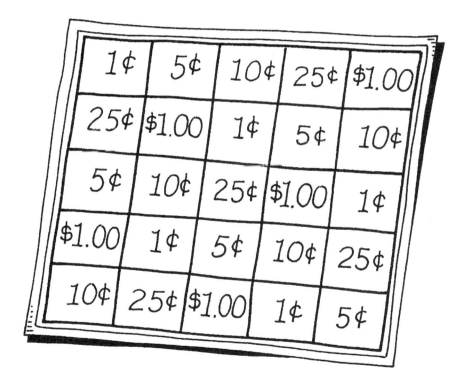

Computation

PARENTS: You probably don't remember a time when you didn't know that adding two groups of things gives you one larger group, while taking away something from one group leaves you with a smaller group. But these fundamental mathematical concepts may be new to your kindergartner.

The activities that follow use real objects to help your child understand what happens when groups of things are added together or taken away. By working with real objects, your child will learn that addition requires counting forward, while subtraction requires counting backward. The activities also introduce the + and − symbols. Some children can make an immediate connection between joining or separating groups and using symbols to describe what happens. Other children need a little more time to see this connection. Also, while some children might memorize specific addition and subtraction facts such as 2 + 2 = 4, don't expect or demand it of all kindergartners. That ability will come after your child understands the basic concepts.

Activity 1: ADDITION: FINDING TOTALS

PARENTS: *Before you begin this activity, it may help to read aloud the following introduction to addition with your child:*

When two groups of things are put together, it's called addition.

There are 3 flowers in a vase. If you pick 2 more flowers and put them in the vase, how many flowers are in the vase now?

This is an addition problem, because you start with 3 flowers and add 2 more. After the flowers are added, there are 5 flowers. To show what happens, you can write

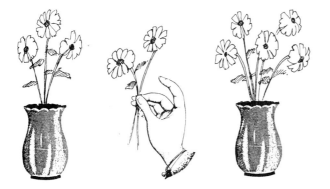

3 + 2 = 5

The sign + means "plus." It shows that you are adding.

The sign = means "equals." It shows that two amounts are the same:

3 + 2 is the same as 5
3 + 2 = 5

Get Ready: Gather 10 objects
of the same kind, such as crayons,
blocks, pebbles, or pennies. Put
some of the objects in one pile and
some in another pile. (When you
start out, you do not have to use all
10 objects.) Draw a large plus sign
on a slip of paper and place it between the two piles. Tell your child
that the two of you are going to play
an addition game.

Go: Have your child count how
many crayons are in each pile and
tell you how many. Tell him that
you are going to add the two piles to
make one new pile. Point to the plus
sign between the piles to show what
you will do. Then put the piles together. Ask your child to count the
crayons and tell how many there are
now.

Talk and Think: After you make the new pile, ask:
• "How did we make the new pile?"
• "How many crayons are in the new pile?"
• "Were the other piles bigger than this pile?"
• "Is this the biggest pile?"
Repeat this activity several times with different-size piles so your child can practice
adding various combinations up to 10.

Go a Little Further: Ask your child to do some simple addition mentally.
Here's how: Display two groups that each contain just one or two items. Have your
child count the items in each pile. Ask him to put both groups into a bag. Close the
bag. Ask him to tell you how many objects are in the bag. Then he can open the bag
and count the new group. Repeat this several times with different-size piles.

Activity 2: SUBTRACTION: THE TAKE-AWAY GAME

Get Ready:
You will need:
a small group of no more than 5 objects of the same kind, such as buttons or pebbles

Go: Tell your child that you're going to play a number game. Put the buttons on a table and ask your child to count them. While she watches, cover some of the buttons with your hand and slide them a few inches away (keeping them under your hand). Then ask:

- "How many buttons did you count before?"
- "How many buttons do you see now?"
- "Can you tell how many were taken away?"

Talk and Think: After she tells you, lift your hand to show the missing buttons. Tell her that when you took away some of the buttons, you were *subtracting*. Ask:
- "How did you know how many buttons I took away?"

If your child has trouble with these questions, put all the buttons back on the table. Have her count them again. Then take one button away while she watches. Ask:
- "How many buttons am I taking away?"
- "How many are left?"

Go a Little Further: As your child begins to understand subtraction, you can use more than five objects in the group. You can also try reversing roles, and let her take away the items. For fun, you can occasionally "guess wrong" and have her tell you how many items she removed.

As your child repeats this activity, remind her that when you take away buttons, you are *subtracting* a number.

Activity 3: ADDITION AND SUBTRACTION STORIES

Get Ready:
You will need:
5 to 10 index cards
a pencil or a marker

Write a plus sign on one of the index cards, a minus sign on one, and an equals sign on another.

Tell your kindergartner that you're going to tell some number stories. Show each sign to your child and remind him what each symbol means.

Go: As your child listens, tell a number story about a family event. For example, you might tell about the time that Uncle Ralph was a boy and ordered five hot dogs but could eat only four.

Parents: Put your hand over 4 of the hot dogs to show "taking away" the hot dogs that Uncle Ralph ate.

Talk and Think: Use the plus, minus, and equals signs as you tell the story. Ask:

- "How many hot dogs did Uncle Ralph order?" (Put a 5 on one card.)
- "How many did he eat?" (Put a 4 on a card.)
- "How many were left?" (Put a 1 on a card.)
- "How could you use a plus sign [+] or a minus sign [–] to tell the story?"

Using the index cards, help your child write an addition or subtraction sentence that tells his story, for example, $5 - 4 = 1$. Have him read the numbers and symbols aloud: "Five minus four equals one," as he points to each card.

Go a Little Further: Have your child tell another story using the same addition or subtraction sentence. The story can be about something that really happened or something he makes up.

Measurement

PARENTS: Your kindergartner probably uses words that describe size and degree such as "big," "smaller," "long," "tall," and "taller." These words show that she recognizes size relationships. This important skill is fundamental not just to mathematics but to science, geography, and even storytelling.

Children need to learn that measuring is one way of describing something—for example, how big, hot, heavy, or tall something is, or how long something takes to do. Children also need to learn that measuring is a way to compare objects in terms of such qualities as size, weight, and capacity.

Kindergartners generally have little trouble comparing things by placing them next to each other, but they are only beginning to understand measurement. The activities that follow will help your child recognize the standard measuring tools. Don't expect your child to be able to use the tools to measure. Your child should, however, be given opportunities to use arbitrary units, such as paper clips or footsteps, to measure length.

Activity 1: MEASUREMENT TOOLS

Get Ready: Let your child help you gather some household measurement tools such as a ruler, tape measure, thermometer, clock, and bathroom scale.

Go: Tell her that these are all tools used to measure things. For each tool, ask:

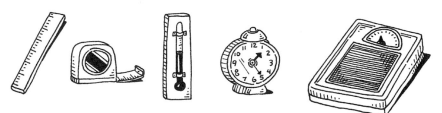

- "Do you know the name of this one?"
- "Do you know what we use this for?"

Talk and Think: To help her focus on how these tools are used, ask:
- "Which tool tells what time it is?"
- "Which tool tells us how hot or cold it is?"
- "Which tool tells how heavy something is?"
- "Which tool tells how long something is?"

Activity 2: MEASURING WITH PAPER CLIPS

PARENTS: When children first learn to measure, many of them have difficulty measuring with rulers that use standard units such as inches or centimeters. To help a child understand concepts of measurement and why we measure using units like inches, it is generally helpful to begin by asking your child to use a set of identical objects, such as paper clips, to measure the length of an object.

Get Ready: Get together a few pairs of similar items to measure, such as two books, two cereal boxes, or two toy trucks. The items in each pair should be of different sizes. Also have ready a bunch of paper clips (all the same size) to use as measuring tools.

Go: Tell your child that the two of you are going to measure some items. Show him the pair of books and ask:

• "Which book looks bigger?"
• "How can you find out which is bigger?"

Your child may say that one book looks bigger, or he may hold the books next to each other to compare. Give your child some paper clips. Help him measure the book. Line up the clips one by one along the binding side of one book until you reach the end of the book. Do the same with the other book. Ask:

• "How many paper clips long is this book?"
• "How many paper clips long is that book?"
• "How can you tell which book is longer?"

Go a Little Further: Have your child hook the paper clips together after measuring each of several items. Then ask him to arrange the paper clip chains in order from shortest to longest.

You can also have your child make a paper ruler by tracing a paper clip several times, end to end. Have him use his new ruler to measure length. As he becomes familiar with using the paper ruler, provide an inch ruler and help him investigate how to measure small objects with this tool.

Activity 3: MEASURING WITH HANDS AND FEET

Get Ready: Tell your child that you're going to measure some items using your hands.

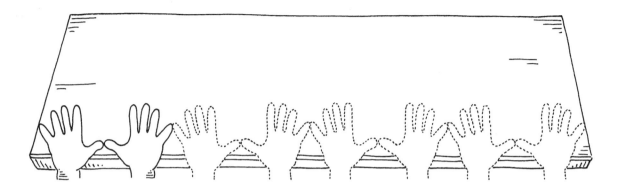

Go: Spread out your hand and have your child do the same. As your child watches, measure a table by alternating hands the length of the table. Ask her to count the number of hands it takes to measure the table. Ask:

- "How many hands long is the table?"
- "Will the table still be [number of] hands long if I measure it again?"
- "How long is the table if we use *your* hand?"
- "Why does it take more of your hands to measure the table than mine?"
- "What about our feet? Do you think it takes more hands or more feet to measure the table?"

Go a Little Further: Show your child how you can use your feet to measure an item, like a small rug, by counting as you place one foot in front of the other. Then have your child use the length of her foot to measure the table by cutting out a paper foot length, using your child's foot as a model. Show her how to use this paper foot to measure the length of the table. She can also measure other furniture and spaces using this paper tool.

Activity 4: FULL, HALF-FULL, AND EMPTY

Get Ready: You will need four identical glasses and a pitcher of water.

Go: Arrange the glasses in a row and fill up one glass with water. Fill another glass half-full. After that, pour a small amount of water into the glass next to the half-full glass. This glass should be less than one-quarter full. The glasses should *not* be in order from full to empty.

Talk and Think: Have your child compare the water levels. Ask:

- "Which glass is full?"
- "Which glass is half-full?"
- "Which glass is empty?"
- "Are the glasses in order from full to empty?"
- "Can you put them in order?"

Go a Little Further:

Add another glass that is half-full. Have your child decide which glass is "as full as" the new one.

Activity 5: HEAVY AND LIGHT

Get Ready: Ask your child to help you pick out several different items of different weights, such as books, pebbles, and blocks. You can also use grocery items of different weights.

Go: Put all the items on a table. Ask her to pick something heavy from the group.

Talk and Think: To help your child recognize the difference between heavy and light, ask:

Which child is holding something light?
Which child is holding something heavy?

- "Why did you pick this [name of item]?"
- "Is it hard to lift? Can you find something that is harder to lift?"
- "Can you find something that is easier to lift?"
- "Can you find something that is light? Is it very easy to lift?"

If your child has difficulty understanding which object is light, you can pick up a light object and say, "This is not very heavy at all—it's light; it's very easy to lift." This will help her recognize that heavy things are hard to lift, while light things are easy to lift.

Then ask your child to choose two items. Ask:

- "Which item is heavier? Why?"

Go a Little Further:

Choose three items of obviously different weights. Ask your child to arrange the three items in order of weight, from heavy to light.

Activity 6: LONG AND SHORT EVENTS

Get Ready: Gather some photos or picture books that convey the idea of things that take a long time. For example, they might involve a car or train trip that takes all day or the growth of a pet or plant.

Go: Ask your child to listen as you tell about something that takes a long time. Show the pictures you've gathered as you tell your story. Then, ask your child to tell about something that he thinks takes a long time. Next, give one or two examples of things that take a short time, such as snapping your fingers, clapping, or eating a cookie. Ask your child to tell about some other things that take a short time.

Talk and Think: To help him become more familiar with long and short events, you can ask questions like:

- "Which would take longer: combing your hair or going from our home to school?"

- "Which would take longer: pouring a glass of water or reading a whole story?"
- "Which would take a shorter time: eating a raisin or eating dinner?"

Activity 7: BEFORE AND AFTER; MORNING, AFTERNOON, AND EVENING

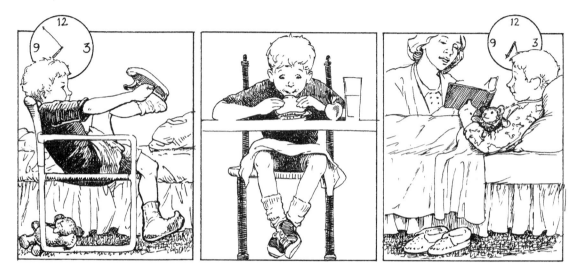

Get Ready: A good time to begin this activity is in the evening, before your child's bedtime. Ask your child to tell about some of the things she did today.
- "Did you play today?"
- "Did you eat lunch?"
- "Did you brush your teeth?"

Go: Tell your child you want to talk about the parts of the day—morning, afternoon, and evening. Then ask:
- "What do we do in the morning?"
- "What do we do in the afternoon?"
- "What do we do in the evening?"

Talk and Think: To follow up, you can ask:
- "Did you eat breakfast in the morning, the afternoon, or the evening?"
- "Did you eat breakfast *before* or *after* you got dressed?"
- "Did you come home from school in the morning, the afternoon, or the evening?"
- "Did you eat supper *before* or *after* you came home from school?"
- "What part of the day is it now? Is this the morning, the afternoon, or the evening?"

Activity 8: WHAT TIME IS IT?

Get Ready:

You will need:

a sheet of colored paper

scissors

a paper plate

a marker or a crayon

a brad

To make clock hands, cut two narrow strips from the colored paper: one strip should be longer than the other. Then, have your child help you turn the paper plate into a clock face by numbering around the rim from 1 to 12. Finally, use the brad to attach the ends of both strips to the center of the clock face. Your child can use this home-made clock face to show different times.

Go: Put a real clock on a table. Use a clock with two hands and twelve numbers rather than a digital clock. Discuss the clock with your child. Point out the twelve numerals. Tell him that the short hand is the hour hand. It tells what hour it is. The long hand is the minute hand. It tells the minutes.

Set the clock to show 4 o'clock. Point out how the short hand points to the hour and the long hand points straight up, to 12. Tell your child that you can tell what hour it is by looking at the short hand. Go over another example, such as 5 o'clock: point out that the long hand points straight up, to 12, while the short hand points to the 5. Then ask:

- "Where is the short hand pointed?"
- "Where is the long hand pointed?"
- "Can you name the time?"
- "Can you show the same time on your clock?"

Talk and Think: Set the clock to show 8 o'clock and then 9 o'clock. Each time, ask:

- "Where is the short hand pointed now?"
- "Can you name the time?"
- "Can you show the same time on your clock?"

You can continue the activity by having him name the time shown as you move the short hand to other numerals on the clock. Show only whole hours. Don't expect your child to recognize parts of an hour, such as 5, 10, or 30 minutes before or after the hour.

Go a Little Further: Have your child help you keep track of the time until it's time for a snack or a story. About ten or twenty minutes before the hour of the activity, tell him that you will have a snack at (the next hour) o'clock. Several times before the hour, ask your child if it's time yet. You can also tell your child to let you know when it's time.

Activity 9: THE CALENDAR

Get Ready: You will need a calendar, preferably one with big, easy-to-see numbers.

Go: Show your child the calendar. Remind her that a calendar is a way of keeping track of time and of showing what day today is. Explain that every day is part of a week and also part of a month. Have her touch the line of days that make up a week. With your help, have her point to and say the names of the days of the week, starting with Sunday. Then have her touch all the weeks that make up the month.

Show her today's date on the calendar. Identify today by the day of the week, the date, and the month; for example: "This is Wednesday, the fifth of October." Have her mark an "X" in the box for today's date on the calendar. Explain that tomorrow you will mark tomorrow's date. Set aside a regular time each morning to mark the calendar.

Talk and Think: When you and your child mark the calendar every day, have her tell you what day of the week it is. When she answers, follow up by telling her the more complete date: "Yes, today is Wednesday. Today is Wednesday, the fifth of October." Then say:

- "Today is Wednesday. Do you know what day it will be tomorrow? What day was it yesterday?"
- [*On a Friday*] "Today is Friday. What things do we usually do on Friday? Tomorrow is Saturday. What things do we usually do on Saturday?"

Most kindergartners don't have a good sense of long-term time, so ask about events that happen on a single day or on the same day every week.

Go a Little Further: As your child becomes familiar with the calendar, ask:

- "Can you name the days of the week in order, starting with Sunday?"
- "How many days are there in a week? How can you find out?"
- "How many days are in this month? How can you find out?"

Geometry

PARENTS: Kindergartners need to learn to recognize and name various shapes, and to use words of position and direction to tell where things are. The activities in this section will help you introduce basic shapes and words of position and direction to your child. Beyond these activities, you can use lots of everyday opportunities to give your child practice with shapes and words of position and direction. For example, you might ask, "What shape is that piece of pizza? That's right, it's a triangle." Or, while reading aloud, you can point to a picture and ask, "Can you tell me where the troll is? That's right, he's *under* the bridge."

Activity 1: WHAT'S THAT SHAPE?

Get Ready:

You will need:

cardboard

scissors

markers or crayons

a brown grocery bag

With your child, look at these pictures of the four basic shapes. Say their names aloud as you point to them and run your finger around their outlines:

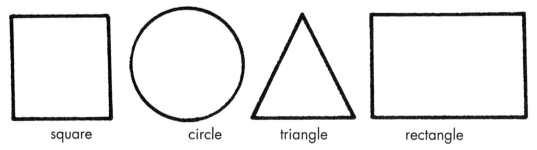

square   circle   triangle   rectangle

You can point out that a square and a rectangle are alike: they both have four sides. But in a square, the sides are all the same.

Now tell your child that you are going to make shapes like these and play a game. Cut from cardboard several of each of the four basic shapes. They should be about three inches by three inches. Your child can color or decorate the shapes as you cut them.

Go: Let your child put the shapes in the bag. Then hold the bag so your child cannot see into it. Ask him to reach into the bag (with one or both hands) and, without looking, to pull out a circle. If he brings out one of the other shapes, show him the picture of a circle and try again. Repeat this game with all the shapes.

Think and Talk: After playing with all the shapes, ask your child, when he pulls out a correct shape, how he knew it was a (shape name).

Activity 2: SHAPE AND SIZE

Get Ready:

To make sixteen shape cutouts, you will need:

stiff paper, poster board, or cardboard

scissors

markers, crayons, or other decorations like stamps or stickers

Cut out four of each shape. Two of the cutouts of each shape should be the same 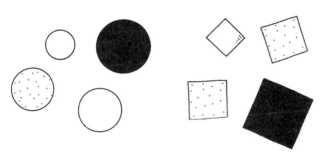 size, a third should be smaller than the others, and a fourth should be larger than the others. As you make the shapes, ask your child to tell you the name of each shape. Your child can color or decorate the shapes as you cut them.

Go: Put the shapes on a table and mix them up, turning some at different angles. Choose one and ask your child to find another cutout that has the same shape.

Talk and Think: To help her compare the shapes, ask:
- "Are the two shapes the same size?"
- "Is the shape you chose larger or smaller than the first one?"

Go a Little Further: You can extend the game by picking up a shape and asking your child:
- "Can you find another piece that's the same shape and size as this?"
- "Can you find another piece that's the same shape as this but [bigger or smaller]?"
- "What is the name of this shape? Can you pick out all the other pieces that are the same shape?"

Activity 3:
WHERE IS IT? USING WORDS OF POSITION AND DIRECTION

PARENTS: Direct your child's attention to the pictures below. Ask questions that will encourage your child to use position words in his answers. You can model the use of position words by answering the first two or three questions yourself.

- "Where is the lamp?" (The lamp is *on* the table.)
- "Where is the cat?" (The cat is *under* the table.)
- "Where is the balloon?" (The balloon is *over* the table or *next to* the lamp.)
- "Where is the girl?" (The girl is *next to* the table.)

- "Is the door open or closed?" (The door is *open*.)
- "Is the window open or closed?" (The window is *closed*.)
- "Is the girl in front of the house or behind the house?" (The girl is in *front* of the house.)
- "Is the boy in front of the girl, or is he behind the girl?" (The boy is *behind* the girl.)
- "Are the children inside the house, or are they outside the house?" (The children are *outside* the house.)
- "Do you see where the path goes?" (It goes *around* the house.)

- "Do you see the cow?" (The cow is *between* the pig and the sheep.)
- "Is the pig to the left of the cow, or is the pig to the right of the cow?" (The pig is to the *left* of the cow.)
- "Is the sheep to the left of the cow, or is the sheep to the right of the cow?" (The sheep is to the *right* of the cow.)
- "Is the rooster above the pig, or is the rooster below the pig?" (The rooster is *above* the pig.)
- "Is the pig below the rooster, or is the pig above the rooster?" (The pig is *below* the rooster.)
- "Does the tree look like it is near the animals or far from the animals?" (The tree looks like it's *far* from the animals.)
- "Is the pig near the fence, or is the pig far from the fence?" (The pig is *near* the fence.)

Activity 4: SIMON SAYS

Get Ready: This game emphasizes right and left, but you can also use other directional words, such as "behind," "beside," "between," "above," "below," "under," "far from," "near," "inside," "here," and "there."

Go: Tell your child that you are going to play a game of Simon Says. If she does not know the game, explain that she is to do what you say only if you use the words "Simon says." If you tell her to do something without saying "Simon says," she should not do it.

Play the game by giving commands that use directional words, especially "left" and "right," such as:
- "Simon says: Put your right hand on your hip."
- "Simon says: Put your left hand on your chin."
- "Simon says: Put your left hand on your tummy."

Occasionally give commands that do not begin with "Simon says."

Talk and Think: To get your child to focus on directional words, after playing for a while, ask:
- "Which commands were hard to follow?"
- "Which were easy?"

Go a Little Further: If your child has no difficulty with left and right, make the commands harder by using more directional words. For example, instead of saying "Put your right hand on your neck," say "Put your *right* hand *behind* your neck." Or, "Put your *right* hand *beside* your *left* knee."

VI.
SCIENCE

INTRODUCTION

Children gain knowledge about the world around them in part from observation and experience. To understand the world of plants and animals, or of seasons and the weather, or of physical forces like magnetism, a child needs firsthand experience with many opportunities to observe, experiment, and get her hands dirty. In the words of *Benchmarks for Science Literacy* (a 1993 report from the American Association for the Advancement of Science): "From their very first day in school, students should be actively engaged in learning to view the world scientifically. That means encouraging them to ask questions about nature and to seek answers, collect things, count and measure things, make qualitative observations, organize collections and observations, discuss findings, etc."

While experience counts for much, book learning is also important, for it helps bring coherence and order to a child's scientific knowledge. Only when topics are presented systematically and clearly can children make steady and secure progress in their scientific learning. The child's development of scientific knowledge and understanding is in some ways a very disorderly and complex process, different for each child. But a systematic approach to the exploration of science, one that combines experience with book learning, can help provide essential building blocks for deeper understanding at a later time. It can also provide the kind of knowledge that one is not likely to gain from observation: consider, for example, how people long believed that the earth stands still while the sun orbits around it, a misconception that "direct experience" presented as fact.

In this section, we introduce kindergartners to a variety of scientific topics, consistent with the early study of science in countries that have had outstanding results in teaching science at the elementary level. The text is meant to be read aloud to your child, and it offers questions for you and your child to discuss, as well as activities for you to do together.

Suggested Resources

Animals Born Alive and Well by Ruth Heller (Grosset and Dunlap, 1982)

Chickens Aren't the Only Ones by Ruth Heller (Grosset and Dunlap, 1981)

From Seed to Plant by Gail Gibbons (Holiday House, 1991)

Me and My Body by David Evans and Claudette Williams (Dorling Kindersley, 1992)

My Five Senses by Aliki (HarperCollins, 1989)

What Will the Weather Be Like Today? by Paul Rogers (Greenwillow, 1990)

Recycle That! by Fay Robinson (Children's Press, 1995)

Plants and Plant Growth

Plants Are All Around Us

This orchid grows in a hot, wet place.

This cactus grows in a hot, dry place.

I'm going to say a word and you tell me what you think of. Ready? Here's the word: "plants."

Did you think of something like a green bush or blooming flower or tall tree? Can you tell me two more things about plants?

We live in a world full of plants. Some plants grow big, like the California redwood trees. Some redwoods stand over three hundred feet tall—that means almost one hundred children your size would have to stand on each other's shoulders to reach the top!

Other plants stay tiny. A plant called duckweed grows in lake water. It's so tiny that it just looks like a green speck.

Thousands of different kinds of plants grow all around the world. Some plants, like tropical orchids, grow only in steamy jungles. Some plants, like cactuses, grow where it's hot and dry. Some plants can grow just about anywhere: the dandelion grows in the cracks of city sidewalks just as easily as in fields and yards.

Some plants smell wonderful, like a rose in bloom. Some plants stink, like the plant with a name that says a lot about its smell: skunk cabbage! Have you ever smelled a sweet-smelling flower, or a plant you didn't like at all?

All the food that you eat comes from plants. Peas and potatoes, carrots and cucumbers, the wheat that gets ground into flour and baked into bread—they all come from plants. But wait a minute. What about meat—like a hamburger or

sliced turkey? And what about fish? Cows, turkeys, and fish are not plants—they're animals! That's right—but all those animals eat plants.

And that's not all: without plants we would have no paper for writing and drawing, no lumber for building houses, and no cotton cloth for clothes. We couldn't live without the plants in our world.

Plants have different parts. Look at the pictures and put your finger on each part of the plant as you say the name of the part.

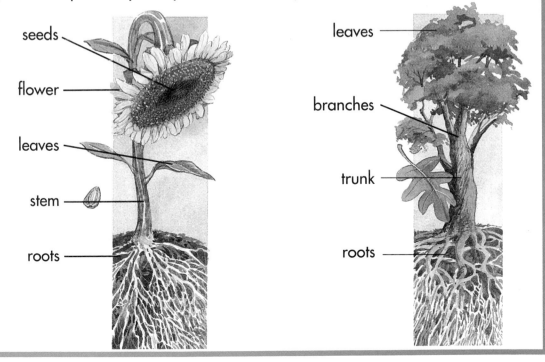

seeds

flower

leaves

stem

roots

leaves

branches

trunk

roots

Seeds Grow into Plants

Many plants grow from seeds. Have you ever seen the little seeds inside an apple? Or have you eaten a slice of watermelon and had to spit out a lot of seeds? Have you eaten a peach, which has one big seed in it? (Don't eat the seed!)

Many plants have flowers, and these flowers make seeds. Flowers bloom in all the colors of the rainbow: yellow tulips, orange marigolds, red roses, purple lilacs, blue forget-me-nots. A bouquet of colorful, sweet-smelling flowers is one of the nicest presents a person can give.

A little seed can turn into a giant plant. Even big trees start from little seeds. Have you ever found an acorn, then looked up to see the big oak tree that dropped it? That little acorn has all it needs to start growing another oak tree.

"Great oaks from little acorns grow."

An acorn is the seed of an oak tree: only an oak tree can grow from an acorn. Do you think a peach tree can grow from an apple seed? No—only an apple tree can grow from an apple seed. And only a sunflower can grow from a sunflower seed. What can grow from a pumpkin seed? That's right: only a pumpkin.

If you put a seed in dirt and water it, it will usually sprout into a baby plant.

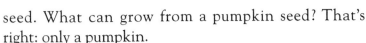

This bean is a seed. Let's look at what happens when it's planted and watered. After a little while, a small root pokes out and grows down into the ground. Then a tiny shoot with leaves grows up in the other direction.

Just like a human baby, a baby plant needs food. Where does the baby plant get its food? From the seed, which is like a little lunch box. As the baby plant grows, the seed gets smaller because the plant is using the food inside the seed.

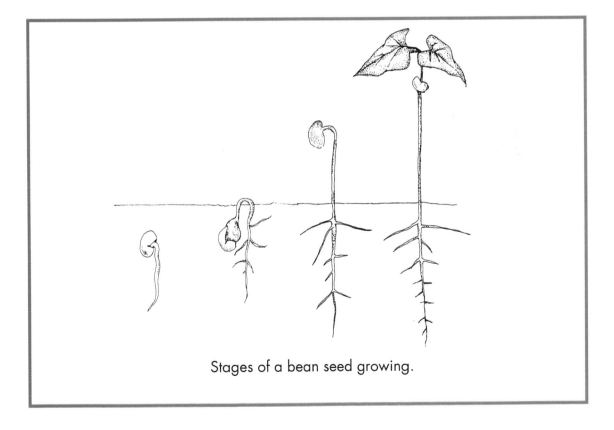

Stages of a bean seed growing.

Watch a Seed Grow in a "See-Through" Planter

PARENTS: Here's an activity you can do with your child that will let you see a seed grow into a plant. Tell your child that you're going to make a "see-through" planter. Have your child do as much as you and he are comfortable with. You'll need to be in charge of the first steps of making the planter, which require cutting a milk carton with strong scissors or a utility knife.

Get Ready:

You will need:

a half-gallon milk carton

scissors or a utility knife

clear plastic wrap

tape (masking tape or transparent tape)

a big rubber band

potting soil

some bean seeds (not beans to cook and eat from the grocery store,
    but the kind that come in a sealed package for growing)

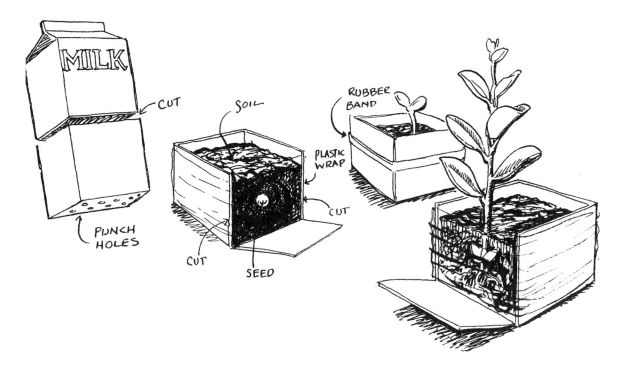

Go: First, cut the milk carton to about one half of its height. Now you have a box with no top. Poke some holes in the bottom, for drainage.

Now cut straight down along two corners of the milk carton. This will allow one side of the carton to fold down, like a flap, while remaining hinged at the bottom.

Leave the flap down so that you have an open side. Cover this side with a sheet of clear plastic wrap. Pull the wrap taut and tape it securely to the outside of the milk carton. Now raise the flap and slide a big rubber band around the milk carton to hold the flap up in place.

Fill the carton about three-fourths full of soil. Now take some of the bean seeds and put them in the soil, next to the clear plastic wrap. Cover these seeds with just a little more soil (about a half-inch).

Put the carton on a plate and sprinkle in just enough water to make the soil moist, not dripping wet.

Put the plate and carton in a warm place. Check the soil daily and add water as necessary to keep the soil moist. Every day, remove the rubber band and let down the flap. This will let you look through the window of clear plastic wrap and see how your seeds are growing "underground"! Pretty soon you should see roots poking down, and sprouts growing up through the soil.

What Plants Need to Grow

What's the difference between a plant and a person like you? Well, both you and a plant start out small and then keep on growing. But you can walk around. Most plants stay put. As a plant grows, its roots sink deep down into the soil and hold on tight. A plant may sway in the wind, but it stays rooted, growing in one place for all its life.

Another big difference between you and a plant is how you eat your breakfast, lunch, and dinner. Have you ever seen a plant eat breakfast? Plants don't sit down for a meal, but they do need food. In fact, plants make their own food.

To make their food, plants need air, light, and water, and also minerals from the soil. The plant's leaves take in air and sunlight. The plant soaks up water and minerals through its roots. (These minerals are dissolved in the water, the way you can dissolve sugar in a cup of water.) The plant uses the air, light, water, and minerals to make its own food. Don't you wish you could do that when you're hungry?!

You can grow a plant in a pot of soil if you give it enough water, air, and light. What do you think would happen to a plant if it doesn't get enough water or light? Let's find out.

What Do Plants Need?: An Experiment

PARENTS: Here is a simple experiment you can do with your child to show what a plant needs to live. Have your child do as much as you and she are comfortable with.

Get Ready:
You will need:

3 paper cups

a sharpened pencil

potting soil

9 bean seeds (not beans to cook and eat from the grocery store,
but the kind that come in a sealed packet for growing)

a cookie sheet or tray

Go: Tell your child that you're going to do an experiment together that will take several days. In this experiment, you're going to plant some seeds and see what they need to grow.

Poke a tiny hole (you can use a sharp pencil point) in the bottom of each paper cup. Let your child fill each cup with potting soil to about a half-inch from the top. Then show her how to plant the seeds: have her use her finger to poke three holes in the soil in each cup, about half a finger deep. Then put one seed in each hole and cover them all with soil. (You need only three bean plants for this experiment, but you're planting more in case some of the seeds don't germinate.)

Put the cups, once planted, on the cookie sheet or tray. Water the plants sparingly, so that the soil is damp but not muddy. Take the tray to a spot near a sunny window. Help your child water the seeds (just a bit) every day until the seeds sprout and the first leaves begin to spread. If more than one plant has sprouted in a cup, then carefully pull out the other plants and leave only one plant per cup in order to proceed with the experiment.

When you have a plant growing well in each cup, write numbers on the cups: 1, 2, and 3. Now explain to your child that you're going to do something different with each of these plants.

Plant 1. Leave this plant where it is and continue to water it every day. Talk with your child so that she can see that this plant is getting everything it needs to live: water, air, light, and minerals from the soil.

Plant 2. Leave this plant where it is but do not water it anymore. Ask your child what this plant won't be getting. Help her see that it won't be getting water but that it will be getting air and light.

Plant 3. Have your child put this plant in a dark place, such as in a kitchen cabinet or a closet. Tell her to keep giving this plant a little water daily. Ask your child what this plant will not be getting. Help her see that the plant will be getting air, water, and minerals but no light.

Check the plants with your child every day. As changes in the plants become noticeable, you can ask your child:

- "What is happening to each plant?"
- "Which plant seems to be doing best?"
- "What does a plant need for healthy growing?"

Seeds to Eat

You've learned that a baby plant sprouts from a seed and then uses the seed for food as it grows. Did you know that you get food from seeds, too? Here are some seeds you might eat.

Corn is the seed of the corn plant that grows tall in the farmer's field. When you eat corn on the cob, you are eating rows of seeds.

Wheat is the seed of the wheat plant. Wheat seeds are so hard that if you tried to eat them, they would almost break your teeth. So we grind wheat seeds into flour to use for baking bread.

Peas are the seeds of the pea plant. Peas grow in long green pods.

Green beans are the seed pods of the bean plant. When you eat a green bean, you are eating a pod and a seed. If you pull one apart very carefully, you can see the little seeds inside.

Peanuts are the seeds of the peanut plant. Next time you eat a peanut, pull it apart very carefully. You can see the start of a tiny new peanut plant inside.

We Eat Many Plant Parts

Seeds aren't the only part of plants that we like to eat. We eat roots, like radishes, onions, and carrots. We eat stems, like celery. We eat leaves, like lettuce and cabbage. We even eat some flowers. For example, when we eat broccoli, we're eating the flower of the broccoli plant just before it blooms.

And of course, we eat the fruit of many plants. Apples, pears, and oranges are fruits. For us, these fruits are food. For a plant, the fruit protects the seeds that grow inside the fruit. In the plant world, by the way, tomatoes, green peppers, and pumpkins are also fruits, even though most of us call them vegetables. They are fruits because they hold seeds inside them as they grow.

Growing Food Plants

You may think that fruits and vegetables come from the grocery store. But that's just where we go to buy them. Somebody has to *grow* most of the fruits we eat. Many of the fruits and vegetables at the grocery store grew on plants at farms and orchards.

The food you buy at grocery stores often comes from really big farms. There are different kinds of big farms. There are poultry farms (where they raise chickens). There are dairy farms (where they raise cattle and where your milk comes from). There are grain farms (where they grow big fields of wheat, corn, barley, and other grains). There are "truck farms," where they grow—no, not trucks!—but lots of different vegetables, like lettuce and broccoli.

Other farms grow important crops, but not for eating. For example, cotton comes from farms. You may be wearing something made of cotton.

LOOK WHAT PLANTS PROVIDE US!

Many of your favorite foods come from plants. Can you add to this list?

French fries	come from	Potatoes
Sugar	comes from	Sugarcane plants
Cereal	comes from	Wheat, oats, corn, and rice
Maple syrup	comes from	Maple trees
Chili beans	come from	Bean plants
Chocolate	comes from	Cocoa trees
Bananas	come from	Banana trees

It takes a lot of work to grow all the plants we eat. Farmers work all year round to raise food. They plow the earth and plant the seeds. They try hard to keep weeds and animals away from their crops. Some farmers figure out ways to *irrigate*, or bring water to, their crops so the plants will grow even if it doesn't rain.

Each farm or orchard packs its vegetables or fruits into crates and boxes so trucks can carry them to grocery stores across the country. Some trucks have refrigerators inside so the food stays fresh until it reaches the store. Some fruits or vegetables are cooked in factories, then canned or frozen to keep even longer.

Seasons and Weather

The Four Seasons

A year is divided into four parts, called the four seasons. Do you know the names of the seasons? They're spring, summer, fall, and winter. (Fall is also called autumn.)

What is each season like? That depends on where you live. In many places, spring is warm, and flowers bloom. Then comes a hot summer. Then comes a cool fall, when the days get shorter. Then comes a cold winter, and maybe lots of snow.

In other places, the seasons change in other ways. Some children live in places where it never snows. In some neighborhoods, the leaves stay green all year round.

But no matter what the weather does where you live, the year still cycles through four seasons—spring, summer, fall, winter—over and over, every year.

What are the seasons like where you live? When you think of each season, what do you hear or see or smell? What different things do you like to do during the different seasons?

TWO KINDS OF TREES

In many parts of our country, the leaves on many trees and bushes turn from green to red, gold, and brown, and then fall off. This happens in the season called—you guessed it—*fall.*

Trees and bushes whose leaves fall in the fall have a special name. It's a big word, so hold on: deciduous (dee-SIJ-oo-us). It's almost a tongue twister: try saying "deciduous" four times very fast! "Deciduous" means "falling off." Even though deciduous plants lose their leaves in the fall, they grow new leaves in the spring. Maples, oaks, and apple trees are all deciduous trees.

But you may have noticed that some trees and bushes stay green all through the winter. They lose some of their leaves every year, but because they seem to stay green forever, we call this kind of plant *evergreen.* Pine trees and holly bushes are evergreens.

The tree in the middle of this picture is a deciduous tree. Look at all the leaves it has in the summer!

Here's the same tree in the winter, after its leaves have fallen.

Talking About the Weather

I'm going to ask you the same question in two different ways. Here's the first way: "What's it like outside?" Here's the second way: "What's the weather?"

The weather is what it's like outside. Did you think about the weather today? Maybe you did, without even realizing it. What kind of clothes did you wear today? The weather had a lot to do with your choice.

No matter where people live, they talk about the weather. It's something everybody shares. When it's cold outside, we shiver. When it's pouring rain, we need rain-coats or umbrellas. When it's hot and humid ("humid" means the air is moist and sticky), we sweat and want a cold, icy drink.

What do we talk about when we talk about the weather?

Temperature. Is it hot or cold, cool or warm? The temperature goes up and down. When the sun comes up, it warms the air and the temperature goes up. When the sun goes down, the air gets cooler and the tempera-ture goes down.

The temperature changes with the seasons. In many places, summer

> To tell what the temperature is, people use a thermome-ter. Many thermometers, like the ones in the picture here, have a colored liquid inside a tube. As the tem-perature goes higher, the liquid rises in the tube. As the temperature goes lower, the liquid goes down in the tube.

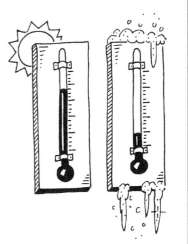

days are usually warm or hot. In most places, the temperature in summer is much higher than in the winter. Winter days are usually cool or cold.

Clear or cloudy? Look up in the sky. Is it a clear day? On a clear day, the sun shines in a bright blue sky. Or is it a cloudy day? Or a "partly cloudy" day—which means, some clouds, but also some blue sky?

A partly cloudy sky.

Clouds are made of very tiny drops of water or tiny bits of ice. Clouds come in different shapes, sizes, and colors. Are there any clouds in the sky now? Are they big, white, and puffy? Or are they white streaks, or dark gray stripes? Or is the sky covered over with a blanket of gray clouds so thick that you can't see through to the sun? A thick blanket of gray clouds sometimes means that rain is coming.

The wind. Is the air calm and still, or is the wind blowing? The wind is moving air. You can't see the wind, but you can see the way the wind moves the branches of trees, or carries a kite higher and higher, or blows your hat off your head. Sometimes the wind blows gently and feels good. Sometimes the wind blows hard and brings stormy weather.

I DO NOT MIND YOU, WINTER WIND

by Jack Prelutsky

I do not mind you, Winter Wind
when you come whirling by,
to tickle me with snowflakes
drifting softly from the sky.

I do not even mind you
when you nibble at my skin,
scrambling over all of me
attempting to get in.

But when you bowl me over
and I land on my behind,
then I must tell you, Winter Wind,
I mind . . . I really mind!

The Wind Blows in Many Directions

PARENTS: This activity can help your child see which way the wind is blowing and understand that the wind blows in different directions. The activity requires some cutting and stapling. Have your child do as much as you and she are comfortable with.

Get Ready:

Tell your child that together you are going to make a weather vane that she can use to see which way the wind is blowing.
You will need:
an empty plastic milk container
scissors and a stapler
a plastic straw
a pen or marker
a pin
a pencil with an eraser

Go: The weather vane will look like an arrow. Cut two small squares out of a side of the plastic milk container. Staple one square to one end of the straw. Cut a triangle out of the other square, then staple the triangle to the other end of the straw.

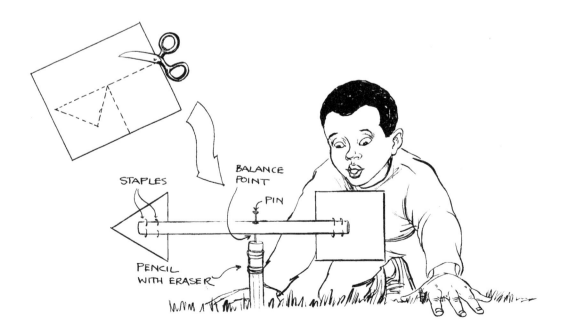

Now, hold out your index finger and put the straw across it. Move it until it balances on your finger. With a pen or marker, mark this balancing point. Push a pin through the straw just at the balancing point.

Now, take the straw with the pin through it and carefully push the pin into the eraser of the pencil. Push the pencil into the ground, straight up and down.

The weather vane will point in the direction the wind is blowing from. Check your weather vane every day for a few days or more. Does the wind change directions?

Rain and Snow

Rain can pour down hard.

> ### RAIN
>
> *by Robert Louis Stevenson*
>
> The rain is raining all around,
> It falls on field and tree,
> It rains on the umbrellas here,
> And on the ships at sea.

Rain. Rain falls from clouds and soaks into the earth, filling up the lakes and streams and helping the plants grow. Sometimes you may not welcome the rain: you know the poem, "Rain, rain go away, come again another day." But without enough rain, the ground becomes dry and hard. When that happens, then the roots of plants cannot soak up enough water and the plants can die.

Rain can fall in fine, tickly droplets, called mist or drizzle. It can come down in a short, friendly shower. Or it can pour down hard. Have you heard the funny expression

Have you ever seen a rainbow?

people sometimes use to describe a really heavy rain? They say, "It's raining cats and dogs!" If it rains too much for a long time, then that can cause a flood.

If you're lucky, then sometimes when it's raining, or just after a rain, you'll see a rainbow. Rainbows look like magic, but they appear naturally, when sunlight shines through raindrops in the sky. Have you ever held a prism up to sunlight and seen how it breaks the light coming through it into bands of color? Raindrops do the same thing to sunlight—they break it into bands of color—and that's why you see a rainbow.

Snow. In winter, if the temperature drops low enough, then instead of rain we get snow. When just a little snow falls, we call it a snow flurry. If a big snowstorm dumps lots and lots of snow, we call it a blizzard.

When snowflakes fall, they may look like little bits of white, all of them the same.

But did you know that every snowflake is different? Each snowflake is its own beautiful design of tiny ice crystals.

It's snowing!

These are snowflakes. Almost every snowflake is different, but they're all six-sided. Can you count the sides?

Make a Snowflake

PARENTS: Children like the lovely snowflake designs they can cut out of folded paper. The folding is a bit complicated, and some cutting is required.

Get Ready:
You will need:

white paper

scissors

Go: Tell your child that, though almost every snowflake has a different design, all snowflakes have six sides, and that you're going to cut some six-sided snowflake designs out of white paper. Proceed as follows:

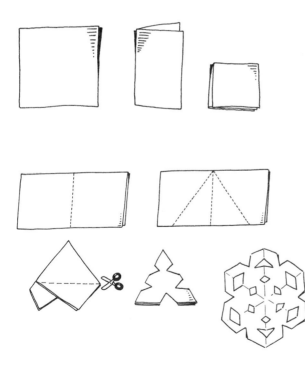

1. Begin with a *square* sheet of paper.
2. To fold this sheet into six parts, first fold it in half.
3. Then fold it in half again, but just crease that fold lightly.
4. Open the fold you just made.
5. Folding from the point where the two fold marks meet, make three overlapping pie slices. You might have to try this part a couple of times to make sure the two outer pie slices match up.
6. Cut off the edges as indicated.
7. Now, each time you clip through your folded piece of paper, you are making six cuts. Snip here, snip there.
8. Open it up—you've got a six-sided snowflake!

Storms

On any day, the weather can change quickly. You might be playing outside on a sunny day, and then suddenly a storm will blow in.

What's the sound of a thunderstorm? Rumble! Boom! Snap! Crack! Boom again! You hear the thunder roaring. You see the bright, jagged streaks of lightning in the sky. Thunder and lightning might scare you, but they're part of nature during a thunderstorm.

You don't have to be scared of lightning if you follow some simple rules. If you're outside when you hear thunder and see lightning, go inside quickly. Never stand under a tree during a lightning storm. Never stay in a swimming pool or lake during a lightning storm. Find your way to a dry shelter and wait for the storm to pass by. Lightning storms usually don't last long.

During a thunderstorm, rain can fall fiercely. Sometimes the rain can even freeze before it comes down. Then it becomes hail—balls of ice that can be as small as peas or as big as golf balls!

Bolts of lightning light up the sky.

Animals and Their Needs

What's your favorite animal?

Is it a wild animal, like an owl or a bunny?

Is it a little creature, like a ladybug or a toad?

Is it an animal at the zoo, like a monkey or a hippopotamus?

Is it an animal on the farm, like a cow or a horse or a goat or a chicken?

Or maybe your favorite animal is one that lives at home—a pet dog or a cat, a goldfish or a hamster.

We share the world with many different animals. Some are wild, like lions and wolves and bears. Can you name some wild animals that live near you? Have you seen squirrels in the park or the woods? Have you seen robins or bluejays in the trees?

This is a beaver. Is he wild or tame?

Some animals are tame, like pet dogs and cats. Whether animals are wild or tame, they need certain things to live. They need water to drink and food to eat. Do you remember that plants can make their own food (from water, minerals, air, and sunshine)? But animals can't do that. Some animals, like rabbits, eat plants. Some animals, like lions, eat meat. Some animals, like bears, eat both plants and meat.

Animals also need safe homes. Wild animals find or make their own homes. Some rabbits make their homes in holes in the ground. Bald eagles build their nests way up high, on mountain ridges or in the tops of tall trees.

GO ON AN ANIMAL SEARCH

PARENTS: Wherever you live, you can find evidence of animal life all around you. Go on an Animal Search with your child. Look for different animals and the evidence of animal life: birds, feathers, caterpillars and other bugs, webs, footprints, even droppings!

Taking Care of Pets

Wild animals can take care of themselves. But pets need special care. You can learn a lot about animals by taking care of a pet. Owning a pet is almost like being a parent. Think about what your pet needs. You provide food and water and a safe home. You teach your pet and you love your pet. If you do all these things well, you'll have a healthy pet.

Some people like dogs best. They give them food and water and a place to sleep. Dogs love to take walks. Some dogs can learn tricks, like fetching a ball or rolling over or catching a Frisbee in midair!

Some people like cats best. They give them food and water and a place to sleep. Cats curl up on the sofa or at the foot of the bed. When cats feel content, they purr. When they're frightened, they arch their backs, their hair stands on end, and their tails puff out like a big brush!

Some people like birds best. They give them food and water and a clean, dry cage. Some birds sing. Some birds even "talk." People teach parrots to say funny things like "Hello, Sugar!" and "What's up, Doc?"

Some people like to keep more unusual animals as pets, like tropical fish or snakes or iguanas or ferrets or monkeys. No matter what kind of pet a person chooses, the animal will always need food, water, a safe home, and loving care.

Animals Care for Their Babies

Have you ever held a kitten? It's so tiny, it fits inside your hands. It's soft and furry, just like its mother. It has two ears and two eyes, four paws and one tail, just like its mother.

How is a kitten different from its mother? Well, it's smaller. It may have the same color and markings as its mother, or it may have very different color and markings. An orange-striped mother cat could have a kitten with gray stripes or black and white spots. Or she could have orange-striped kittens. Even though the kittens may not have the same color or markings as their mother, the kittens are definitely cats! Can a mother cat have a puppy? No way!

If you've ever seen a mother cat with kittens, you know how much attention she pays to her babies. She washes them by licking them clean (imagine if you took *your* baths that way!). She plays with them. She makes sure they get enough food, by letting them drink her milk. She even teaches them how to hunt when they get bigger.

Many animal parents take special care of their babies. Mother robins bring bugs and worms back to the nest, and then they help their babies learn to fly. Mother whales help their babies learn to swim down deep and come up for air above the water. Baby animals need these special lessons because one day they will have to take care of themselves.

Just like baby animals, human babies also need special care and attention from their parents. Think of all the ways adults help a newborn baby. Babies can't feed themselves. Babies can't dress themselves. Babies can't clean themselves. Babies need adults to help them learn how to walk and talk. Sometimes you still need help from adults, right? But you're not a baby any longer, and there's a lot you can do for yourself.

This mother robin is feeding her babies a worm. Yum!

The Human Body

Your Five Senses

Look up. Look down. What part of your body do you use? Your eyes.

Listen very carefully. What part of your body do you use? Your ears.

Sniff. What do you smell? What part of your body do you use? Your nose.

Lick your lips. Can you taste anything? What part of your body do you use? Your tongue.

Rub the top of your head. Use your fingertips to feel your hair.

Your body can *sense*, using your *five senses:*

sight   hearing   smell   taste   touch

You see with your eyes. With your eyes you can see how big things are, and what colors things are. Did you know that some animals can't see colors? Cats, for example, can't see colors. But their eyes can see better in the dark than your eyes can.

You hear with your ears. You hear pleasant sounds, like a bird singing or someone reading to you. You hear loud sounds, like the siren of a fire engine. You hear quiet sounds, like a whisper. You can hear a lot, though some animals can hear more than you: a dog, for example, can hear a special whistle that puts out a very high-pitched squealing sound that you may not be able to hear. Some animals can't hear at all: you may hear a bee buzz, but the bees never hear their own buzzing, because they don't hear anything.

You smell with your nose. Smells can be pleasant, like the scent of a rose or the aroma of bread baking in the oven. What smells good to you? Smells can be unpleasant, like the smoke from a car's exhaust or the odor of a rotten piece of fruit. What smells bad to you? You can smell a lot, but dogs can smell even more. Have you noticed how dogs like to sniff, sniff, sniff around almost everything? Have you ever heard of dogs who can help find people who've gotten lost in the woods or the snow? The dogs do this by using their sense of smell.

Your sense of smell also helps you taste things. Have you noticed that it's hard to taste things when you have a bad cold? Why do you think that happens? What's your nose like when you have a bad cold?

You taste with your tongue. Look in a mirror and stick out your tongue. See how it's covered with little bumps? Those little bumps have tiny parts that tell you what things taste like. They tell you whether things are *sweet*, like ice cream; *sour*, like a lemon; *salty*, like potato chips; or *bitter*, like some medicine you might have to take when you're sick.

You touch things and feel them. What do you feel if you pick up an ice cube? If you pet a cat or dog? If you rub a piece of sandpaper? If you step barefoot on the grass? You feel by touching with your hands, and with the skin all over the rest of your body.

Taking Care of Your Body

Okay, get ready to use your body. Ready? Then . . .

Put your arms over your head and reach way up to the sky. Stretch!

Jump up and down!

Bend at your waist and touch your toes.

Curl up in a little tiny ball.

Lie down and be absolutely still. Close your eyes. Shh! Don't move!

Your body can do so many things. It can bend and jump and run and sleep. It can see and hear and smell and taste and touch. It can talk and sing. It can draw and paint.

It's important to take good care of your body. Your body needs special care. You need to keep clean by washing your hands before eating and after going to the bathroom, by taking baths regularly, and by brushing your teeth. You need to help your body grow stronger by eating good foods, by getting plenty of exercise, and by getting a good sleep every night.

Taking Care of the Earth

The Forests and the Trees

Imagine that you're climbing a high tower. When you reach the top, you look out over a great forest. You see trees stretching for miles, like a big blanket of green—so many trees that it might seem as though we could never run out of them.

Think about the forest and the trees. Why are they important? If you were an animal in the forest—a bear, raccoon, owl, or deer—the forest would be important to you because it's your home! Many people like to hike through forests and camp out in the woods, where the air is fresh and clean. Those are some reasons why forests are important: because they are homes for many animals, because people enjoy hiking and camping in the woods, because the trees help keep the air we breathe fresh and clean.

These toys are made of wood.

But people cut down trees. Think how many ways we use the wood from trees. We burn wood in fireplaces. We use wood to build houses. We use it to build furniture: chairs, tables, dressers, and more. Pencils are made from wood. Paper comes from wood. It takes a whole forest—almost half a million trees—just to make the paper that goes into the newspapers that Americans read every Sunday. Think of all the other paper we use: paper towels, cardboard, the paper you use for writing and drawing, the paper that makes up the pages of this book.

So, trees are important to us when we cut

them down and use them to make things we need: houses, furniture, paper, and more. But trees are also important to us when they're standing tall in the forests. We have to be very careful not to cut down too many trees. And we should grow new trees to take the place of the ones we've cut down. Some logging companies—companies that cut down trees—are careful to plant new trees after they have cut down the old ones.

Conservation: Saving and Protecting the Earth

It's not just trees that we have to be careful about. We have to be careful about how we use other riches of the earth, too.

For example, the earth has only so much fresh water for us to drink and use. So it's important not to waste water. You can help save water if you don't let the water run in the sink when you're not using it, and if you turn off the faucet firmly whenever you're finished.

When you don't let the faucet run and you make sure to turn it off firmly, you're helping to *conserve* water. To "conserve" means to use something carefully. It means to save and not to waste. There's an old saying that people use: "Waste not, want not."

> "Waste not, want not."

That means, if we're careful not to waste what nature gives us, then we will have enough of what we need. But if we waste what nature gives us, then someday we may want something—like trees or fresh water—but be unable to find what we need.

It's Smart to Recycle

One good way to waste less is to recycle. Recycling means using things over and over instead of throwing them away. Lots of families already recycle clothing: when one child grows up and gets too big for a shirt or pair of pants, then the clothes are passed on to a smaller child—maybe a brother or sister, or cousin or neighbor—to be worn again.

By using things over instead of throwing them away, we help conserve what the earth gives us. "Waste not, want not!"

Many cities and towns have recycling centers to collect materials that can be used over and over. Is there a recycling center in your

You can recycle, too.

town or city? Do you know where it is? Here are some things that you shouldn't throw away: instead, take them to a recycling center.

Paper. Factories can recycle newspapers and lots of other kinds of paper with writing on it. They grind it up and make it into new paper. You can recycle paper, too. How? You can take a piece of paper that you or someone else has already used, turn it over, and draw or write on the back.

Cans. Factories can recycle most metal cans. They clean them and melt them and use them to make new cans. Recycling centers will ask you to separate two different kinds of cans. One kind is made of aluminum, like the cans that soda comes in. The other cans are often called tin cans: these cans hold fruits and vegetables, dog food and cat food, beans and spaghetti with sauce, and lots more.

Glass. Factories recycle glass jars and bottles. They wash them, then grind them up and use them to make new glass. If you want to save your glass jars and bottles to recycle, you should separate them into colors: clear glass, green glass, brown glass. Most recycling centers have different bins for the different colors.

Plastic. Factories recycle plastic, like milk jugs and soda bottles. They melt the plastic and reshape it into other things, like chairs and picnic tables. You can recycle plastic jugs at home or at school. You can use them for all kinds of things: as paint jars, as pots to grow plants in, even as musical instruments.

Keep Our Earth Clean

It's hard to live without making a mess. When you paint a picture, you make a mess. When you cook dinner, you make a mess. When people work in factories, making cars or clothes or televisions, they make a mess, too. But we all have to learn to clean up our messes.

People who work in factories today are studying the problem. They are trying to figure out how to make the things we need without making messes. They are trying to keep unhealthy smoke from polluting the air. They are trying to keep dangerous chemicals from going into the streams and polluting the water.

We can help, too. There's a place to put our garbage. Not on the floor. Not on the sidewalk. Not in the street. Not in the woods.

You know where garbage belongs, right? Garbage goes in the garbage container. People who throw garbage wherever they want are littering. "Litterbugs" are thoughtless, lazy people. Don't litter: that's one way to help clean up the earth.

HERE ARE THREE THINGS YOU CAN DO TO HELP CONSERVE.
Can you add to this list?

1. Turn off water faucets firmly.
2. Recycle paper, metal cans, glass, and plastic.
3. Turn off the lights when you don't need them.

An Invisible Force: Magnetism

PARENTS: We recommend that you obtain a simple magnet and some paper clips to use with your child as you read this section. (But keep magnets away from computers and floppy disks.)

 This is a paper clip. It's made of metal. Can you pick it up without touching it? Don't use tweezers or pliers—you're not allowed to touch it with anything. So, can you pick it up?

Yes! How? With a magnet. If you hold a magnet close to the paper clip—which is made of metal—the clip will come flying up to the magnet.

Now, if you slowly pull the paper clip off your magnet, what do you feel? You feel the magnet pull back. Hold your magnet close to a refrigerator door: can you feel the pull? Let the magnet touch the refrigerator and it won't fall. It sticks to the door. Put a pencil or shoe up against the refrigerator, and what happens? It just drops to the ground. But the magnet sticks.

It seems almost like magic, but it's not: it's *magnetism* that pulls the paper clip to the magnet and makes the magnet stick to the refrigerator door.

We cannot see magnetism, but we can see what magnetism does. We can see the

magnetic force attract a paper clip. We can see how a
magnet holds a note or picture on the refrigerator
door. In some cabinets, you
can see how little magnets
keep the cabinet doors
closed. And if you were to
visit a junkyard, you could
see how huge magnets pick
up things as big as a whole
car!

Can Magnetic Force Pass Through an Object?

PARENTS: Here is an experiment you can do with your child
to find out whether the invisible force of magnetism can pass
through another object.

Get Ready:

You will need:
a piece of paper
a paper clip
a magnet
a piece of construction paper
a book

Hold the paper thumb-up like this.

Go: Have your child start with the plain piece of paper. Show
him how to hold it flat in front of him, with one hand. Put the
paper clip on top. Now have your child put the magnet under
the piece of paper. Tell him to move the magnet under the paper clip, and to keep moving the magnet while he watches the paper clip move.

Talk with your child about what's happening. The magnetic force is passing right
through the piece of paper. See if it will pass through thicker objects. Try the same experiment with a piece of construction paper and with a book.

What Do Magnets Attract?

A magnet is made of metal. It feels cold and hard, like a doorknob or a spoon. A doorknob and spoon are also made of metal, but they're not magnets. Only magnets have that special magnetic attraction.

What do magnets attract? Let's do an experiment.

PARENTS: Tell your child that she's the scientist, and she can do an experiment to figure out what materials magnets will attract.

Get Ready:
You will need:
a crayon or marker
2 boxes
a magnet
a variety of objects and materials, such as:
   a sheet of paper, a piece of wood, a safety pin, a plastic toy,
   a key chain, an apple, a ruler, a staple, a pencil,
   an aluminum soda can, a penny, a thumbtack,
   a small rubber ball, a nail, a feather

Go: Use your crayon or marker to label the two boxes. On one write "Yes"—this means, "Yes, a magnet attracts these materials." On the other write "No"—this means, "No, a magnet does not attract these materials."

Now have your child hold the magnet close to a variety of materials. Does it attract? Does she feel a pull? As she tries each material, have her put it in the appropriate box. (Be careful with sharp objects, like the thumbtack and staple.)

You can also have your child try the magnet on some objects too large to put in one of the boxes. Does the magnet attract a car door? A tree trunk? A tabletop?

So, what has your scientific experiment shown? Do magnets attract paper, wood, or plastic?

No. But magnets do attract safety pins, thumbtacks, staples, nails, paper clips, the car door, and the refrigerator door. What are all these different things made of? They're made of metal. So, magnets attract things made of metal.

But not *everything* made of metal. Some metals are not attracted by magnets. If you try to make your magnet stick to a soda can, it won't. Soda cans are made of a metal called aluminum. Try to pick up a penny with a magnet: it won't work. Pennies are made of a metal called copper. Magnets attract some metals, but not aluminum and copper. The most common metal that magnets *do* attract is called iron. All the things your magnet picked up before—the paper clip, safety pin, nail, and other things—they all have some iron in them.

Sometimes people say that a person has "a magnetic personality." Can you figure out what that means?

Stories About Scientists

George Washington Carver

George Washington Carver was a scientist who helped farmers learn how to grow new crops and take better care of the soil. He studied many different plants and crops, but some of his favorites were peanuts, sweet potatoes, and pecans.

We don't know exactly when George Washington Carver was born, but it was probably sometime in the 1860s. His mother was a slave, owned by a farmer in Missouri named Moses Carver. (If you don't know about slavery, you should find out more about it in the American History section of this book.)

Young George Carver was fascinated

George Washington Carver.

by plants and flowers. He tended his own little garden. People began to see what a gift he had for growing things. They called him the "plant doctor" and asked him to help them grow their gardens better.

George longed to go to school. But in those days most schools only taught white children. So, George had to move to a town eight miles away to attend a school for black children. Imagine, having to move just to be able to go to school, all because some people back then wrongly believed that a black child should not get an education.

His determination carried him all the way through college. In 1894, George Washington Carver graduated from Iowa State University. Soon he was invited to come teach at Tuskegee Institute in Alabama, a college created especially for African-American students. It was just what Carver wanted: a place where he could study plants and agriculture, and help educate other black men and women.

Carver wanted to help farmers in the South. They had been raising cotton for many years, and the crops weren't growing strong and healthy anymore. Carver said they needed to improve the soil by growing other crops, like peanuts. People laughed and called peanuts monkey food. Nobody ate peanuts back then. So Carver invented ways to use peanuts, just so people would listen.

One evening a group of important people came to dinner at Tuskegee. George Washington Carver planned the menu. What do you think he served? Peanut soup, peanut bread, peanut loaf, creamed peanuts, peanut cookies and peanut ice cream for dessert!

In his laboratory Carver learned how peanuts could be used to make shoe polish, ink, oil, cattle feed, shampoo, soap, and shaving cream. Altogether, Carver discovered over three hundred ways to use the peanut. People started calling him "the Wizard of Tuskegee."

Next time you eat a peanut butter sandwich, remember George Washington Carver.

Jane Goodall

Did you ever try to sit very, very still and watch an animal? Maybe you looked out the window and saw a bluejay at a bird feeder, or you watched a mother dog lick her puppies clean. Or maybe you sat very quietly and looked at a fly as it landed on your arm. You can learn a lot about animals by watching closely, especially if you take care not to scare them.

When she was a little girl, Jane Goodall loved watching animals. She crouched in a hen house quietly for hours, hoping to see how a chicken lays eggs. She brought earthworms into her bed to see how they move. When she read *The Story of Dr. Dolittle*—about an imaginary doctor who goes to Africa and learns to talk with the animals!—she decided, "That's what I want to do."

When she grew up, Jane Goodall went to Africa. She was especially interested in the apes and chimpanzees. Since their bodies are so much like human bodies, she thought that we could learn a lot from the chimpanzees.

Goodall went to the African country of Tanzania (tan-zuh-NEE-uh). She lived in a part of the country where hunters were not allowed and where a group of a hundred chimpanzees lived. She was very patient. Every morning at five-thirty she would climb a hill and look through her binoculars, trying to see how the chimpanzees lived. For months the chimpanzees were scared of her, but they slowly came to trust her. After a year the chimps let Jane Goodall come close to them, but not close enough to touch. After two years they knew her well enough that they would eat the bananas she put out for them near her house.

The more the chimpanzees trusted Jane Goodall, the more she saw how they really lived. She learned a lot about chimpanzees that people didn't know before. She saw chimpanzees holding hands, hugging, and kissing. She saw them fighting. She learned the sounds and the facial expressions they used to communicate with one another.

Jane Goodall and a friend.

Perhaps most important of all, she saw chimpanzees making tools. For example, chimpanzees know how to make tools to catch red termites, which they love to eat. They break off long, thin twigs or pieces of grass and poke them down into the holes where the termites live. The termites climb on, then the chimpanzees pull the twigs or grass out of the holes and lick off the termites. The chimps had invented something like a fishing pole for termites! Before Jane Goodall saw this, no one believed that chimpanzees made tools.

Jane Goodall has now spent almost forty years living in Africa and watching the chimpanzees. She recognizes the chimps, and even calls many by name, like David Greybeard, Goliath, and Honey Bee!

Wilbur and Orville Wright

Nowadays, thousands of airplanes and jets fly across the country and around the world every day. But it wasn't very long ago that people thought that human beings would never fly. They thought that flying was something that birds, bats, and some insects could do—but people? No, they said, that won't happen. But it has happened; and it took two brothers, Wilbur and Orville Wright, to prove that human beings could build a machine to fly.

When they were young, Wilbur and Orville Wright were known by their friends as boys who could build and fix things. Together they opened a bicycle shop. They built, sold, and rented bicycles. In the 1890s many people wanted one of those new two-wheeled traveling machines.

At night the Wright Brothers used their brains and tools to study the possibilities of flying. They heard about a German engineer who had built a glider. A glider is a plane with no engine; it's carried by the wind, like a kite. Even when the Wright Brothers heard the sad news that the German engineer had been killed when his glider crashed, they kept on trying to find a way to fly.

They built their own glider. It had two big wings, one on top and one on bottom, and a place for a person to lie down in the middle. They found a special place to test it,

The Wright brothers and their plane. Orville is in the plane and Wilbur, on the right, is holding the wing.

on the windy sand dunes near the Atlantic Ocean at Kitty Hawk, North Carolina.

That first glider flew low to the ground, but then it crashed. Wilbur was discouraged: "Man will not fly in a thousand years," he said.

But he was wrong. He and his brother kept working and kept coming up with new ideas. Soon they had built another plane, but not a glider: this plane had an engine, to turn the propellers.

On December 17, 1903, the Wright brothers stood on the Kitty Hawk sand dunes and tossed a coin to see which one of them would fly their new plane first. Orville won. Wilbur helped him climb into *Flyer I*, as they had named their new machine. The engine started. The plane rolled along the dune. Then it lifted into the air! Orville flew *Flyer I* a total of 120 feet, staying in the air 12 seconds.

That doesn't sound like a very long flight to us today, but to the Wright brothers, 12 seconds meant success! They flew *Flyer I* three more times that day, and on the fourth flight the plane stayed in the air 59 seconds—almost a minute—and flew 852 feet—almost the length of three football fields. The Wright brothers had proven it: human beings could fly in a flying machine!

Only five other people saw them fly that December day at Kitty Hawk. Only a few newspapers even wrote about it. No one seemed to understand how important the airplane would be. But the Wright brothers kept on flying. They built new airplanes and flew them for audiences in France and the United States. Once Orville flew circles around the Statue of Liberty.

In five years of practice flying, they had only one accident, but it was a bad one. Orville was hurt, and a friend flying with him died. It reminded the Wright brothers how dangerous flying could be, but it didn't stop them from continuing to build and fly airplanes. By 1908 they were famous around the world for their flying machine.

Illustration and Photo Credits

Animals Animals/Earth Scenes
   © Hans & Judy Beste: **131(a)**
   © Ken Cole: **265**
   © Bruce Davidson: **125(b)**
   © Richard Day: **257(a)**
   © 1988 John Gerlach: **259(a)**
   © Mickey Gibson: **130(a)**
   © Johnny Johnson: **125(a), 263(d)**
   © Breck P. Kent: **129(b), 134**
   © R. Kolar: **269**
   © Terry G. Murphy: **137(a)**
   © 1982 John Nees: **268(a)**
   © Alan G. Nelson: **136**
   © C. M. Perrins: **122(b)**
   © 1990 Reed/Williams: **145**
   © Leonard Lee Rue III: **169(b)**
   © Tim Sheperd/Oxford Scientific Films: **255(a, b)**
   © Michael Stoklos: **262**
   © Jim Tuten: **126, 129(a)**
   © Doug Wechsler: **244(a)**

Archive Photos: **137(b)**
   © Jeff Greenberg: **170(b)**
   © Anna Kaufman: **260(a)**
   © L.D.E.:   **264**
   © American Stock: **123(b)**

Art Resource, NY

Erich Lessing: Pieter Bruegel the Elder, *Return of the Hunters.* 1565. Oil on oakwood, 117 cm × 162 cm. Kunsthistorisches Museum, Vienna, Austria: **159(a)**

Erich Lessing: Pieter Bruegel the Elder, *Children's Games.* 1560. Oil on oakwood, 118 cm × 161 cm. Kunsthistorisches Museum, Vienna, Austria: **165**

The Bettmann Archive: **127(b), 140(a, b), 141, 144, 146, 147, 148, 149(a, b), 151, 244(b), 260(b)**
UPI/Bettmann: **276**

From *Bob Books for Beginning Readers* by Bobby Lynn Maslen, illustrated by John R. Maslen. Copyright © 1976 by Bobby Lynn Maslen. Reprinted by permission of Scholastic Inc.:   **10**

Alexander Calder, *Lobster Trap and Fish Tail.* 1939. Hanging mobile: painted steel wire and sheet aluminum, about 8′ 6″ × 9′ 6″ diameter (260 cm × 290 cm). The Museum of Modern Art, New York. Commissioned by the Advisory Committee for the stairwell of the Museum. Photograph © 1996 The Museum of Modern Art, New York: **171(b)**

Mary Cassatt, *The Bath.* 1891/92. Oil on canvas, 39$\frac{1}{2}$″ × 26″. Robert A. Waller Fund, 1910.2. Photograph © 1994, The Art Institute of Chicago. All Rights Reserved: **167**

   C.C.I.:   **7, 8(a, b), 11**
   Comstock: **252(b)**
   Culver Pictures, Inc.:   **150, 277**
   Leslie Evans: **258(a)**

Text Credits and Sources

Poetry

"April Rain Song" by Langston Hughes from *The Dream Keeper and Other Poems* by Langston Hughes. Copyright 1932 by Alfred A. Knopf, Inc., and renewed 1960 by Langston Hughes. Reprinted by permission of the publisher.

"I Do Not Mind You, Winter Wind" from *It's Snowing! It's Snowing!* by Jack Prelutsky. Copyright © 1984 by Jack Prelutsky. By permission of Greenwillow Books, a division of William Morrow and Company, Inc.

"The More It Snows" from *The House at Pooh Corner* by A. A. Milne. Illustrations by E. H. Shepard. Copyright 1928 by E. P. Dutton, renewed © 1956 by A. A. Milne. Used by permission of Dutton Children's Books, a division of Penguin Books USA Inc.

"My Nose" by Dorothy Aldis, reprinted by permission of G. P. Putnam's Sons from *All Together*, copyright 1925–1928, 1934, 1939, 1952, © renewed 1953–1956, 1962, 1967 by Dorothy Aldis.

"Tommy" from *Bronzeville Boys and Girls* by Gwendolyn Brooks. Copyright © 1956 by Gwendolyn Brooks Blakely. Reprinted by permission of HarperCollins Publishers.

Stories

All Aesop's Fables in this text adapted from *The Fables of Aesop*, retold by Joseph Jacobs (c. 1900); our version of "The Grasshopper and the Ants" also draws upon the retelling in *Everyday Classics: Third Reader* by F. Baker and A. Thorndike (1917) and *The Natural Method Readers: A Second Reader* by H. McManus and J. Warren (1915).

"The Bremen Town Musicians" adapted from versions in *Everyday Classics: Third Reader* by F. Baker and A. Thorndike (1920) and *The Progressive Road to Reading: Book Two* by G. Burchill et al. (1909).

"Casey Jones" is an original retelling by John Holdren, copyright © 1996. Reprinted by permission of the author.

"Chicken Little" adapted from versions in *The Merrill Readers: First Reader* by F. Dyer and M. Brady (1915); *The Progressive Road to Reading: Book One* by G. Burchill et al. (1909); and *New American Readers: Book One* by L. Baugh and P. Horn (1918).

"Cinderella" is primarily based on the version by Charles Perrault, in *The Blue Fairy Book*, edited A. Lang (1889), and incorporates elements of the Brothers Grimm version (translated by L. Crane, 1886), as well as details from the retelling by F. Baker and A. Thorndike in *Everyday Classics: Third Reader* (1920).

"Goldilocks and the Three Bears" adapted from versions in *The Natural Method Readers: A First*

Reader by H. McManus and J. Haaren (1914) and *Story Hour Readers Revised: Book Two* by I. Coe and A. Dillon (1914).

"How Many Spots Does a Leopard Have?" from *How Many Spots Does a Leopard Have and Other Stories* by Julius Lester. Copyright © 1989 by Julius Lester. Reprinted by permission of Scholastic Inc.

"Johnny Appleseed" condensed and adapted from "Johnny Appleseed, Planter of Orchards on the Frontier," in *Tall Tale America: A Legendary History of Our Humorous Heroes* by Walter Blair (Coward, McCann & Geoghegan, Inc., 1944).

"King Midas and the Golden Touch" condensed and adapted from "The Golden Touch," in *A Wonder-Book for Boys and Girls* by Nathaniel Hawthorne (1852).

"Little Red Riding Hood" adapted from "Little Red-Cap" in *Household Stories from the Brothers Grimm* (translated by L. Crane, 1886) and from "Little Red Riding Hood" in *Everyday Classics: Third Reader* by F. Baker and A. Thorndike (1920).

"Momotaro: Peach Boy" adapted from *The Adventures of Little Peachling*, retold by A. B. Mitford, in *The Children's Hour: Folk Stories and Fables*, edited by Eva Tappan (1907).

"Pooh Goes Visiting and Gets into a Tight Place" by A. A. Milne, illustrated by E. H. Shepard, from *Winnie-the-Pooh* by A. A. Milne, illustrated by E. H. Shepard. Copyright 1926 by E. P. Dutton, renewed 1954 by A. A. Milne. Used by permission of Dutton Children's Books, a division of Penguin Books USA Inc.

"Snow White" adapted from *Household Stories from the Brothers Grimm*, translated by Lucy Crane (1886).

"The Story of Jumping Mouse," text only, a story from *Seven Arrows*, copyright © 1972 by Hymeyohsts Storm. Retold and illustrated for children, copyright © 1984 by John Steptoe. By permission of Lothrop, Lee & Shepard Books, a division of William Morrow & Company, Inc., with the approval of the Estate of John Steptoe.

"The Three Billy Goats Gruff" adapted from versions in *Popular Tales from the Norse* by Peter Asbjornsen (translated by G. W. Dasent, 1908); *The Elson Readers: Book One* by W. Elson and L. Runkel (1920); and "The Three Piggy Wigs" in *The Progressive Road to Reading: Book Two* by G. Burchill et al. (1909).

"The Three Little Pigs" condensed and adapted from "The Story of the Three Little Pigs" in *English Folk Tales*, retold by Joseph Jacobs (1892).

"Tug-of-War" is an original retelling based on many versions of this tale, including: "A Tug of War" in *Yes and No: The Intimate Folklore of Africa* by Alta Jablow (1961); "The Tug of War" in *African Village Folktales* by Edna Mason Kaula (1968); and "Tug of War" in *African Myths and Legends* by Kathleen Arnott (1962).

"The Ugly Duckling" adapted from the original story by Hans Christian Andersen (translated by C. Peachey, 1861) and from retellings in *Third Year Language Reader* by F. Baker et al. (1919) and *Everyday Classics: Third Reader* by F. Baker and A. Thorndike (1920).

"The Wolf and the Seven Little Kids" adapted from *Household Stories from the Brothers Grimm*, translated by Lucy Crane (1886).

While every care has been taken to trace and acknowledge copyright, the editors tender their apologies for any accidental infringement where copyright has proved untraceable. They would be pleased to insert the appropriate acknowledgment in any subsequent edition of this publication.

Index

ABOUT THE AUTHORS

E. D. Hirsch, Jr., is a professor at the University of Virginia and the author of *The Schools We Need* and the bestselling *Cultural Literacy* and *The Dictionary of Cultural Literacy*. He and his wife, Polly, live in Charlottesville, Virginia, where they raised their three children.

John Holdren has been a teacher of writing and literature at the University of Virginia and Harvard University, and is now Director of Research and Communications of the Core Knowledge Foundation. He lives with his wife and two daughters in Greenwood, Virginia.

"The best year of teaching I ever had. This year has
been so much fun: fun to learn, fun to teach."
Joanne Anderson, Teacher,
Three Oaks Elementary School
Fort Myers, Florida

Collect the entire Core Knowledge series

ISBN	TITLE	PRICE
31841-3	What Your Kindergartner Needs to Know	$12.95/17.95 Can
48119-5	What Your First Grader Needs to Know (Rev. Ed.)	$24.95/34.95 Can
31027-7	What Your Second Grader Needs to Know	$11.95/16.95 Can
31257-1	What Your Third Grader Needs to Know	$11.95/16.95 Can
31260-1	What Your Fourth Grader Needs to Know	$11.95/16.95 Can
31464-7	What Your Fifth Grader Needs to Know	$11.95/16.95 Can
31467-1	What Your Sixth Grader Needs to Know	$11.95/16.95 Can
31640-2	Books to Build On	$10.95/14.95 Can

READERS:

The titles listed above are available in your local bookstore. If you are interested in mail ordering any of the Core Knowledge books listed above, please send a check or money order only to the address below (no C.O.D.s or cash) and indicate the title and ISBN with your order. Make check payable to Dell Consumer Services (include $2.50 for postage and handling). Allow 4–6 weeks for delivery. Prices and availability subject to change without notice.

Please mail your order and check to:
Dell Consumer Services, Dept. CK
2451 South Wolf Road
Des Plaines, IL 60018

SCHOOL DISCOUNTS FOR BULK ORDERS:

For bulk orders of quantities of 100 or more books in the Core Knowledge Series (*What Your Kindergartner–Sixth Grader Needs to Know*), schools receive a discount on orders placed through the Core Knowledge Foundation. Call 1-800-238-3233 for information or to place an order.

FOR MORE INFORMATION ABOUT CORE KNOWLEDGE:

Call the Core Knowledge Foundation at 1-800-238-3233.

THE CORE KNOWLEDGE SERIES

From the author of The Core Knowledge Series comes the essential reading resource for your child

BOOKS TO BUILD ON

A Grade-by-Grade Resource Guide for Parents and Teachers
Edited by John Holdren and E.D. Hirsch, Jr.

Do you know what books your kindergartner through sixth grader should be reading? Building on the fundamentals of the popular Core Knowledge Series, this invaluable grade-by-grade guide helps parents and teachers choose the best books for children on a wide range of subjects, from fiction to fine arts, science to Shakespeare.

IN TRADE PAPERBACK AT BOOKSTORES EVERYWHERE

Delta
Trade Paperbacks